5GATEWAYS

a profound spiritual routemap

by Open

Openhand Press

5GATEWAYS: a profound spiritual routemap
by Open

Second edition: printed 3rd September 2015
First edition: printed 29th November 2007
Published by Openhand Press

ISBN 978-0-9556792-4-7
Cover design: Trinity Bourne

for friends on the path...

"Be a lamp unto yourself.
Don't search for light anywhere else;
the light is already there, the fire is already there.
Just probe a little deeper into your being, enquire.
Maybe much ash has gathered around the fire...
Just probe deep inside, and you will find the spark again.
And once you have found a single spark inside you,
you will become a flame, soon you will be a fire...
a fire that purifies, a fire that transforms,
a fire that gives you a new birth and a new being.
Be a lamp unto yourself."

Last words of Gautama, the Buddha

Contents

Foreword

I incarnated somewhat unusually, via what's termed in spiritual circles a 'soul exchange' or 'walk-in'. I come from the higher dimensions where I work as a catalyst. My soul is naturally drawn to convolution and density; I thrive on the challenge of realignment, bringing energy back into harmony with the universal flow. For me, working in this way, is the juice of life itself. It fires my soul to witness others breaking free of limiting density, unravelling injustice and inequity.

I have enjoyed a close connection, over a number of past lives, with the soul who incarnated here as Chris Bourne. I have been his mentor and guide, just as you all enjoy Benevolent Guidance from higher dimensions. The Universal Law of Attraction drew us close, both impassioned by an allied yearning: to assist in this great shift of consciousness now taking place across the Earth. His calling was to shake off the sleepy and distorting delusions of the past, unravel the divine being within himself, and to evolve – *to ascend* – into a New Paradigm of being: a heavenly place that he could sense, intuit and feel in the depths of his heart. It was my destiny to come here and share greater clarity on what exactly is taking place in this great shift: to provide an invaluable spiritual routemap – the 5GATEWAYS – so that people can more accurately navigate the path of Enlightenment and Ascension - a destiny which is now beckoning all.

Such is the challenge of life on Earth right now. In a universe of great diversity, change is the only constant. Realities form for the purpose of exploration, education and growth. But their 'shelf-life' also then expires at some point. Life is constantly working to find higher harmonies of balance and equity; so these old realities unwind and new ones take shape. Earth is ascending into the Fifth Density of Being – a frequency of experience we can all access when we shed the layers of the old density attachments. Many across our planet are feeling this great shift, which is causing them to act and live differently, from a place of greater unity, compassion and respect for all life. It is a feeling that is, as yet, going unheeded by the majority, who continue to speed towards the precipice; fear-based control, that fuels ever escalating consumption, is driving them to the edge of oblivion. Paradoxically, this control based ignorance and intransigence - *the fear of letting go* - is bringing their reality ever closer to meltdown. As I said in the 5GATEWAYS documentary:

> *"we're not living in one world but two. The lower world is based on a system of inequity and injustice. It's a world of of rich and poor, of profit and loss, of winner and loser - it's an outdated system long past its sell-by date; and yet there's another world of interconnectivity with all - it's where all life is cherished and respected. Now these two world's are beginning to separate - the energy is moving from the old world and into the new. As that energy moves, the old systems, the old structures are fracturing and breaking apart. One world has a future, the other does not."*

There is a very clear path from the old world to the new. It is one that has been shared by masters through the ages from the Buddha to Jesus. It is a path that you can navigate successfully through the old reality as it begins to break down, and live the Higher Paradigm here and now. That is exactly how new realities form – we must live them, and be the change, for only then, can change truly happen.

This is exactly what happened for Chris. His soul yearned for the Higher Paradigm. He'd had enough of the old world values of inequity and greed, the pointless struggle to live a lesser life based on the notion of separation, trying desperately to control that which ultimately cannot be controlled. Across the Earth, life is moving on; a universal flow is gathering pace into the Higher Paradigm of being, and it is your invitation to dive fully in, to surrender, and come home to the loving embrace of the divine. For

Chris and myself, this allied yearning caused our souls to literally exchange places via a sacred agreement. It was, and is, my passion to share this routemap with all who might hear. Time is running out. To truly advance and succeed as a universal being, is to dive into the centre stream of your own evolution. What could possibly be better than rediscovering the miraculous being that you truly are? What could replace that sense of completeness and majesty in the depths of your own soul? How might you then sew a path of divine destiny, helping others unfold into the New Paradigm?

Many in our world are already feeling and speaking about this new harmony that we must unveil, if the Earth and all life on it, are to thrive again. Just like blossoms in springtime, many wonderful philosophies and spiritual practices are springing up to support, heal and evolve people. But how do they all connect together? How can they truly lead to the new reality as the old one falls around us? I put it to you, that what mankind desperately needs right now, is a common sense of purpose and destiny. We need to motivate, inspire and uplift people to all pull in a similar direction. Yes, we are all brilliantly unique, all having a unique experience of life. But nevertheless, I have observed that as people ascend the evolutionary mountain, they tend to pass through key altitudes – *key densities* – which impact everyone in very similar ways. Capturing the essence of these shifts within this routemap, can remove much unnecessary confusion and suffering. It can shine the light forwards, in a world that is often beset by hazy darkness.

So I commend the 5GATEWAYS routemap to you as an inspiration for your journey. It is not offered as dogmatic gospel, rather as a template to catalyse greater understanding. Sometimes, at the right moment, a glimmer of light is all it takes to catalyse a self-realisation shift, that can greatly enhance your life - to inspire a new way of being. That is the benevolent intent behind this book. I wish you great joy and success on your journey.

From my heart to yours
Open

Prologue

"Humanity is now faced with a stark choice: evolve or die. . . . If the structures of the human mind remain unchanged, we will always end up re-creating the same world, the same evils, the same dysfunction."

Eckhart Tolle

The Message

From Chris Bourne's Memoirs...

At the age of 12 I realised something was deeply wrong with life; the soul in me became active, desperately looking for a deeper meaning and purpose. I searched everywhere - academia, high intensity sport, business, even the military - and although I was successful in a worldly sense, none of this made me happy or contented. Each achievement, each fulfilled goal, only managed to quench the thirst of a deeper longing for just a fleeting moment. Then it would quickly begin again – the seemingly endless quest for the intangible – something I knew was there, somewhere, but what to find? How to find it?

Then one day, at the age of 40, I stopped struggling. I had had enough. I was ready to give it all up; to give in. Maybe even to die. What point was there any longer? I had 'achieved' much more than most, yet none of these accolades brought any real meaning. As I surveyed my life, it felt like I had been abandoned, cast adrift, in an endless ocean we call the mind. The truly sad part was, I didn't even know who I'd been abandoned by!

Like many across our planet today, I was consumed within society's ultimate deception: the delusion that we are all separate from one another; that we have to fight and struggle in life to get what we want; that there is no benevolent guiding hand leading us to our ultimate salvation. Then suddenly, just as all seemed lost and I had reached the end of my tether, this veil of deceit was, for me, forever shattered.

Through a sequence of miraculous experiences, I was fully awakened to our absolute authentic reality. A universal orchestra of co-creative activity sang its sweet melody loud and clear. Higher consciousness was speaking to me through the synchronistic pattern of life, leading me on a journey of self-realisation. Situations, events, circumstances and chance meetings conspired to reveal an inner pathway through consciousness itself. I was taken through five "Gateways of Light" leading to my Enlightenment and Ascension. Frequently painful, sometimes terrifying, it was a magical journey of unfolding, flowing as one with my soul, experiencing ever finer tastes of universal unity and harmony. In short, I was reacquainted with our birthright, to know ourselves as what we really are - the unfathomable "Seer" - that exists in and through all things.

Through that journey of inner unfolding, I was reconnected with the place of universal knowing, a vast cosmic library of divine energy I have come to know as "Unity Consciousness"; an imperishable flow of unconditional love that we can all gain access to by letting go of the governance of the mind and surrendering into the heart.

In so doing, it has become abundantly clear to me that my purpose here is to help bring a message. Not a channelling, it was rather a 'download' of energy, of consciousness, which infused directly into my being and became a part of me. Although the message may have originated at a higher source, I now recognise it as my own. So rather than just simply speaking it, I live it and it animates my being.

Initially, it was difficult for me to fully process the message through the veils of distorted human thinking, and even more difficult to put it into words. However, the energy would not go away, and so I persevered and with the patient help of Benevolent Consciousness, I finally unveiled the truth as a deep inner knowing. Now, after much dedicated soul searching, I am comfortable that I have found the right vocabulary to capture the true essence of it.

I know the message is of vital importance to all humanity at this time of great turmoil and transition. I know in my heart it provides the solution to every single problem we currently face. It is one which has been gifted to us before, but it has been much misunderstood and maligned. Time is running out, we need to dust off the pages of history and look at the message with fresh eyes. We need to open our minds and unlock the hidden code buried in our hearts. So what was the message? It was, and continues to be, this...

"We stand on the brink of a miraculous new evolution for mankind. A higher vibrational reality is beckoning us founded on unconditional love for all life and synchronistic co-creativity; it is a 'heaven' which exists here and now all around us. In this New Paradigm, we are completely at one with each other and all life. There is no killing, manipulation, or exploitation of any sentient life form or natural resource. All is shared and experienced in harmony without fear. There is absolute trust in our at-one-ment with the divine. Indeed we experience ourselves as the divine, not separate from it. Our living purpose is self-realisation and spiritual enrichment.

The New Paradigm is already unfolding all around us, but it is difficult to see, taste and feel as the old world values crumble and collapse. All life and all structure are formed from universal life energy - from pure consciousness. Nothing is stationary, the underlying fabric from which all life is woven is naturally evolving to ever higher states of harmony and at-one-ment. It is a river of life flowing ceaselessly through every single moment and nothing can resist its eternal flow. Anything that is of lower vibration, lower harmony, anything that sustains inequity and the selfish exploitation of life, will, over time, literally fall apart.

That is what is happening to our society right now. To many, it is an inequitable and unjust system based on exploitation, fear and greed. It is one that has unceremoniously shunted our existence out of harmony with our planetary system and our universe as a whole. Industrial consumerism, the supposed 'virtuous' building block upon which the very fabric of our society has been founded, is now tumbling. It has become an insatiable beast that has been raping Mother Earth in this realm, stripping her bare of natural resources to fix humanity's ever burgeoning addictions. We have built a society on false promises and written countless blank cheques which can no longer be cashed. We have founded our lives on sand and the tide is now fast coming in.

As this turbulent transition takes place, we are each being invited to join the New Paradigm; we each have a ticket for that journey. To get on board, we have to go within, peel away our attachments to the material world, process out our fear-based thinking and dissolve distorted behaviour patterns that limit us. It is these that constrict and confine us in the lower level of consciousness. We are being invited to separate out the authentic characteristics of our soul from the conditioned beliefs, illusionary needs and false agendas that have been programmed within us. We have to let this darkened veil fall from our eyes so that the new world can unfold into view.

So in this eleventh hour, we are each being presented with a choice: either we continue to buy into the collapsing fear-based mentality of division and struggle or we step into the heart and reconnect with our divine birthright.

Benevolent Consciousness is drawing ever closer to help those prepared to listen. We are being provided with a routemap through the inner landscape. The map guides us through Five Gateways of consciousness leading to our Enlightenment and Ascension into the Higher Paradigm. It is a process that has been followed by spiritual masters throughout the ages, and has the power to unite evolving people everywhere.

We each follow a unique pathway as we ascend the spiritual mountain, but those who have climbed before us, report similar experiences, challenges and opportunities as we pass through key 'altitudes' en route to the 'summit'. The map is a gift to humanity in these times of profound change. It offers the priceless opportunity to come to know ourselves experientially as what we truly are - the "Seer" - an eternal presence through all creation. In so doing, we move back into harmony with the natural flow of the universe and unfold the magical lives we were born to live."

The message came with an experiential exploration of how to tune into higher guidance and what may happen as we follow our inner journey of Spiritual Evolution - our 'Ascension'. It is not an easy journey, there are many distorting and manipulating influences that would attach us to the external drama of life and thereby divert us from our path. However, if we apply ourselves diligently to the task of unveiling our inherent beingness, then a beautiful adventure of self discovery unfolds before us, full of mystery, miracles and magic.

I know, beyond a shadow of doubt, that success is open to every single one of us who ventures honestly down the path. Are you ready to make that journey? If so, from my personal experience, 5GATEWAYS is a profound spiritual routemap, that can guide you on your way.

The Five Gateways

- introduction -

What is Ascension?

Our planetary system is undergoing an entirely natural evolutionary process called "Ascension". In other words, it is moving from a lower vibrational reality into a higher one. It is an underlying flow of energy, which is affecting every single thought, emotion and feeling we are currently having. Whether we know it or not, how we process this inner movement of consciousness, influences every choice we make, and shapes the outer circumstances of our lives in a most profound way. The experiences on the inside, although frequently quite subtle, are nevertheless having an instrumental effect in our outer world. Our spiritual evolution - our Ascension - is not something we can conveniently sweep under the carpet whilst we get on with the day-job; in every moment, the underlying flow of energy is influencing and shaping our lives in an amazingly profound way.

So what is Ascension? Imagine, for one moment, the creation of the universe observed as the Big Bang with a radiant explosion of light. With subdivision, relativity happens, and with that, conscious awareness, what we might call "Separation Consciousness". As the light spreads outwards from the centre, its vibrational energy decreases, whereupon the pull of "Unity Consciousness" drawing back to the centre, intensifies. The resultant dynamic causes the Separation Consciousness to condense into waves of form; in other words 'densities of consciousness'. We could perhaps imagine ourselves as "The Source" of a universal pond, with waves spreading outwards from the centre. We might consider each wave represents a density (what some call a "dimension"), clustered into realms of existence. Humanity currently lives in the Lower Realm, a particularly dense collection of vibrations at the outer edge of the pond, quite removed from The Source.

On the surface of our imaginary pond, it appears as though the water is flowing outwards - in fact it is only the disturbance of the waves flowing, the water itself moves only up and down. You might consider the water to be held in place by an undertow to counterbalance the outward flow. Again, this phenomenon represents a wonderful analogy for the universe as a whole, where on the surface (in physical time-space), it appears as if the universe is spreading outwards to ever greater separation, which we experience as greater disconnection from the Source and therefore greater 'dis-ease'. It is probably this feeling of separation for example, which causes ignorance and the inconsiderate exploitation of other sentient life forms, such as Mother Earth. Quantum science observes this as an increase in 'dis-order' known as an increase in "positive entropy", meaning the flow from a higher, more harmonious vibrational state, to a lower, more scattered one.

However, 'under the surface of the universe', in what we might call "Unity Consciousness space" (quantum science calls it "negative time-space"), there is a flow back to The Source to ever greater degrees of order, harmony and ease. We can actually feel this pull when we get out of the mind and into the heart, which guides us in a way that brings increasing inner peace, greater self acceptance, ever expanding joy and at-one-ment with all life. Science refers to this as an "increase in negative entropy", but to me, "unconditional love" seems a much more appropriate description!

> *This 'condensation' of consciousness has formed the known universe into the shape of what science and spirituality call "The Torus". It approximates to the shape of an apple, with an axial core, around which the dimensional layers of reality are formed.*

Within this universal Torus, the flow back to core - *to The Source* - is called Ascension. Specifically, it is where the centre of consciousness of a sentient being is flowing to ever higher vibrational states of existence. Using our pond analogy, it is moving from one wave at the edge of the pond to those closer to the centre. It is a heavenly process which is naturally unfolding for all sentient life forms including "Gaia" - *the Soul of the Earth herself.* The problem for humanity right now, is that resistance to this process, is causing immeasurable pain and suffering, from poverty and disease, to isolation, fear and despair.

Why is it that society seems not to accept, or even observe, the process of Ascension? Why is it that so many people are resisting the movement to ever higher vibrations of love, harmony and at-one-ment with all life? Why is it that most people do not currently experience this expanded reality, which can be sensed and felt in Unity Consciousness space? It is because the physical aspect of the human being, which many identify with, is only designed to tune into the lower densities of reality. We are each bombarded with literally billions of bits of information about our reality every second, and yet the average human brain can only process a very tiny proportion of this. To cope with the overload, the brain forms a map of the reality it has come to expect, and filters out the rest of the information. Since our outer world is shaped by our inner configuration of consciousness, our experience of reality can become severely limited. In other words, the risk is, we confine ourselves only to what we experience at the edge of the pond.

However, when we let go of our conditioned thinking and programmed behaviours, then our soul unfolds into other layers of consciousness and we become increasingly able to tune into a much wider array of the available information. We get to experience higher densities beyond what we are used to. This is not theory; people right across our planet today are experiencing many of these other densities. It is like tuning into different stations on the radio. All radio bands exist in the same space and time, but at different frequencies. The problem for humanity right now, is that most have become too used to just one frequency - one station on the radio...

If you want to experience the full complement of life, and prosper in this great shift that is now taking place, then you have to tune the dial to get to the higher vibrations.

As you access more of this expanded reality, it often comes with profound joy as you rediscover your interconnectedness with the whole of life. It is then that you may get tastes of the Fifth Density, which is a part of the next higher realm of existence and is mankind's immediate destiny. In short, the more familiar you become with the guiding patterning of all events, the more it dawns on you that we are not living in one world, but two. There is a higher realm of existence overlapping this one. Whilst your day-to-day, five-sense experience, still resides in the lower physical realm, your psychic and intuitive senses enable you to interpret physical phenomena as symbolic representations of the next higher one. Some people are already able to centre their consciousness in the new realm and taste the flow of divine oneness and unconditional love that is omnipresent there. Others have profoundly clear visions of this 'New World' (perhaps more appropriately 'Renewed World').

This new reality can only be accessed however, when you have found a good degree of inner stillness, which in itself arises from becoming more surrendered and at one with our natural planetary ecosystem. When you do this, Gaia begins to speak to you, quietly at first, but as you tune in more consistently, her sweet voice becomes increasingly clear and undeniable. Your consciousness is drawn to the underlying - pre-eminent - message of our times, and a story begins to unfold before your very eyes. The story is a double-sided coin: on the one side, there is the beauty, joy and harmony of the unfolding higher existence; on the other, there is the fear, pain and struggle of the lower reality crumbling all around us. The two strongly contrasting stories are happening in the same place, at the same time, and you have a choice as to which one you invest your energy into.

Currently, society's approach to humanity's problems is one of technological evolution, but the evolution of consciousness is our natural pathway, unfolding skills and sensitivity many people never dreamed possible. It happens when you surrender and let go of the conditioned reality you have come to expect - the darker side of the coin. As you do so, slowly but surely, you are guided to the higher story - the brighter side. More of the universe unfolds before your eyes or, put more appropriately, *you* unfold into the new realm; you reconnect with your inherent divinity and rediscover yourself as a multi-dimensional being.

When you become fully multi-dimensional, you are no longer constrained by the crumbling old world reality. No matter what distortion and darkness is taking place, you are centred in the New Paradigm of expanded consciousness. You become a beacon of light, influencing everything around you, catalysing the shift for those also ready to experience it. You are breaking down the matrix of conditioned thinking, so that ever more people may be liberated...

> *Slowly, but surely, the higher vibrational paradigm will dawn all around; the old world reality will be peeled away, just like a worn out skin.*

In order to raise your consciousness to the required vibrational frequency, you must go inwards and 'open up' by acknowledging your genuine feelings, releasing tightness and tension caused by your attachment to the physical drama of life. It is where the soul has identified with life's illusion...

> *Fragments have broken away from the soul's mainstream and shipwrecked themselves on the beach of some broken reality. You have to get into this wreckage by honouring the experience of it, owning up to it, and becoming as one with it. It is only then that you can reclaim the lost fragments of soul that became detached and abandoned.*

The more you open into these blockages and feel the unconditional love, joy and harmony, the more you understand what distortions of consciousness are limiting your Ascension and how to process them out. As you do so, your vibration rises and you transition through the Five Gateways of inner consciousness.

So when you have passed through these Gateways, does that mean you automatically leave the physical body? The answer to this question depends on what your purpose here is. Many people are here to assist in the Ascension of others, so may still remain in physical incarnation to be able to help more effectively. Although we still maintain physical presence in the lower world, our soul is centred in the higher one. In short, we are already ascended.

Gaia continues to live in the two realms (*for a while longer*), although her centre of consciousness has now shifted into the Fifth Density, a process which completed with the galactic alignment of 2012. It was a profound shift of energy, which catalysed her rebirth into the new density (I have described this momentous occasion in "DIVINICUS": rise of the divine human). Following this completion, she is now steadily unfolding the new reality. What is crucial for evolving people to understand, is that her energies are now being progressively drawn into the higher density, which will, over time, fracture and fragment the fragile biosphere we are currently living in. Humanity is being compelled higher, to ascend 'upwards' (actually inwards) across her multi-dimensional, superconscious bridge. Although gathering in strength, the movement of energy is still compassionate. However, because many are still resisting this natural flow, there is a growing polarity between the higher and lower realms, between light and dark. This is why those who are still locked in the old fear-based mentality, are experiencing increasing doubt, fear and worry, as they try to manipulate and control ever dwindling natural resources in the lower realm. This is why anger, frustration and resentment are also on the increase, as people struggle for security. Instinctively, they can feel the draining away of energy.

This fear-based reality cannot exist indefinitely. That would be to contradict the natural evolutionary flow of the universe. Hence humanity is being invited inwards, through the internal layers of consciousness - the Five Gateways - to the next chapter of the human story.

What are the Five Gateways?

Since my incarnation here, I have been fully engaged in helping others through their own spiritual evolution. Thus I have witnessed at first hand how people's experiences closely match ancient spiritual teachings shared by masters through the ages. I have observed through many real life encounters, the reoccurring pattern of the five key expansions of consciousness, as people unfold internally. Whilst I consider the evolutionary pathway for each soul to be unique, to me it is clearly consistent that those ascending the 'spiritual mountain', tend to pass through these five key 'altitudes' en route to 'the summit' (even though people might not always recognise them).

Since the release of the 5GATEWAYS documentary on the web in 2011, thousands of people around the world have commented on how it accurately mirrors their own experiences, providing great reassurance and encouragement, as they witness their own journey reflected through these clearly identifiable shifts of consciousness. It is proving to be of great comfort and support to have a reasonable idea – *a routemap* - of where your current level of evolution stands, for it helps you identify what challenges and influences you might be engaged in. If you know how and why your life is being affected by the momentous shifts now taking place, then you will likely find it easier to venture inwards with confidence and discernment. It is also greatly encouraging to know that you are not alone; evolving brothers and sisters everywhere, are joining the ascending group by their soul integration through these Gateways. Indeed, it helps to know what others have experienced in their respective journeys, for it can shed light on the issues you are currently facing; why sometimes you might experience powerful life upheavals and ultimately how to catalyse the unfolding transitions. In so doing, it can remove much unnecessary doubt, fear, pain and anguish. It is for these key reasons I offer my interpretation in this book.

However, I do not offer my views as 'The Absolute Truth', for it is my observation that each of us is influenced to a greater or lesser degree by inner distortions of reality. I do not believe anyone has a perfect perspective of reality, no matter how enlightened they may be. So, I offer these sharings as an interpretation of my truth, which may resonate with you at least in part, and thereby help you unfold a deeper understanding of your own truth.

So how might you best use this book and the guidance contained within it? My purpose has been to provide a text book, offering a routemap, through the major transitions of the human evolutionary journey. It is something you can continually refer to on your path of unfolding. I have noticed plenty of people highlighting key phrases and sections, which speak loudly to them, at their current phase of evolution. And they will often dip back into the book to find new resonances as their consciousness progressively shifts.

This book is not a light – storylike – read! It is meant to be deeply considered, and felt, in relation to your own journey.

5GATEWAYS excludes no particular religion, belief system or spiritual practice, providing they are allied to the universal driving force of unconditional love, and operating as I believe they were always meant to - as doorways into our own direct experience. My descriptions should not be considered as dogmatic gospel. They are personal viewpoints, which I trust are good enough to raise awareness as you encounter similar experiences and wonder why you life is taking the twists and turns it is. Each of us is unique, walking a unique pathway, and yet those who have walked before us have left signposts - milestones - which many seem to encounter and describe in similar ways. I trust therefore, that for those who are able to hear and integrate these realisations, they will prove of value.

I know in my heart that 5GATEWAYS provides the blueprint for mankind's Ascension. I have come here from the higher densities purposefully to share it. It is a routemap with which the supportive forces of benevolence are helping souls align. In my reality, the process is a universal truth, which is now beginning to unveil itself within humanity's collective consciousness, and is intended to be of profound benefit to people in these times of tumultuous change.

It is a sharing that has been many thousands of years in the writing, which is already perhaps the most celebrated in human history. Up to this point however, it has been concealed behind veils of misunderstanding, manipulation and misinformation.

Now the time has come to dust off the pages of history, to read with fresh eyes and open hearts. It is time to stand up and reclaim your divine birthright, the gift that has been denied humanity for so long.

The time is now. There is no other time!

The 5GATEWAYS routemap
-overview-

The Five Gateways on the road to full Enlightenment and Ascension are expansions through internal layers of consciousness. They are each accompanied by a quantum shift in our perception of reality, which is mirrored in the outer world by an equally poignant life changing circumstance - *a synchronistic, unplanned and unforeseen "ceremony"* - to mark the event. For example, it could be the ending of a relationship, which although may have been difficult, nevertheless unleashed a new sense of liberation; or it may be the end of a career, which no longer serves; or perhaps a change in geographical location to a more uplifting environment.

These occasions bring you to a Gateway between the old consciousness and the new. You are invited to seize the day, release the outdated patterns of behaviour, unveil a more authentic way of being and thereby step through the Gateway. The 5GATEWAYS routemap can be summarised as follows...

Gateway 1: *"Awakening" - you awaken to the magic of the soul and your interconnectedness with all life.*

Gateway 2: *"Realignment" - you attune to the soul and completely surrender to its supreme governance in your life.*

Gateway 3: *"Transfiguration" - a dramatic shift of perception from identification with the personality, to being the Seer, expressed as the soul, through the bodymind.*

Gateway 4: *"Enlightenment" - any 'fragments' of soul still identifying with karmic filters are released and 'reconnected'. The soul becomes fully integral within your being.*

Gateway 5: *"Resurrection" - your seven bodily vehicles of expression are finally cleansed, reactivated and re-energised. The soul unfolds into multi-dimensional living.*

Each expansion unfolds over a period of time, which although can last many years, is currently being accelerated in this critical period of human evolution. A quickening is happening all around us where Benevolent Consciousness is affording an opportunity to step onto the fast track of guided, spiritual Enlightenment...

> *In short, you are being offered a rapid reacquaintance with your divine birthright.*

When you begin to watch yourself, in and through all your interactions in life, you begin to notice every moment seems to have a natural energetic flow directing you. If you stay attentive, you are caused to see how inner tightness, generated by conditioned programming, disrupts this flow by projecting disharmony into your outer life...

> *It may seem like you have reached a crossroads, where it can be difficult to rationalise the best way forwards. Fear of the unknown may cloud discernment and dim the senses.*

At such a crossroads, the universe is inviting you to confront and let go of these inner constraints, limitations and expectations that bind you, and instead, express your highest truth. If you can summon the courage to follow the guiding flow of the universe, events will be carefully crafted to maintain focussed attention on your limiting patterns of behaviour. As you are caused to expose and then release attachment to the external drama, the inner constriction is eased, the soul infuses into your being more fully, and you experience expansion through that particular Gateway; you release that which was previously limiting the radiance of your soul.

The Gateway transitions themselves should not be considered as simple doorways, but perhaps better as specific 'corridors of expansion', each with an entrance and exit. They can be transitioned relatively quickly or take many years to complete; it all depends on your recognition of what is going on, and your degree of surrender to the process. The more you fight or deny the truth, the more prolonged the transition becomes. However, the expansions cannot be planned or manipulated; although you can accelerate them, you cannot shortcut them. Unless you have consciously integrated what you are meant to, you cannot truly transition the Gateway. This does not mean that you must have an intellectual understanding of the transitions for them to take place; however, there will be a marked inner knowing that something has changed within - you will feel the shift of consciousness.

The key is to always be in observation of your inner motivations towards external events, until you recognise how and why your beingness is shaping the events in the first place. Each consequence, that your attention is specifically drawn to, is an outward reflection of your internal configuration of consciousness. As you step into the corridor of expansion, the key aspects for you to realise confront you with increasing intensity. You are in effect drawing these circumstances to you. It is what some refer to as "The Law of Attraction". It is vital to state though, if you truly wish to evolve and access the New Paradigm, it is not about manipulating your inner thoughts to attain a supposedly more desirable outer reality. Our destiny is not so much a creation, but rather an authentic way of being, which then manifests creative vehicles of expression for this beingness – *such as a New Earth!*

How do you know if you are making a Gateway transition?

If you surrender to the destined flow, you will soon recognise that you have entered a specific period addressing repetitive cycles of actions and corresponding reactions. Synchronicity is the underlying code, and when you begin to read it, you are caused to see where you may be acting out conditioned and distorted behaviour programs arising from fixed neural pathways in the brain. These are formed from the perceived need for a particular outcome in life – where the soul is not 'self-realised' (realising of the One Self). Thus it attaches to the drama, and generates a 'source pain', from which the conditioned behaviours then grow.

These "distortions" prevent spontaneous authentic action by the mainstream of the soul; it is veiled by them and unable to radiate its full brilliance. As you bring conscious awareness to the distortions, you notice they generate tightness throughout the bodymind - they tend to suck you into de-energising programmed loops of activity - like a doubtful or worrying mind for example.

You cannot simply write over these by programming more desirable thoughts, as is frequently suggested in the spiritual mainstream; it is possible to paper over the cracks, as many do, but only for a time. The universe is tirelessly challenging such programmed and distorted identities, to help souls surrender into the free flowing spontaneity of the One, where such control is rendered redundant.

If you can soften into the tightness caused by your conditioning, then you become able to touch the source pain, deep in your consciousness (which will likely be based on past-life karma). You may then become as one with this trauma, release the identification with it, and so integrate the lost fragment of soul. You can then change your surface level thoughts and behaviours in a truly meaningful, lasting way. A new way of expressing is revealed to you - *a gift of beingness* - which helps you interrupt the old behaviours. If you keep attuning to this new sense of beingness, the old constrictions dissolve, the soul infuses more fully, your vibration rises and your consciousness expands through the Gateways.

How do you know if you have passed through a Gateway?

The passing of each Gateway is marked by a ceremony of one form or another (also known as an "initiation"). The ceremony can be very dramatic and alter the outward experiences of one's life permanently. It could shatter and break apart existing relationships; it may feel as if you are going through a crisis or some kind of breakdown (sometimes called "spiritual emergence"); or it may feel as if life is bringing you to the very threshold of endurance. It is as if you have studied a new facet of beingness and are now being examined to see if you have gained the necessary experience to sustain that new way of being.

However, it is not that you are being judged in some way, for the expansion is self-determining. Although the event might be testing and painful, if you can summon the courage to confront your fears, you will pass through the Gateway, whereupon the sense of release, expansion and liberation can be truly breathtaking and divinely magical. So when you feel the fear arising, instead of turning your head away, my advice is to look it square in the eyes, walking courageously into the jaws of uncertainty. Then the bubble of illusion will miraculously explode and you will emerge, just like a resplendent dragonfly, bathed in a new, radiant light.

Although often quite dramatic, it is also possible that you may have transitioned one or more of the Gateways in previous lifetimes. In which case, you may recreate much milder repetitions in the current lifetime to remind you. Neither should you consider that having transitioned a Gateway, your consciousness is then somehow fixed in the new expansion. It is also possible to slip backwards if you do not remain self-vigilant. The journey forwards requires continual commitment, perseverance and attention to your inner state of being.

It is also important to say, that although the Gateway ceremonies themselves are sequential, and their completion happens each in turn, the Gateway realisations themselves are not simply linear. It could be for example, that even though your consciousness is centred in Gateway 1, you may also begin to process karma, which would not normally be fully engaged until Gateway 4. Likewise, although you may begin to experience multi-dimensionality quite early in your journey, this would normally be associated with opening Gateway 5. Indeed, perhaps for this reason, I have observed a definite tendency for most people to overestimate where they are in the process. True and lasting progression depends on non-attachment, especially to the need for progress!

There are also plenty of anomalies for "starsouls" – those who have travelled here from other constellations (as opposed to human souls, who have only incarnated so far on Earth). Starsouls tend to reconnect quickly back to the higher densities early in their journey here. So they may have mostly felt their higher connectedness from early in their life. Indeed, I have observed many living with their consciousness already centred in the higher densities. However, each soul is drawn here to this physical realm for a reason, and many such souls often access the higher dimensions, but without first being fully integrated in the lower ones. Such souls may have had partial kundalini activations (see Gateway 3) and already have processed karma (see Gateway 4), but they have not necessarily fully completed the Gateways because of the need to integrate through the lower densities. In these cases, the Gateway ceremonies may be much lighter or inconclusive. There is a strong encouragement to continue and persevere with the journey here - *to master full integration of lower and higher self.*

For these various reasons, the Gateways could perhaps best be considered as a multi-dimensional spiral staircase, with each higher Gateway enfolding the earlier ones. It is therefore of value to read and digest all of the Gateways information, even though you might be at an earlier stage in your journey or perhaps believe that you are already in the latter stages.

If you inquire with complete self honesty, and watch where the ego or spiritual identity might want to raise its head, then you will truly perceive where you are on your path, thereby gaining deep understanding of how and why your life is being influenced as it is. Thus 5GATEWAYS can smooth your evolution and prevent any unnecessary meanderings down blind alleyways!

In the following five sections, we will look at these divine expansions in detail, including invaluable tools, tips and advice for transitioning the 5GATEWAYS shared from real life experiences.

Gateway 1

"Awakening"

*"Know that this universe is nothing but a dream,
a bluff of nature to test your consciousness of immortality."*

Paramahansa Yogananda

Key: Surrender

From Chris Bourne's memoirs...

My life was changed forever on 29th November 2002 by an event that would be etched in my consciousness for all eternity. A benevolent presence was with me as I sat behind the steering wheel of a smashed car obstructing the fast lane of the M40 just north of Oxford. It was a typically busy day, with cars travelling at their usual breakneck speed. I looked up through the driver's side window to see the yellow driving lights of a fast-approaching car only yards away. In the next moment, a mere blink of the eye, it would career headlong into mine and I would be dead. Yet I did not mind, it felt like this was meant to happen. A part of me was already in heaven, the rest was about to join it.

Why was I so at peace? Why was I positively looking forward to my own death? Up to that point, I had been living a lie: a forty year old business man with a wife and two children leading a rapidly expanding web development company, an executive lifestyle with an executive car and house to match. I had all the trappings of a successful consumeristic life style, everything we in society are conditioned to aspire to. Yet nothing seemed to satisfy me. There was always the search for something else, but as yet unknown. Earlier, I had managed to momentarily pacify my discontent with better cars, gadgets, clothes or music. When these failed, adrenaline sports took over and most Sundays you'd find me careering down a rocky mountain pass on my top-of-the-range mountain bike or deeply engaged in my other form of reality avoidance - the martial arts.

In truth I was clinically depressed. My thirteen year marriage had been on the rocks for some years. Unlike the tired Friday night movies, we were not "living life happily ever after". We had long since lost genuine interest in each other and the vacuum of true soul connection had been filled by predictable mutual dependency. My life was determined by pleasing others because, in truth, I lacked the courage to be genuine and speak my honest feelings: pleasing my children on a Saturday at Whacky Warehouse because I had lost the ability to do something original; pleasing my friends by fulfilling their conditioned expectations of me; pleasing ridiculously demanding customers because I needed that ever burgeoning pay cheque. I was truly lost in the rat race, climbing the endless property ladder to nowhere. Something just had to give... and finally, just when all hope seemed to be lost, life did give. It gave more than I could ever - in my wildest dreams - imagine possible.

It had begun a few weeks earlier with an email, "the chance of a lifetime", an-all-expenses paid trip to Comdex, the international technology conference in Las Vegas. There was just one more vacant place available to the first applicant. The thought of winning never entered my mind, but something deep within caused me to apply anyway. Surprise, surprise! I won the last place and a few weeks later, just like Alice, I was whisked off to a magical wonderland. As the plane steadily emerged out of the dark, billowing clouds shrouding Heathrow International Airport, there was a deepening sense that I was leaving the darkness and density of my past behind. Mid-flight entertainment was the film "The Bourne Identity", the story of a betrayed man, shot several times in the back and cast adrift in the ocean. Miraculously discovered by the crew of a fishing trawler, he is rescued and healed, but left suffering amnesia, unaware of his true identity. Comfortably numb I may have been, but even so, I could not miss the startling synchronistic parallel with my own life. Indeed, from the very beginning, there was a sense of magic in the air, a presence, seemingly able to shape events and circumstances, like my encounter with Maria, a wonderfully warm and sharing soul who helped me to let go

- just for a moment - of the depression and hopelessness of my meaningless life, which now seemed many worlds away.

One of the Seven Wonders of the World, the Grand Canyon, is but a short flight from Las Vegas and in my current mood of surrender, a trip there with Maria seemed infinitely more appealing than back-to-back seminars courtesy of corporate America. As we stared together into the majestic void, the feeling that we were standing on the very precipice of life itself, gripped the core of my being. Perhaps it was this infinite stillness that sparked off the inner alchemy to finally abandon the annoying chatter of my childlike ego. Perhaps it was the growing feeling of a guiding presence or the deep yearning of my long-abandoned soul cast adrift in the ocean of life. Whatever it was, something had called me from my bed early the following morning to the roof top of the Hilton hotel where we were staying.

Martial Arts were a passion of mine, they had always seemed to keep my head above the engulfing tide of mass human subconsciousness. So it was, I found myself practising gently flowing movements in the early morning darkness high above the crisscrossing matrix of city streets far below me. But this was quite unlike any other practice I had ever experienced. What began quite casually, became increasingly sublime; somehow, each move was drawing me deeper inside myself.

Suddenly, I became both the movement and the moved, dissolving into a new effortlessness, where flow happened spontaneously. There was no longer anyone inside saying "go" or "stop", "turn" or "block". Crystal clear clarity was arising from within, as the inner and outer worlds unfolded into one. Then, on the horizon, attention (at this point I cannot even say 'my' attention) was drawn to the sky beginning to lighten, the blackness becoming purple and indigo, as dawn gently kissed the distant panorama. At the sun's first appearance, I was compelled to stop. Frozen in time, I noticed the early morning chatter of traffic far below me receding further and further into seemingly distant galaxies, until there was no sound at all. Nothing was worthy of this stillness, of this beauty, of this peace.

*Time ground to a halt, and yet simultaneously accelerated. Within the apparent blink of an eye, the sun was fully up and radiating golden warmth. Suddenly, I was being washed through with wave upon wave of unconditional love, seemingly from a source of infinite benevolence. Release after release, unfolding upon unfolding, surrender into surrender. I was being loved completely and wholly just for me. There was no judgment in the love and no need for anything to be reciprocated. It seemed to penetrate every fibre of my being, seeing me with complete openness, honesty and clarity. It saw my darkness and loved me unconditionally; not in spite of it, like another human might. No, it loved me **because** of it. For the first time in all the forty years of my life, I was totally accepted and worthy. Being 'me' in that moment was entirely and completely right. No one was criticising, questioning, abusing or judging. There was not even the requirement for a payback, no need for me to reciprocate. I was allowed to swim in it, to sink in it, to breathe it into every pore. This was my initiation to the magical, universal flow of divine love I have come to know as the "Awakening". My very own soul had begun to infuse into me - this was the reason I had no fear of death that day.*

In the following ten days, leading up to the crash, it was as though time was moving in slow motion; my consciousness had expanded and it felt like I was co-existing in two places at once. In the higher one, I could feel the benevolent presence and the sense of infinite peace, indicating at-one-ment with the whole of creation; in the lower, a movie was playing, the story of my life thus far. The presence helped me see how every event in our lives has but one purpose: to help us reveal an aspect of truth about ourselves to ourselves. A magical orchestra of synchronicity shapes and forms ceaseless patterns of activity, with just one purpose: to wake us up to the glorious magic of everlasting divine union.

*With each moment of my life's review, the presence invited me to see that we shape every experience according to our inner tightness. Whatever we fear, whatever we are attached to, whatever sense of lack we may have, we recreate in our lives time and again until eventually we get the message: that we are **already** whole and complete; that we do not need anything, but that inner sense of contentment; that there is no need to effort or struggle in our lives; that we do not have to control or intentionally manifest. Simply by letting go, our inner constriction unwinds and the negative patterns of our lives can dissolve. In so doing, our vibrational energy rises and our consciousness expands to fill the universe. This is why I was fully prepared to die that day, because I knew I could not die! Death was merely a doorway into another more expanded state of being.*

During the final moments of my life's review, directly leading into the crash itself, I was treated to a sequence of spectacular visions: an event of such cosmic proportions that it is impossible to properly justify in words. I saw two overlapping worlds separating through a brilliant galactic sunrise - a stunning supernova - which seemed to fill the night sky to eternity. The light body of our planetary system was ascending into a higher, more evolved state of being. She was positively pulsating with universal life energy. The old world, on the other hand, was becoming darker and denser. As Gaia expanded into her glorious new form, her old body was crumbling away like a tired, worn-out skin; she was shaking off that consciousness still lost in the control, manipulation, doubt, fear and denial. I was ready to join the new dawning. The visions were so impactful, outstanding and surrendering, that during the crash, I was able to completely let go of everything in my life and surrender to the inevitable. As I awaited the smash of the fast-approaching car, I was in a state of ecstatic bliss.

What happened next was beyond the realm of any 'normal' comprehension. No, I did not ascend into some heavenly nirvana and neither did the fast-approaching car career headlong into mine. Instead, the car door opened and an 'angelic' individual helped me out of the crumpled wreckage. As I was guided across the motorway to the hard shoulder, I looked to my left to see that every car on the busy midday motorway had miraculously stopped, forming a perfect parting line along which I was now walking. Mine was the only car involved in an incident which, under normal circumstances, would have resulted in a multi-car-pileup.

Neither I nor anyone else was meant to die that day. The presence made me aware that it was my purpose to continue, to help share a message with those prepared to listen. "5GATEWAYS" is that message, and I had just passed through Gateway 1.

(Author's note: it was during the crash that I began the process of soul exchange with Chris, by descending into his Fourth Density field and supporting the realisations of the Awakening.)

Gateway 1
- overview -

*Breaking through attachment
to the physical density; dealing
with existential matters.*

For countless lifetimes, many will have lived completely unaware of the presence of the soul and their magical at-one-ment with all life. This happens because as the infinite presence of the One explodes into being, Unity Consciousness is working to flow into, and illuminate, Separation Consciousness. It is a universal process of light flowing into the dark, mirrored by souls disconnecting from the One, losing themselves, and then reconnecting again. Fortunately, there is a vast army of evolved, benevolent beings on hand to support and assist in this re-awakening process.

This process of forgetting one's inherent nature and remembering it again, creates the experience of relativity: we cannot know what we truly are, unless we have first known what we are not. Just as we cannot know hot without knowing cold, we cannot partake of the infinite, unbounded liberation, unless we have first been confined and constricted. And so the physical universe provides an incredible mirror: it offers the opportunity to have an experience of the infinite perfection of Pure Presence – the One - which precedes all experience.

The One is right-there now, in the background of your every thought, emotion and feeling. It is the blank canvas, upon which, the story of your life is painted. It is the absolute of who you are, and your soul is the streaming consciousness of experience that constantly flows from it, and back to it. As the One, at the Big Bang, we subdivided into a multiplicity of flowing energies, and universal awareness arose from the relativistic interplay. The outward flow ultimately condensed into form, which we can call "Separation Consciousness". However, since everything came from infinite potential – *from nothing* - the outward flow must be balanced by an equal and opposite inward one, which we can call "Unity Consciousness". Although nothing is actually separate, the notion of relativity (and therefore individual form) was created from the two opposing flows of energy...

The Unity Consciousness acts like a gravitational force, condensing the energy of Separation Consciousness into what we now experience as physical form.

Over eons of time, Unity Consciousness evolved into flowing waves returning to the Source – souls, providing the possibility of unique and varied experience. The early story of a soul's existence, is to lose itself in a state of false identification. An unevolved – *non-realised* – soul, attaches to the notion of physical separation and ties itself into the external drama, believing that the answer to its questions, needs, fears, hopes and desires, can somehow be found by shaping (or at least trying to shape) Separation Consciousness...

"A human being is a part of the whole called by us
the 'universe', a part limited in time and space.
He experiences himself, his thoughts and feelings
as something separated from the rest -
a kind of optical delusion of his consciousness.
This delusion is a kind of prison for us,
restricting us to our personal desires
and to affection for a few persons nearest to us.
Our task must be to free ourselves from this prison
by widening our circle of compassion
to embrace all living creatures
and the whole of nature in its beauty."
Albert Einstein

Eventually you begin to surrender and give up chasing soullessly through the external world of consequences. You tire of continually trying to shape, control and manipulate, because even if you manage a tenuous degree of security, absolute control is always frustratingly just beyond your grasp. There will always be something to rock the foundations of your precious existence no matter how financially secure or sensually satisfied you might think that you are. Eventually, you abandon the fruitless torture of trying to please others, realising that it is only they who can find their own pleasure as a result of their inner state of being. It is at this point, the inner world of causality beckons - that which truly governs the outer circumstances of your life.

As you begin to relinquish the struggle, the Gordian knot of attachment begins to unwind of its own accord. Sometimes this can be sudden and dramatic, as in a life-threatening car crash for example. Or, it could be the stunning recognition of the awesome majesty of Mother Nature: sitting down on a park bench, quietly watching the sun streaming through gently waving branches. It could be looking out into the star-filled night sky, touching the vastness of space, finally realising the shocking inconsequence of your "storm-in-a-teacup" life.

It is just as you surrender the need to shape, manipulate and control, that the first key to the true nature of our authentic reality materialises. Frequently, the door of the prison cell is unlocked as the result of a curious or even dramatic occurrence. It could be an event that causes you to question the very nature of reality or an unusual phenomenon that seems to connect you to life in a way you have not tasted before. Maybe for an instant, you feel your interconnectedness - you do not just see an animal through the clouded haze of a tired memory, but feel its very life essence coursing through your veins. It might be staring at the clouds and dissolving into them; it could be the experience of timelessness; the sense of spiritual presence or waves of unconditional love irradiating your being. Suddenly, you are no longer lost in the prison cell of the mind, *you realise your mind is inside of you!*

All such experiences indicate that your consciousness has

expanded – *a reasonable amount* - out of the teacup and into the universe. You taste the magic of the soul for the first time. When this happens, it tends to be, that many then embark on another journey in search of more of that taste and paradoxically, the quest often ratchets up the internal efforting once more, so you may slip frustratingly back into the previous slumber. However, unlike previously, you now have a memory of the soul, so although you may not be directly experiencing the expanded consciousness of the Awakening itself, it could be that you think you are. This period in the soul's journey is called the "pre-Awakening": the soul is seeking, but never quite breaking through.

This pre-Awakening can last many years, until you tire yet again, give up the quest for the 'Holy Grail', and settle once more into the awesomely ordinary and profound simplicity of your own self-awareness. It is then, in your surrendered solitude, that the constriction of life's unfulfilled promises can finally burst wide open. That which you have always sought, was always present. Although you may have pilgrimaged to the ends of the Earth, the pot of gold at the end of your life's rainbow was there all the time, *right under your very feet!*

When this new dawn arises, no matter what then transpires, whatever tightness you may once more project yourself into, there is always a way back to this experience. You may frequently submerge yourself back into the depths of delusion, but somehow, eventually, you keep remembering to just let go, and then bob refreshingly back up to the surface again, gasping for a few welcome breaths of crystal clear air.

It is when you are able to continually do this, that you can say you are truly "Awakened". The experience of soul has been initiated within your being and you enjoy its presence on a frequent basis. You have expanded through Gateway 1, to the magical taste of Unity Consciousness, that awesome awareness that unites all.

Transitioning Gateway 1
- essential tools -

1. **Be ready to let go:** *be absolutely clear that you are ready to relinquish the struggle to shape external circumstances – "the drama".*

2. **Be the Observer:** *move to the place of the Observer of yourself as much as possible.*

3. **Regaining the Observer:** *develop a technique for continually returning to the place of the Observer.*

4. **Surrender into complete self-acceptance:** *let go of self judgment and surrender into complete self-acceptance.*

5. **Mark the Awakening:** *notice the internal shift of consciousness that is the Awakening and watch for a memorable ceremony marking the event.*

1. Be ready to let go: *be absolutely clear that you are ready to relinquish the struggle to shape external circumstances – "the drama".*

It seems like an obvious point, but although many people say they are not fully content with life in the day-to-day activities of the drama, and even though they say they have tired of seeking external gratification to fulfill the lack of inner completeness, they are not ready to change. Their conditioning and strength of addiction to conditioned behaviours is too strong for them to overcome at the moment. For example, the fear of giving up a job that is crushing the soul; reluctance to end an unfulfilling and restrictive relationship; the fear of spending time alone in stillness; fear of change and what that might bring. It may be that they are simply not ready to let go of such constriction. In which case, probably the best approach is for them to keep doing these things, until finally there is complete acceptance: that the path of self-realisation will provide the only route to true liberation. So they may continue to give in to the conditioned behaviours until they realise they can never gain that external fulfilment and sense of completeness they are really looking for.

> *When you have finally tired and sickened of the struggle and internal efforting caused by the perceived need to shape the circumstances of your life, then you are ready to embark on the inner journey of self-discovery.*

At this point, be absolutely clear with yourself, that the ONLY game going on in the universe is self-realisation, and that you might as well finally take an active part in that game, rather than trying to conveniently ignore it, while it plays with you! So accept that ALL events, happenings and circumstances have but one purpose... *to reflect our absolute completeness - our "absoluteness" - beyond all circumstances.* Realise the aim of the game is to be completely free inside, WHATEVER happens.

2. Be the Observer: *move to the place of the Observer of yourself as much as possible.*

When you have finally made the choice to venture inwards, the next step is to begin watching yourself in all activities, events and circumstances. In other words, you become the Observer of yourself. We may define the Observer as a soul-inspired intention (perhaps the only aligned intention) to relinquish identification with the drama. It is to notice where you lose your temper; where you become tight inside because of other people's behaviour; where addiction to the physicality of life may cause you to act in predictable ways. For example: you are not able to follow a spontaneous pull of the soul because you are hungry and feel you must eat at all costs; or you are not able to sit in stillness, because you are attached to distraction; or when your behaviour is dictated by the perceived need to please or placate someone else.

> *If you become attentive internally, you will start to notice a sense of 'tightness', caused by such circumstances that you attach to.*

When you notice these kinds of occurrence, firstly, it is important just to watch them, and accept them as the internal, reactionary tightening to conditioned behaviours; and although it is your responsibility to deal with them, is not your fault for them being there in the first place - they came from the circumstances of your upbringing and the society we live in.

In this way, it is important not to judge yourself for giving in to the behaviours initially; this very softness and self-acceptance begins to liberate you from the identity that has formed around the behaviours – *you begin to realise you are not them.*

At this point, it is vitally important that you do not try to overwrite the attachments by using some form of positive programming, for all you really end up doing, is cementing yourself as an identity, albeit a different one. For example: "I am the identity that has covered up my lack of inner completeness by forcing myself to give up smoking or binge eating"; or "I am the identity that has cloaked my lack of self esteem by continually reminding myself to be confident"; or "I am the identity that has to control my body language in order to appear empowered ". When you are able to watch yourself in these dramas and not need to change them, paradoxically, you are actually **already** beginning to free yourself from them.

When you are being the Observer of yourself in all arising experience, this is really what it means to be meditating. Whilst some may like to engage in a particular meditative practice such as chanting, breathing or sitting in stillness, others find it just as effective to be engaged in everyday activities.

> *The key question is: are you lost in activity? or observing yourself in it? To me, the latter is meditating.*

In this state, ultimately, the Observer itself will dissolve into the experience of non-identified Pure Presence – "the Seer" - which is to be in an enlightened state; in which case, life itself becomes meditation.

3. Regaining the Observer: *develop a technique for continually returning to the place of the Observer.*

In the beginning, everyone loses the place of the Observer to a greater or lesser degree. It could be that you spend complete days lost in the "Matrix" of conditioned behaviours and controlling thought forms. At some point however, the realisation will dawn once more, that you have become identified again and need to recover your centre. It could be, for example, that you have gone through a very difficult experience, which has pushed all your inner buttons. Maybe you have endured a particularly stressful time at work or difficulty in family relationships.

To help release yourself from the drama again and recover the place of the unattached Observer, it helps to have a tool or technique to recover that place. It could be a visualisation, deep breathing or a mantra of some kind. It could be simply catching yourself, taking a brief pause, and connecting once more with the fullness of the moment. It could be something very basic: for example, someone I know placed post-it notes saying "let go" all around her flat. For her, something so simple was yet extremely effective!

In the work that I currently do, helping people evolve, I frequently advocate asking oneself the following questions. I have found they can be of great help...

i. Who am I? Answer: "I am"

We are everything and nothing - the absolute beyond all definition. We are eternal, we cannot die and we cannot go anywhere because we exist everywhere. We created everything we are now experiencing and there is nothing we cannot cope with.

ii. Why am I here? Answer: "to experience who I am"

There is only one true purpose of the universe - *to experience ourselves as the Absolute*, whole and complete, without need of anything. Every moment reveals this to us, and there is absolutely nothing else going on.

iii. What time is it? Answer: "the time is now"

Nothing before this moment matters (apart from the influences we carry forwards), because we can do nothing to change it; and since the future unfolds out of what we do in the present, we need not lose ourselves in that either. Therefore, the only thing to do, is be fully present in the landscape that is landing now.

iv. What do I need? Answer: "nothing I do not already have"

We do not need anything but ourselves to be whole and complete in this moment, because if we did, we would not be here! We will always have EXACTLY what we need to be who we truly are. It is only when you are being the false self (*in other words when you are identifying with your physicality*) that you experience a sense of lack, loss, neediness or desire.

4. Surrender into complete self acceptance: *let go of self judgment and surrender into complete self acceptance.*

Most are conditioned from birth that a sense of completeness and wholeness comes from an external 'fix'. For many souls, the love felt in the womb comes with conditions in the external world. So you are rewarded if you are being 'good' and chastised if you are being 'bad'. You learn how certain behaviours bring fulfillment and others bring pain. As you grow, society teaches you that you are somehow not quite good enough as you are, that there is something you need externally to fulfill yourself. These patterns of behaviour develop into a fixed neural-web-program called the *"inner child"*. You then tend to respond to all external occurrences through this identity filter. It negatively affects every decision you make, locking you into a limited and restricted reality.

As you transition puberty, powerful flows of hormones through the body cause you to rebel against this victimisation (or else retract into a shell). You develop new techniques and behaviours for protecting the inner child, and another web of fixed neural pathways forms in the brain acting as a second filter, which is called the *"inner teenager"*. Indeed, it is possible for multiple identities to develop (including spiritual ones), especially where there has been an extremely influential experience. All of these identities can influence your every choice in life, if you allow them to.

The key to releasing yourself, is to begin to notice when they are active by watching when you become tight or stressed out. It tends to happen when you feel you are being judged by another or by society in general - for example, that there is something wrong with what you feel is inherently right. In truth, you are judging yourself, because in some way, it is you who has acquiesced to the external viewpoint and thus judged yourself. You can release yourself from these programs by realising that whilst it is your responsibility to deal with this condition, it is most definitely not your fault for it being there in the first place. It is certain that it came from your upbringing and society in general...

This mirrors the universal process of light infusing, getting lost in, and then illuminating, the darkness.

So it is vital not to descend into blame - those who influenced you were themselves conditioned by society (*reflective of the darkness of the universe*). This opens the path to forgiveness, both for them and yourself. When you can accept that no one is to blame, then you can truly accept your 'faults', not needing to change them (at least for the moment), and eventually settle into absolute self-acceptance.

The key is SURRENDER: surrender the need for an outcome; surrender the need for it to go a particular way; surrender any resistance to the way the moment is clearly shaping itself; surrender the attached need to defend yourself in any given situation; become awesomely okay with whatever happens, knowing that it is the unbounded liberation on the inside which really counts.

Surrendering in this way, at whatever apparent personal cost, is a powerful catalyst for the Awakening.

5. Mark the Awakening: *notice the internal shift of consciousness that is the Awakening and watch for a memorable ceremony marking the event.*

When you finally release yourself from attachment to the external drama, it comes with quite a dramatic shift of consciousness - what begins in the mind, is experienced throughout the body. So, for example, you may feel a growing sense of release, expansion, timelessness or opening up. You will experience surges of energy or waves of unconditional love flowing through you. These are all signs that the Awakening has taken place. In which case, you may fully accept and embrace the new consciousness as your new state of being by completely immersing yourself in it. Watch for a major event coinciding (a divorce for example) inviting you to mark the occasion, and take full part in it with total commitment and energy, even though it may be bitter sweet. Thus your Awakening ceremony takes place.

Transitioning Gateway 1
- general misconceptions -

1. **Striving:** when people hear about the path to Spiritual Enlightenment, and get an initial taste of it during the pre-Awakening, there frequently arises an attached striving for success. This simply pushes the 'objective' further away, in the same way a small child might try to grasp and chase a balloon. However, if you can purposefully rest in awareness, the 'objective' instead moves to you. In other words, you realise it was there all along.

2. **Not seeing the Seer:** becoming an intentional Observer of yourself, is a good first step to dissolving into that which you ultimately are – the unidentified, non localised "Seer" of all things. It is often erroneously imagined, that when you ultimately soften into this place of Pure Presence, then you should see or feel something different (apart from the relaxedness of non-attachment). This misbelief often pushes people away from their destiny. So my advice is to keep being the Observer of all arising thoughts, emotions and feelings, but let go of any expectation of the ultimate state this will bring you to. One day, you will simply know: "I am the One", the Absolute, resting in presence in the background of all events. Without seeking, you have arrived.

3. **Curing the tightness:** when you initially become the Observer and feel tightness, efforting, injury, illness or dis-ease in the bodymind, there is often the misconceived desire to want to immediately heal it - to take the pain away. The genuine function of the disorder (the darkness of the universe) is to act as a mirror to you as the One Self - to realise that you are infinite freedom, totally unidentified with such things. Trying to heal the pain simply gives it more energy and sucks you – *as an identity* - into it. To truly awaken, is to become awesomely okay with whatever is arising in the bodymind.

Paradoxically, it is when you are free of the need to be healed, that true healing can actually take place.

4. **Discipline:** we are truly blessed by the abundance of many excellent spiritual practices helping people to awaken. However, all too often, we erroneously hear that only a strictly disciplined approach, such as a particular meditation done at particular times, is the only way forwards. Whilst persistent commitment to the path is of paramount importance, rigid discipline can also become a doctrine, which can remove you from the spontaneous authenticity of the soul, expressed uniquely in each living moment. If you keep attuning to the soul - *in other words the sense of 'rightness' within* - then you are likely to find discipline being replaced by a continually evolving natural rhythm.

5. **You must get rid of the personality:** it seems to be a commonly held misconception, that in order to fully awaken, you must get rid of your personality - defined (by me) as the uniqueness of our soul. Rather, it is attachment to your personality - which becomes ego - that you must dissolve. It is the ego - or 'false self' - that identifies with the personality and therefore limits you. But once the ego has been unwound, the personality is now magically liberated to express uniquely in the moment according to your 'soul-ray-harmonic' (the innate configuration of your soul - see Gateway 4). Take a look around at the natural world - is not each species of plant and animal displaying a widely varied characteristic of The One Life? So it is with us: our souls are uniquely crafted and configured to express the many varied faces of the One. It is not our personality we must get rid of, rather our attachment to it. It is only ego that tries to get rid of personality.

Transitioning Gateway 1
- indicators of beginning -

Typically the Awakening is a kind of bitter, but then sweet, experience. Awakening souls tend to grow increasingly dissatisfied with society and their life in it; feelings of frustration, stress, anger or depression may arise as you begin to notice the seeming pointlessness of all the struggle in the external drama.

As you begin to give up trying to shape the drama, frustration may give way to listlessness and many become increasingly distracted in day-to-day activities. You may notice that you are becoming increasingly at odds with the people around you, especially if they are still deeply engaged in the struggles of society. It becomes ever more challenging to summon the energy to remain in these places of lower vibration.

This progressive surrender causes people to begin to break down - tears will likely flow quite frequently. If this happens to you, the key is to allow them to flow, for they release pent up frustration, negative energy and even deep-seated trauma. They will help cleanse and wash away the convoluted energy that has built up within. These feelings may be accompanied by an inner yearning to 'go home' without fully understanding what this really means. It is often because you are now reconnecting with Unity Consciousness, our at-one-ment with the whole of life. And it may also have a deeper reason...

You may have the sense that you have incarnated here from elsewhere in the cosmos, that you have a soul family from another constellation that is perhaps beginning to connect with you through 'the ether'. And for many, it will be the increasing shift into the New Paradigm, in a higher vibrational state, which they begin to feel beckoning them.

Although this yearning to go home could, in extreme cases, lead even to suicidal feelings, it is quite understandable because you may have recognised there is a much more appropriate place for you to be. If these kinds of feelings do arise, it is vitally important to remember that you incarnated here for a reason – probably to explore the dense physicality of life and to master the sense of separation. It may also be about learning to remember that beauty lies all around us and maybe you have disconnected from that. It is this reconnection that feels like coming home. It is then that a state of hyper-awareness may spontaneously arise, precipitating reconnection to the soul.

As this commences, you may begin to have unusual dreams, both sleeping and waking, challenging the very essence of what you have come to know as reality. Often these dreams are of a prophetic nature, guiding you on the journey of Awakening.

In summary, typical signs that the Awakening may be commencing are as follows...

- *a growing realisation that nothing in the external world seems to fully satisfy*
- *frustration or underlying depression at the state of one's life*
- *an arising feeling of disconnection from society*
- *feelings of listlessness and lack of direction*
- *prophetic, reoccurring dreams questioning the nature of reality*
- *feelings of hyper-awareness*
- *noticing strange coincidences*
- *a sense of 'magic' in the air*
- *a yearning to 'go home'.*

Transitioning Gateway 1
- indicators of completion -

Someone who has passed through Gateway 1, will be feeling the soul and its magical presence in their lives most of the time; they will be frequently tasting the wonder of at-one-ment with all things. The intensity of experience through the five senses will have made a dramatic leap, as though the 'volume' was suddenly increased. No longer are you viewing life through the tired mental filters of memories and ideas; rather you are now reinvigorating your magical connection with its essence. For example, in encountering a creature like a horse, you can no longer simply pass it by as some ordinary, everyday experience. Instead, you find yourself increasingly brought to tears by the sheer magnificence of life itself. Such 'ordinary' moments become extraordinary.

Those involved in the moving arts such as dancing, gymnastics, athletics, yoga or tai chi, find themselves no longer simply performing a repetitive practice, rather they are feeling through the body into deep conscious awareness, tuning into the soul and allowing it to speak for them. Such depth and intensity of experience can frequently bring one to tears. The same may be said for music, painting, writing and singing. All are now opening channels directly to the soul.

Conversely, it becomes increasingly challenging to witness the suffering of another, be they human, plant or animal; you begin to feel their pain as your own. Whilst you may recognise that all experiences are designed to bring about self-realisation, it does not prevent deep empathy and compassion arising within. Sometimes, these feelings may be lost within the daily routine of life, but someone who has successfully made this first transition, will have discovered ways of reconnecting, whether it be a few moments breathing, a favourite meditation, or a walk in the countryside, for example.

In summary, this reconnection to the soul that marks the Awakening may be typically experienced as follows...

- *feelings of awesome okayness, sense of lightness or floatiness*
- *dissolving of the sense of want, ambition and need*
- *sense of expansiveness and timelessness*
- *feelings of interconnectedness and at-one-ment with all things*
- *increased intensity of experiences through the five senses*
- *observation of magical and/or 'miraculous' events*
- *initial unveiling of psychic sensitivity and intuition*
- *tingling sensations or pulsations in the hands and body*
- *feelings of joy and waves of love flowing through the body.*

Gateway 1
- summary -

The Awakening is one of the most profoundly beautiful experiences that the miracle of creation has blessed humanity with. Prior to it, in most cases, you will have blindly accepted your separateness from all things. Whilst you may have held the notion of a greater truth beyond what you see, most will have experienced themselves as separate from that Source of All Life, not the integral whole everyone is.

Many will have endured countless lifetimes in this delusion, totally engrossed in the alluring seduction of the external drama, until finally one day, you awaken to the first realisation: that nothing 'out there' ever seems to fully satisfy; you are always left wanting more of one experience or less of another. You know there is something you are ultimately looking for, but you are not entirely sure what it is or how to find it: perhaps a new job, a new living environment or that perfect partner that never seems to quite materialise?

With the realisation that the solution to your problem is continually eluding you, finally you give up the chase and paradoxically, just when you stop trying to grasp the balloon, dancing continuously just out of reach, suddenly the illusion bursts. An awesomely simple inner knowing arises over you: that you are everything; that you depend on no external thing; that you are - and always have been - already complete.

The love and fulfillment you have ceaselessly chased was there inside all along, and you do not need any one else to give it to you; it is yours already.

I have witnessed many a person finally, laughingly, sob outrageously at their foolishness, as they settle into the stillness of shockingly simple self-acceptance...

"There is one great cosmic joke
that we have been continually having
at our own expense throughout all eternity.
It is the delusion that we may find happiness,
contentment, fulfillment or love, as a direct
result of something at large in
the external universe of effects.
Finally, one magical day, the absolute
truth of causality beckons, that we are
- and always have been -
the creators and therefore masters of our own experience.
At which point, we either laugh or sob outrageously
both at the incredulity of our ignorance
and the awesome majesty of our Being"
Openhand

As you give up the struggle, you surrender internally, thereby releasing inner constriction and tightness. Your consciousness expands as you reconnect with your soul, which has until now faithfully lingered, concealed in the background shadows of your day-to-day experience. At which point, you are awakened to the conscious life force existing in all things. Your divine connection to the nurturing soul of Mother Earth becomes undeniably apparent.

As you taste this beauty and magic of oneness with all things, it is likely to be the case to experience both joy **and** sorrow: the joy of rediscovering Gaia as a long-lost friend; and the sorrow at the recognition of what Humanity's collective ignorance has been doing to her. Frequently, there follows the stunning recognition that society has been like a rabid infestation, a rapidly spreading plague devouring all in its path, destroying plant, animal and human alike.

You will realise that all the while, the guiding hand of Benevolent Consciousness has been speaking to you through the harmonistic orchestra of synchronicity. And you will quickly witness how the

Matrix of mass human subconsciousness has been continually at odds with this natural weave from which the fabric of all events is woven. It is then that you are humbled, brought to your very knees by the simplest of things: a honey bee perhaps; a flowering rose; or the early morning dew, dropping from an open leaf. How is it that such seemingly basic things can be completely at one, when humanity, with all 'his' supposed intelligence, has been so completely lost? (*this is a poignant question I will return to in DIVINICUS*).

When you are truly Awakened (not just at the level of the intellect), it becomes practically impossible to pollute, to damage, to manipulate or to kill ANY LIVING CREATURE, unless to do so is to the benefit of our whole natural ecosystem. It is not about trying to solve accelerating climate change and the break down in the biosphere just to continue to serve your own selfish addictions or delusionary needs; the higher harmony is not about finding more efficient ways to exploit Mother Earth. There is simply the inner compulsion to be as-one with the whole of life, at whatever apparent personal cost to yourself.

Finally, you may come to the realisation that some global meltdown of society might be exactly what is necessary, to bring those who will listen, back to their senses and into alignment with the natural evolutionary path of the planet. Whatever the pain that such an event might bring, whatever the chaos, maybe it is exactly what humanity needs to further his evolution. After all...

destruction is construction,
when it contains the seeds of the future.

In closely witnessing the current flow of world events, it is clearly obvious, that many are still resistant to the changes going on all around. The conditioning of society seems simply too strong for them to break free of their own accord. The world's leaders and governments are still trying relentlessly to manipulate the external drama according to old world agendas, instead of working with people to go into the heart and reconnect with the benevolent life force through all things. This is why we are witnessing an increasing polarity between light and dark on our planet.

If the resistance continues, the tension will increase. Ultimately, nothing will be able to deny the movement into the higher truth. Anything that is of the lower harmony will crumble and fall apart. This is the natural order of life itself. It is inevitable: in the vast cosmos, realities are constantly being created and then unravelled with the underlying compulsion to attain ever higher harmonies.

The movement into the Higher Paradigm is our planet's destiny, and any concentration of consciousness that maintains an eddy current in this gathering flow will ultimately be unwound; just as even the hardest granite gets washed away by the softest water.

If current trends continue, it is likely that many who are still indoctrinated and lost in the drama will not heed the warnings. Does this mean those who are awakening might as well continue to pollute, deforest and destroy anyway? Far from it! Our planetary system is ascending, and to join it, we must become as one with it. This means to cherish it and nurture it as our own selves. As the old world structures topple around us, indeed there will be much difficulty and even chaos, but this old world will provide the mirroring bridge - *the testing ground* - for the new one. If you are to progress into the Fifth Density, you must unfold the higher harmony now, in your own life, and live it fully, no matter what others still languishing in the Third Density may be doing.

Even if you believed the physical world could come to an end tomorrow, would you still plant that apple tree today? An awakened soul almost certainly would.

Gateway 2

"Realignment"

"Between stimulus and response there is a space...
In that space is our power to choose our response.
In our response lies our growth and our freedom."

Viktor Frankl

Key: follow the sense of 'rightness'

From Chris Bourne's memoirs...

I had been living in a profound state of bliss for some months. As others have described before, it was as though I could continue to watch events pass me by without needing to change or shape them. I could rest happily on the park bench of life enjoying the song of the birds, the rush of the wind, the rustle of the trees; there was no need to do, or not do, any particular thing.

Then after a while, I began to feel an inner calling guiding me forwards. Not as before though, this voice was not of the mind. It sang from somewhere much deeper than that. It was the quiet melody of an ancient and yet timeless music, the vibration of a bygone era that was calling me back to my essence - the memory of the original condition of unity. It was my soul singing to me, that which arises from the Source and flows back to it, as a sense of 'rightness'. I had made the journey to the far reaches of the universe - absolute separation from God - and it was now time to make the journey home again, to the living, breathing experience of unity.

My soul was as a mystical siren, singing the sweet song of surrender... "Ride on my wave and I will take you on a magical journey of remembering who you are and where you came from, a journey of such profound joy. It is a story you've been writing for many lifetimes. It is the story of you." "But how do I listen to my soul?" I asked, "How can I be guided forward?"

No answer came. I asked again, and still no answer. For a while I became frustrated and tight, slipping out of the experience of peaceful inner expansion that I had come to know. This was not right. What was the point of guidance if it took me back into the place of confinement? Then it suddenly dawned on me, the silence WAS THE ANSWER. To hear the sweet message of the soul, and to have a chance of even understanding its language, I had to find silence within. I had to be free from the background noise and clutter of distorting influences. I was drawn to the coast to find stillness, and for five days, meditated on the clifftops in Cornwall, looking out over the natural ruggedness to the rolling ocean beyond.

Each day I sat quietly trying to still my busy mind, each time a little longer than before and yet still no message came. All the while, there was only silence. Many times I was close to giving up. What was the point? What was I still searching for? Why not just give up and go back to the blissful state that was just awesomely okay with accepting anything goes?

However, each time I thought to give up, something caused me to persevere, to stay just a little bit longer. I could feel the increasing tightness in my tired body; one that had been battered and bruised by the clenched fists of time; one that was toxic with the poison of modern day living; one that preferred activity to stillness. Even though I knew my body was not me, it was still there, unavoidably in the centre of my reality, like a roundabout with no exits. Perhaps this was part of the message? I persevered, even if I was going in circles, at least I knew I was not attached to the ride!

As I watched these repetitive revolutions of thought, emotion and tired weariness, it suddenly dawned on me, that in the beginning, to listen to the soul, I did not need to effort to cure, heal or quieten them (at least not yet). Whilst I was focussing on my inner drama, I was giving it more attention, more energy, more consciousness. I was making the already noisy base drum of my inner orchestra even louder. If I wanted instead to hear the subtler, quieter instruments in the background, I simply had to notice them, to tune into them, in other words to 'attune' to them. Then in turn, they would get louder and I would be able to hear them more clearly. I realised I had to tune more into life's joy and then follow the sense of 'rightness in the moment'.

This changed the whole experience of my meditation. Instead, I would tune into things that I noticed and then see how I felt about them inside. It might be the sound of the waves, the colour of gently undulating meadows or the movement of clouds. Suddenly I had changed the dynamic. Instead of fighting a continually losing battle, I had found a wonderful game I could always win. What had started as a rigid discipline, for a given period at a set time each day, suddenly sprang into life - now my meditation was a living, breathing experience that came with me everywhere. It was still clear to me that at some point, I would have to work with this inner tightness – this 'source pain' – that had been built up over the eons, but to begin with, I really needed to pick up the breeze of the soul and begin to ride it.

A feeling would come over me to stop and watch the kite surfers sailing the wind and waves; or a bumble bee would grab my attention, as it made its busy yet effortless way from flower to flower; or the rustling bushes along the cliff path. With no agenda, I was completely free to follow. Then, spontaneously, I would find myself just breathing, my eyes would close and I would sink deeply into expansiveness. There was no intention any more, meditation - life itself - just unfolded.

It was the final day of my trip. I felt it had been successful, but somehow, there was still something missing. I hadn't yet received my message, something I could take home to remind me how to follow my soul. My vision quest had not yet been fulfilled. With this in mind, I found myself walking along the cliff path, when I came across a clearing in the shrubs

and brambles, leading to a precipice stretching outwards
like a finger pointing towards the ocean. It was the perfect
spot to sit for a while and it was unmistakably beckoning
me. I settled down, noticed the pull to go inwards, but not
into the aching and tightness of my body, instead this time,
I went into the breath. The meditation quickly intensified,
until breath swept me up onto its silent wings, becoming first
lighter and lighter, then fuller and fuller, harnessing the life
energy of the universe until, like a wave, I swept through the
pain washing over and around the rocks, now powerless to
resist the inevitable flow of my soul. I quietly dissolved upon
the shore of awesome okayness - the place that did not need
answers.

Then a wonderful miracle of nature happened, as if to
reward me for my patience. As I opened my eyes, a bird
of prey, a kestrel, rose up the cliff and hung majestically
in the air right in front of me. Shivers ran up and down
my spine, an intensity of awareness connected me as one
with the bird. I knew this was the message I had come for;
my whole being was suddenly fixated by it. There was a
deep welling up within me and tears began flowing down
my cheeks. The bird connected with the very essence of my
being. For what seemed an eternity, it hung in the air
just a few feet in front of me, skillfully angling its body
and wings to harmonise with the wind, held aloft on the
feather edge of effortlessness. Yet through all the fluid, free
flowing movement of its body, its head was perfectly still,
fixed in time and space, eyes glued intently on its target
below. Suddenly, without warning, without preparation,
without labour of thought or intent, the right moment had
arrived - it dropped out of the sky like a bullet, shooting
swiftly downwards onto its prey. To me, this was the natural
order of things; wind, kestrel, prey, all as one, experiencing
divine union.

I was left speechless. It took me some time to find words for the message, but ultimately they came: "Be in the place of the Observer of yourself and all life without identifying with it; without judging it; without intending or needing it to be a certain way. When you are not identified in this way, your mind and heart open and you begin to feel and flow with the natural order of things. In one hand you receive the energy of the moment in truth, as it really is, without needing to change it; then with the other hand, when the moment is right, give yourself to your highest truth, that which expresses absolutely who and what you are. Everything flows as one to bring Right Action into fruition".

I was blown away. Through the bird, the Soul of the Earth had spoken to me loud and clear. There was no denying, doubting or ignoring. The guiding hand of Benevolent Consciousness had granted me my message and I resolved from that moment on to ALWAYS listen.

In the weeks that followed, I would come to realise that when we make such a resolution to ourselves, we are likewise making the same affirmation to the universe, and when we do so, she will gather the entire force of nature to test our resolve, to hold us to account, to see if we have the courage to really be free. She is not doing it out of spite or malice, not out of some sadistic sense of humour. We have said to her "We are free! Free to follow the divine flow of the universe, the only thing that makes sense in a tired world of humanity's broken promises". She wants that for us, it is our destiny and the only way to live it, is to test it and test it she does. I was soon to discover that when we do unleash soul in this way, it is drawn directly into one's inner darkness, because this is where it is being limited and confined; this is where the 'source pain' is. And that's what the soul must unravel if we – like the kestrel – are to truly be free.

My initiation to test if I was ready to follow my soul materialised almost immediately. My marriage had been on the rocks for quite some time, but in my newly awakened state, it felt like I should make one last effort to resolve things between me and my wife, "for the sake of the children" at least. Hence we embarked on a program of intensive marriage guidance counselling. We raked over the ashes, found common ground and managed to rekindle a few embers of an apparently dying fire. When all the pain, frustration and judgment had been pared away, refreshingly, there remained deep feelings of mutual respect. We had shared much together over the years - joy, love, happiness and not least, two gorgeous children. Perhaps it had been the years of grafting that had taken their toll? Perhaps it was my incessant need to control our lives? Perhaps it was her laissez faire attitude to debt, punctuality and tidiness. Surely in my new state of surrender, I could be more accepting of those things and just let life be?

I was soon to discover that surrender and acceptance are two very different things. To surrender to the universe is not to blindly accept anything goes; it is to recognise the truth of what is, and then follow that. The universe conjured the perfect teaching of this age-old wisdom. My wife and I decided we would make a fresh start and begin it with a second honeymoon, in the village of Deia, on the island of Majorca. It was our favourite retreat destination and we were both keenly looking forward to it. As the plane began to trundle faster and faster towards take off, my wife turned to me, smiled and asked "Do you love me?" A sharp intake of breath overtook me. I was just about to regurgitate the classic "Of course I do, my darling" when something caught me: I could feel a tightening deep in my gut (my sacrum), which I simply knew I had to soften into. As I did, time seemed to slow way down, and suddenly, to my surprise, an image of the hovering kestrel floated into my awareness, a superlative demonstration of absolute truth, beckoning me to do exactly the same.

I paused for what seemed like an eternity. I knew what wanted to be said, what she wanted to hear, what my conditioned behaviours were demanding. The steamroller of controlling thought forms seemed to be gathering strength, just like the now irresistibly rising aircraft. "Of course I do, my darling" was what the crowd wanted to hear, "I will love you forever". But the kestrel would not let me give in. I had to break through the mass human subconsciousness, rise above it and find the truth.

Then they came - the following words, welling up from deep within, without any control or intention... "I love you, but I am not IN love with you". So compelling, so filled with energy, so soulful were they, that their truth could neither be ignored nor denied, no longer swept under the carpet of tired excuses. My wife fell silent, what was there to say? When the soul speaks through you, it needs no interpretation. It has a resonance, that even those still caught in the illusion can feel at some level. To varying degrees, it can be felt by all.

In that moment, as the aircraft rose into the air, flying us apparently to our bright, honeymoon destination, our marriage ended. As painful as it may have been, underneath, I was singing like a bird released. This 'ceremony' marked my transition through Gateway 2. I was now following my soul, soaring on the out-stretched wings of truth.

Gateway 2
- overview -

Confronting and releasing attachment
within the Second Density –
the plane of the emotions.

As your deepening engagement within the layers of inner consciousness strengthens, increasingly, you will notice the natural synchronistic order of life. Chance 'coincidences' reveal the underlying patterning of universal interconnectedness, and the realisation dawns that every event has a natural flow in harmony with a greater purpose. You notice that from time to time, you come into alignment with this movement – *this sense of rightness -* where everything feels totally magical and harmonious.

It is in these moments where you feel completely 'in the groove', that you have truly attuned to your soul, which is aligned with the Divine Flow.

Your very soul is the expression of this universal organising energy, although such internal guidance can be extremely hard to pick up on, and align with, especially in the beginning, because of the filters of conditioning that tend to keep diverting you into blind alleyways. Contrary to mainstream belief, joy, fulfillment and contentment are not ultimately attained by somehow trying to bend the universal organising energy to your will (even though for isolated periods it can be – which some people try to do through a misguided interpretation of "The Law of Attraction"). This simply ratchets up internal non-acceptance and makes you tight. Furthermore, you cannot possibly predict all the various machinations and configurations the impact of your veiled desires will have – *what karma might they create?* It ultimately leads to breakdown and failure – misalignment with the universe - no matter how materialistically successful you might at first appear to be. To be truly successful in life, is to realise the soul has a destined purpose: to express the majesty and the free flowing spontaneity of the One; in the form of the universal organising energy, which has the interests of **all sentient life** at heart…

> *How can you ultimately attain peaceful harmony in life, if your selfish actions consign some other sentient being (which is a part of your greater self anyway), to a lesser manifestation?*

Put simply, our Earth has finite resources, which at some point in our past, were sensitively and finely balanced with the needs of all sentient life here. Because mankind has become so 'successful' at exploiting tomorrow's resources today, and encouraging everyone to compete for them, it has led to over-population and the concurrent destruction of our biosphere. It is an exceptionally powerful mirror to everyone: how moving out of alignment with the natural organising energy, can have disastrous consequences.

The Gateway 2 transition, "Realignment", is all about re-attuning to the soul - the mainstream of which, is aligned with the universal organising flow, with the interests of all life at heart. As your consciousness expands, you find yourself naturally surrendering – *bit by bit, and ultimately completely* - to its supreme governance in your life. As you release the inner tightness of control, concurrently the joy of the divine floods in. It is a priceless feeling, which no efforted manifestation could ever surpass.

> *As the gathering wave of the Realignment sweeps through you, the magical moment arrives, when you go 'down on bended knee', and make the natural inner commitment, that all choices in life, will be those of the soul - **your highest truth** – totally aligned with the divine.*

You may find yourself asking: why is such a Realignment necessary? How did humanity become so far out of alignment?

At birth, the soul infuses into the bodymind and over time, begins to identify with it. Conditioned behaviours develop, forming closed loops of behaviour within the brain. In our dense and often harsh environment, the light of the soul begins to dim. If your parents are not sufficiently awake to continually remind you of your divine essence, or if negative external energies are too overpowering, then the soul begins to fragment and dissipate throughout the bodymind. If this happens (as it does in most cases), you lose connection to Unity Consciousness and the chakras begin to tighten and contract, such that they are no longer fully functioning as they were designed to. Over time, the distorted behaviour patterns further embed themselves in your psyche and you are removed from the experience of divine union...

This very human process of the soul fragmenting within, is mirroring in a microcosmic way, the universal macrocosmic process of light penetrating the darknesss and temporarily getting stuck, before breaking through.

As people awaken, the dissipated fragments of soul begin to reconnect, and slowly but surely, the soul gains increasing influence in one's life. As this reconnection gathers pace, your psychic capabilities begin to reveal themselves, tentatively at first, but then increasingly, as you respond more to your intuitive inner pull to act...

Where does this inner pull guide you to?

It is at this point that confusion can creep in. Sometimes by following the pull, synchronicity furnishes material 'success' in life, and so in the beginning, you may feel the temptation to use the new-found spiritual laws, applying intention to shape the universe to yield a desired outcome. This may indeed seem to work for a while, but the underlying purpose of the universe - *and that of your soul* - is to create learning experiences that you may realise you are already whole and complete, beyond illusionary desires or falsely perceived needs. This is true abundance: to express fully who you really are - *as an experience of the One* - and every incident conspires to help you dissolve more deeply into this sublime way of living...

> *"Desire is a judgment of the moment,*
> *saying "I judge this outcome is better than that one".*
> *It is caused by ignorance and fear,*
> *not trusting what the universe is unfolding.*
> *It is like applying the hand brake to a moving car,*
> *it leads to fate rather than destiny.*
> *Desire requires effort...*
> *Enlightenment requires lack of all effort."*
> *Openhand*

If trying to manifest an outcome, you are denying the absolute truth of the moment. You are, in effect, making a statement to the universe "I am not able to accept things as they are. I am not awesomely okay with life as it is". In which case, you are, **in that moment**, establishing internal separation from the One. You are creating an identity, which is incomplete in some way.

Your authentic being, on the other hand, fears nothing and can locate the blessing in all situations, even those which the ego may consider dark and difficult. The soul (when fully integrated) flows fearlessly as a wave of co-creative universal activity, exploring all darkness with the untainted curiosity of a small child. Whatever the darkness within, the soul will seek it out, so that you may confront, work with, and ultimately relinquish attachment to it; the soul is always seeking to become the master of circumstance, not the victim of it. You will increasingly feel this awesome majesty of authentic beingness as more of the soul reintegrates and infuses within (*providing you are working to open a space for it, that is*).

Mankind's immediate destiny is Ascension (should you choose it), which can only be fulfilled by transcending your attachments and the conditioned behaviours arising from them. If you try to manifest conditioned desires, you may create for yourself an apparently more cosy and abundant existence in the short term. However, if this is based on materialism, or indeed the need for any material outcome, you are likely to find yourself attuning more to denser vibrations that are now being unravelled and broken down, as opposed to the lighter, etheric ones of the New Paradigm which is beckoning you.

Ascension involves confronting the inner constrictions, opening out through them, and thereby continually attuning to the higher, etheric vibrations of the universal orchestra of co-creativity. These are found in every moment by accepting the denseness - *the heaviness of the base drum* - but not needing to change or shape it (at least not initially). In which case we do not identify with it or give it energy. Instead, you will begin to pick up the flow of lightness - the subtler instruments - which transcend the heavier vibrations...

> *"If you want to attune to lightness, you must be light;*
> *to be light, you must become effortless;*
> *to be effortless, you must surrender effort.*
> *The real secret therefore, is one of surrender...*
> *surrendering to the truth of the moment*
> *and being awesomely okay with that."*

So as you increasingly infuse soul, you are guided on a pathway of choices, each offering the opportunity to either gracefully surrender to the path, or give in to the conditioned desires of the ego. When you finally and completely accept that *every* incident is being shaped by what you are being on the inside, and that to struggle to manipulate or control external events is ultimately fruitless, then you are finally ready to step onto the internal super-highway of guided evolution. This "Realignment" happens as you surrender to the will of your soul. And it is one of the most profoundly beautiful experiences - as you truly recognise the real purpose of life, it will likely break you down into tears – *tears of homecoming joy.*

The ensuing pathway that emerges from this Realignment, soon reveals how *every single* incident, event or circumstance in your life offers the opportunity to recognise and release an attachment - where you either need a particular outcome in life or are resisting another. It is just such circumstances that constrict you, fragment the soul, and constrain your infinite liberation; they strangle the very life essence out of you. This tangled web of conditioned behaviours must ultimately be confronted and dug up at the roots.

Attachments arise from 'temporary amnesia' (by the soul), where you believe that a solution in the external world will somehow render the sense of completeness, that was always already present, and yet hidden under veils of illusion. When you suddenly realise the fruitlessness of trying to control circumstances that you have become identified with, and instead go inwards with razor edge honesty, then you bring to the situation the only lasting thing that can truly penetrate and dissolve it – *universal awareness.* You will ultimately discover the root cause of the attachment – *the source pain* - release it, and attune instead to that aspect of wholeness and self-acceptance that was already there in the background. This 'source pain' could be anything from a sense of worthlessness, self-blame, the need to control, being unsupported, being unlovable etc etc. You have to get into that, challenge and unwind it as the One, in order that the soul can then flow freely through it (I go into much greater detail about this inner process of confrontation and unwinding the source pain in Gateway 3 "The Transfiguration").

It is not just simply the case of releasing the attachment in order to proceed - this is another major misconception of the spiritual mainstream. Over the years, the attachment will have built fixed neural pathways of conditioned behaviours in the brain. Just like computer software, these are programs, which once initiated, have almost irresistible cycles of action and reaction that want to be fully played out. They can be sparked off by the seemingly most trivial of things: for example an image or photograph, a thought, a feeling, an emotion, the chance comment of a friend or an acquaintance. Such incidents act as touch points; once activated, these holographic imprints cause the brain to unleash powerful chemicals (neuropeptides) which then flood the body's cells, activating the full spectrum of emotional behaviour, including pleasure, comfort, creativity, security, control, worry, depression, fear, anger, rage, sexual urges, love, joy and the sense of contentment (to name but a few!). Through repetitive – *unconscious* - behaviours, you build networks of these pathways, which together form an 'identity' (see Gateway 3). Written from birth by the controlling thought forms prevalent in society, you end up running inner child programs that can taint your every choice, your every taste of reality.

Each program is animated with mental imagery, emotional essences and energetic blockages, all forming a virtual hologram - a prison cell - in which people then live. Over time, without even perceiving it, you are no longer acting authentically according to the soul's destined way of being. Ideally, as the soul, we should be continually painting our lives on a blank canvas, where the full palette of life's bounteous colours arise spontaneously into form, and then dissolve, without attachment, just as quickly. As the unfettered artist, we are meant to be totally free to create the next masterpiece of higher choice, not limited to painting by somebody else's numbers...

In Gateway 2 - the plane of the emotions - you are mostly confronting emotional attachment by the soul to a particular reality, for instance within interpersonal relationships.

Although you may relatively quickly realise and release the root cause of your attachment, you still have to dissolve the conditioned behaviour and pent-up emotional energy, which has been aligning you with the false path. Freely expressing these emotions and releasing them is very important – perhaps by crying or even letting yourself go into a temporary rage. Once the emotion has gone, then there is still the requirement to unwind the fixed behavioural programs that have caused the build-up of the emotional stress.

There is one sure way of doing this…

*It is to confront the programs, realise where you are being influenced, and then go deeply and honestly into the repetitive cycles of behaviour **as they are happening**. You have to catch yourself, **and interrupt them**, by opening a space through them.*

In that moment, where you may have previously given in to the pattern, if you can pause and centre deeply within the mainstream of the soul, then you will be made aware of an alternative way of being: a 'gift of beingness' will be revealed to you, offering an alternative choice of action – **Right Action** - one that is more aligned with your authentic pathway. For example, instead of always unsuccessfully seeking the right words to win an argument (perhaps because an inner sense of self-esteem was conditioned as 'winning'), you might instead, realise there is nothing to win, that self-esteem exists as a sense of the One, and so let the silence speak more profoundly than your words ever could. Paradoxically, you may find your silent, innate completeness, prospers in the interaction anyway.

Or it may be that you have been living your life to please others, afraid of speaking your truth for fear of how it may upset or harm another. Let us be clear, **no one** can be harmed by the truth. The greatest gift we can give to another, is to dispel an illusion, including one they may be holding about you. If they are living in a lie and you are sustaining that, you are in effect helping them be dependent on something that is an illusion; better to help them burst their bubble and invite them to deal with reality the way it really is. In so doing, you offer them the greatest gift of life itself - *an authentic choice.*

It is in circumstances such as these, that you begin to unleash the divine masculine and feminine energies arising through the soul. These can be equated to the qualities of purpose and surrender. One, the male aspect, furnishes the passion and courage to confront those issues holding you back; the other, the female aspect, invites you to be awesomely accepting of whatever is currently happening.

It is this acceptance that truly enables you to experience the fullness of the moment, without needing to change or pacify it – you are neither needing a particular outcome, nor resisting another.

When you can be quietly surrendered, even in a moment of great danger, and constantly opening into any internal contraction you may feel, then you may notice a spark of divine, synchronistic magic, calling you to act in a uniquely spontaneous way, with great emotional (but unattached) content - one which completely befits the moment.

If you can master the femininity of this vulnerability – *this surrendered openness* - you no longer fear being harmed, nor even death, and therefore you no longer fear life either. Paradoxically then, the very act of surrender, prepares you to act in a much more authentic, focussed and empowered way.

The masculine in you cannot achieve this by itself. It is too insensitive to pick up the subtleties, the purpose too strong to be fully dissolved and emotionally expressive in the moment. It requires the mastery of harmony between both energies...

"A true warrior is wise enough to know
when 'his' purpose is to surrender."

You will likely stumble in the beginning, but sooner or later, you realise you are not here to try to intention some magical new wonderland (*it already exists!*); rather you are here to unfold a way of being, which is completely at one with who you truly are. In this way, choices are made reflecting your highest truth. As the fixed neural pathways begin to dissolve (together with the emotional energy that loads them), your soul, which has until now been fragmented and dissipated throughout the bodymind, once more begins to reintegrate within your being. It is as if you are beginning to 'reconnect the dots' so to speak.

Furthermore, as you fall into line with the orchestra of universal co-creativity, increasingly, you align with the evolutionary path of our planetary system. If you can summon the courage to keep walking the path of transparent authenticity, Gateway 2 will magically yield and open before you. Some call this the "baptism", because it is as if you are being baptised as a disciple of your soul. In other words: you have reconnected and reintegrated enough of the soul to be able to attune to it on a regular basis; the soul's expansiveness becomes the driving force in your life, rather than the limiting ego...

> *Thus, the Realignment has taken place, and whilst you may still frequently go astray, there remains always the underlying conviction to follow the soul's guidance.*

You are now no longer being victimised by events. Instead, you are constantly realising yourself as the creator of every experience you are currently having – *it affords you the opportunity to become the master of life's circumstance.* You are continually remembering that to truly shape a new reality - ***that of destiny*** - you must attune to, and give yourself fully to, the physical, emotional and mental expression of authentic inner beingness, which then shines forth into the world from the depths of your soul. In this way, rather than trying fruitlessly to manipulate external events, you notice increasingly how the world around you begins to take shape as the ***direct result of this beingness.***

You have discovered a new way of creating, one that is truly aligned with the energetic organising flow of the universe: a flow that is ultimately inevitable and irresistible. Increasingly, you feel swept up in a flow of loving joy!

You are now very firmly aligned on the pathway leading to your Ascension, through ever higher levels of consciousness.

Transitioning Gateway 2
- essential tools -

1. **Opening the mind:** *observe yourself in all circumstances; find the lightness and natural harmony through all events.*

2. **Opening the Heart Centre:** *experience as much as possible of the stimulation and energy flowing through the six senses.*

3. **Receive the energy of the universe:** *notice an inner pull to act and follow the natural synchronistic flow of the moment.*

4. **Dealing with blockages and addictive behaviour:** *confront and deal with all exposed blockages and addictive behaviour.*

5. **Give yourself to your highest truth:** *give yourself entirely to the right expression of your highest truth, at whatever personal cost.*

1. Opening the mind: *observe yourself in all circumstances, find the lightness and natural harmony through all events.*

If you are observing yourself as you go through life, you will witness repetitive cycles and fixed patterns of behaviour. If you are to 'open the mind' and attune more to the soul, you must notice more the experiences that generate the following types of inner sensation...

- *completeness, wholeness and contentment*

- *expansiveness and timelessness*

- *joy, laughter and happiness*

- *freedom, liberation, lightness and well-being*

- *an inner warmth or subtle vibrations*

- *strong flows of purposeful and creative energy*

- *the feeling of complete acceptance of the moment*

- *the sense of being in a flow of rightness*

- *when we are feeling completely at one with who we are.*

When learning to follow the flow of the soul, it is important to get to know intimately the activities where you recognise these sensations and allocate as much time to them as possible. It could be sitting in stillness, but it could also be exercising or dancing, walking in the countryside, listening to favourite music or taking a bath with essential oils. It is about following those experiences where you feel completely 'in the groove' so to speak. Let us be clear though, it is not just a case of taking what appears to be the soft option. For example, fasting might cause initial discomfort, but the extraordinary lightness of being arising from it might far outweigh any perceived downside. Or taking a shower in cold water, which will likely cause you to retract sharply at first, but as you open out through the tightness and stop judging the feelings as negative, then a new vibrancy of aliveness will burst through. You must also watch for addictions - so drinking a glass of wine might help you feel expansive, but there are obvious detrimental side effects if you become dependent on it to achieve the soul's natural state of openness (I explore the spiritual way to deal with addictions fully in Gateway 3).

Whilst following your joy, it is essential to watch and connect with your feelings. In so doing, you are 'attuning' to the soul and growing its experience in your life. You become increasingly aware that the feelings are a part of your authentic beingness already; in other words, you do not have to manifest them, rather simply unveil them.

2. Opening the Heart Centre: *experience as much as possible of the stimulation and energy flowing through the six senses.*

We may define the "Heart Centre" as that aspect of the personality that is continually surrendering to the mainstream of the soul. If you like, it is the expanded Observer that now realises there is something much greater at work than egotistical desires and manifestations. It is the Heart Centre that recognises you are an integral part of the overall design. It 'hears' the quiet inner voice of the soul, notices the consistency of its beingness, and compels you to be completely at one with it. Although existing throughout the bodymind, its centre is frequently felt around the heart organ itself. As the Heart Centre activates, increasingly you begin to feel a 'pull', inviting you in a certain direction through life.

In order to strengthen this benevolently directing feeling, you need to open the Heart Centre further, by attuning to the experiences throughout the bodymind that generate the sublime taste of divine oneness: the feelings such as lightness, expansiveness, timelessness and infinite peace, that were discovered in the Awakening; and also those feelings that might move you emotionally to tears. So the key is to follow experiences that bring you joy as much as possible – *those which make your heart sing* – until you are tuning in consistently throughout the day.

During the experiences, it can greatly help to focus individually on those particular senses that are being activated in the moment, then attuning to the soul by feeling the joy, expansiveness, lightness and aliveness through them. Focussing on each sense individually aids concentration and therefore increases the effect. This can be catalysed more effectively by intensifying the sensations in the following ways...

i. **Sight:** expand the breadth of your focus - so when looking towards an object, see not just the object itself, but all in your field of view, especially the periphery, particularly noticing colours, shades and patterns of things.

ii. **Hearing:** notice all of the sounds in your environment - then focus on the ones that feel most aligned and resonant – those that foster a feeling of rightness inside. It is essential to feel the vibrations as well as hearing them.

iii. **Taste:** when eating, turn off as much background activity and external distraction as possible. Take the time to eat slowly, experiencing the texture of the food, chewing and tasting fully before swallowing.

iv. **Smell:** take the time to smell the natural aromas of the environment, such as that of flowers, cooking food or the natural scent of the body.

v. **Feeling:** connect deeply with the feelings within the body as you do things. So whilst walking for example, how does it feel as you place your feet on the ground and transfer your body weight from one foot to the other?

As you open more to the fullness of life in this way, the mind begins to quieten its internal chatter and you begin to feel more present, light and alive in the moment; you start to embrace the magnificent beauty and awesome majesty of life itself...

It helps you to bring more balanced emotional energy to any given situation – more charisma – which unleashes greater creative potential.

What is more, as the Heart Centre opens, your sixth sense - *that of intuition* - begins to strengthen. You notice more frequently how your attention is drawn to particular things: it could be a flower in bloom; the movement of a particular cloud formation; the lyrics of a favourite song. You start to feel the moment has a deeper sense of purpose and meaning, as if it is speaking to you *(like Chris' experience of the kestrel).*

As this begins to happen, instead of struggling to interpret what the situations might mean (which risks closing the soul down), instead simply ask "how does that make me feel inside?" Some signs might alert you to growing internal stress or tightness around a particular situation (or source pain), others will simply be a message of love and support. Your sixth sense is now attuning you to benevolent guidance and its continual outpouring of unconditional love.

If you keep noticing and following, then your intuitive capability expands rapidly. You begin to build a new vocabulary with Benevolent Consciousness, and the sense that you are being looked after intensifies. A deep inner knowing takes root: everything is going to be fine, you will be guided on the right path and you will not have to face anything you cannot cope with. As this inner trust blossoms, uplifting endorphins are released into the body counteracting the programmed addictions of your cellular memory. Endorphins are like the referee, levelling the playing field, ensuring you can express freely, fairly and authentically. Any general sense of tension, stress, doubt, fear and worry begins to dissolve away *(although at this stage, there will still be source pain and karma to deal with – see Gateways 3 and 4).* Your consciousness expands, bringing you ever closer to the Second Gateway.

3. Receive the energy of the universe: *notice an inner pull to act and follow the natural synchronistic flow of the moment.*

As your sixth sense strengthens, you begin to notice the natural synchronistic order of life and your inner pull to Right Action intensifies. Sometimes this pull can be felt as an energy through the Heart Centre; sometimes it is a simple inner knowing "this is what to do now". In which case, it will benefit you to always respond to that pull, because it is like building a reservoir of trust – one which begins to harness the flow within you.

In order to build trust in the universe, it is vitally important to understand where the pull leads. This is frequently where people on the path go astray, especially since so many mainstream philosophies speak of it leading to some destined outcome, or else one which you can intentionally shape. The point is, the soul is seeking out greater self-realisation.

Therefore it will guide you to events, circumstances and experiences that provide an opportunity to expose programmed behaviour patterns formed from an attachment to a desired outcome (or else a resisted one).

These are closed loops of behaviour - *blockages* - causing you to get tight, worried, angry, controlling or frustrated. They are like eddy currents in the divine flow. So the soul is not leading you to some rosy la la land – at least not initially!

How are such blockages created? For each of us, the soul is a unique harmonic of various universal characteristics - what we may call 'divine gifts of beingness' (see the "Seven Rays of Divine Impulse" under Gateway 4). These gifts are innate to the soul, but they need much time and patience to unveil and unleash. If the environment in which you grow is not sufficiently supportive or evolved, distorted repetitive cycles of behaviour form (this is largely unavoidable). So for example, someone who is being controlling of people is expressing the divine gift of will (the 'warrior energy') but in a distorted way - one that is trying to manipulate. Perhaps the love and support they received as a growing child was conditional to them conforming to a particular type of behaviour? In other words, "you'll only get this treat if you behave". Such conditioning can generate lack of trust in the natural flow of the universe and therefore program the need to control events and people.

Another example is someone who is overtly self sacrificing. In this way, they are expressing the divinely feminine characteristic of surrender, which has become distorted because they are dissolving their own truth. Paradoxically, in striving for greater harmony by placating other people's distortions, you may actually disempower them, by giving energy to their illusionary problems. Someone exercising this distortion, may take on too much themselves, thus lowering their vibration, and eventually becoming depleted or washed out. In effect, they are continually dissolving their own truth for the erroneously perceived benefit of another.

It is these blockages that prevent you realising your true potential in life and they must be dissolved out, if you are to unleash the full, unbridled radiance of the soul. So, when unleashed, the soul will begin to guide you on a path through life to confront them, by shaping mirroring situations and circumstances.

In the beginning, it is frequently difficult to feel, hear or intuit the inner pull of the soul, especially if you are not used to following your natural intuition. In which case, stillness is vital. Rather than always approaching your day with fixed ideas of what you must do, it will benefit greatly to spend as much time as possible "free wheeling". In other words, asking the following questions and responding to the answers that arise...

Free Wheeling...

i. **What would you have me do now?** Ask the universe "what would you have me do now?" Be still and wait for awareness to flow. Sometimes it will land as a flash of higher knowing inspiration; sometimes it will be a pull through the heart. Watch what thoughts and feelings arise; notice an inner pull to act. It will always become clear what you are being invited to do (including waiting until further clarity arises).

ii. **Follow the inner directive, observe what happens:** let the flow carry you and then notice what you observe. Usually the universe will reveal one of three things: (a) a distortion you are being invited to deal with; (b) a gift of beingness to unveil; (c) Right Action that now wants to happen.

iii. **Celebrate the synchronicity, feel the unfolding:** it becomes a real joy to witness, and to celebrate the synchronistic interplay that unfolds around you. Commit yourself to the guidance you are receiving; feel the inner expansion.

If you keep practising this technique of listening to and following the soul, then you will notice more and more, your inherent ability to flow with the universe; it is entirely natural, but as with any other skill, you must practice and hone it, if you are to master it. The most important thing to realise is, that flowing with the universe brings you directly to your attachments and judgments of the moment (where you are perceiving the situation as 'good' or 'bad'; where you need a particular outcome or are resisting another). And in Gateway 2, you are mostly dealing with emotional attachments – because you have begun to act on the emotional plane. You are being invited to break through these and unleash authentic beingness, which stimulates the soul more strongly. So if you encounter situations where you are caused to get irritable, angry, frustrated or tight, it is not the universe having some great cosmic joke at your expense! No, you can be absolutely sure that you have made the right choices. These internal barriers and blocked emotional energies are exactly the ones that need to be confronted and dissolved if you are to continue to evolve.

4. Dealing with surface level resistances and attachments: *confront and deal with attachments as they arise*

It is vital to say, that all these surface level attachments have a deeper source pain, which you may not yet be in a place to touch. And getting too wrapped up in the density at this stage can be counterproductive if you have not yet fully felt the flow of the soul, infusing your nature and guiding you. It is important therefore, leading up to Gateway 2, to focus on building the sense of soul (recognising that there will undoubtedly be deeper levels of density to deal with further down the path).

Most surface level attachments are caused by subtle levels of fear: needing to control the inherent uncertainty of life; believing you must achieve a certain goal or attain a particular degree of security; efforting to get your just 'rewards' in life; being attached to an outdated relationship; needing to occupy time; or wanting to be loved. These are just a few of the many and varied examples.

Attachments program people to particular lifestyles. It is these conditioned behaviours that society then 'preys' upon in order to maintain 'business as usual'. Most people consider themselves free to make choices in life, when in actual fact, choices are mostly made to placate these subtle levels of fear and sense of lack...

These attachments create inner tightness and resistance to the natural fluidity of the moment. You know you are in one, when you cannot conceive of flowing freely with another option.

At this point, it is worthwhile to recognise, that you are probably reading this book because you realise, at the very least, some basic universal truths:

i.   That you are the One

ii. That you already have everything you need within

iii. That you do not require the situation to go a particular way

iv. That you cannot ultimately be harmed by the worst possible outcome of any given situation – even death is merely the passing on into another form of life.

You can use these knowings to confront the surface level and emotional, fear-based control mechanisms, in order for the soul to break in and break through. In this way, it can take over more of the natural guidance in your life. Here below is how you can confront such programmed attachments.

Dealing with fear and control:

i.   **If fear or control is arising, directly confront it:** Imagine the worst possible outcome if you did not fulfill the conditioned behaviour which is expected of you (being honest to a work colleague, friend or relative for example). Consider it, and go deeply into it. Ask: "what is the worst possible outcome that could happen?" See the images and feel the emotional reaction. Work to realise that you are the eternal, which will always be unaffected by the outcome; nothing can change your inherent completeness. When you can accept this, it liberates you from the need for the situation to go a particular way. The attachment dissolves.

ii. **Breathing:** When you experience fear, worry, control or the nervousness of desire, the chest tends to tighten and the breathing becomes shallower. It causes you to identify more with the unfolding drama. In this situation, practice deep, rhythmic breathing, bringing the energy of the universe into all areas of the body.

iii. **Tense and relax the body:** In fear, worry or nervousness, the body tightens and builds eddy currents of dense energy, which negatively influence free-flowing action – they restrict the natural authenticity of the soul. A good way to release this tightness, is to tense and relax the parts in which you feel the tightening. This way, the stress can be dissolved and a greater level of relaxation restored.

You will also likely find yourself having to confront addictions, that have been built up due to society's unhealthy lifestyles; such as food and consumables that are purposefully designed to entrap people, causing them to want to consume ever more. However, rather than using a basic approach of excessive discipline, which tends only to create the 'forbidden fruit syndrome' (you crave it more!), it is important to identify and honour the cause of the addiction - they usually overwrite and replace a particular sense of infusing soul...

So if you can access the authentic source feeling of the soul, and give energy to that instead, you are likely to be much more successful at breaking the addiction.

Here then, is an invaluable five step approach for breaking addictions, which incorporates this essential truth...

Soul-based, Five Step Process for Dealing with Addictions:

i. **Accept the programmed behaviour has a purpose:** First, accept the programmed addiction is there for a purpose, which is to help you learn something about yourself *(how to be in the physical, but not of the physical, for example)*. It is also a microcosmic reflection of the wider process of light getting stuck in the darkness throughout the universe and then breaking free. And so it is not your fault that these attachments happen within you. Contemplate this deeply, work to let go of self-judgment, and become accepting of the 'problem' (everyone has similar issues of one form or another).

ii. **Do not fight the program, become 'present with it':** When you are completely accepting of the addiction, and being truthful with yourself about it, you do not tighten around the issue and make it worse than it already is. So, rather than fighting the behaviour, initially experience it as much as you need to. For example, if you cannot resist eating, smoking, drinking, being angry or controlling etc. keep on doing it, be absolutely clear not to feel bad about it; but also be completely honest about the distortion. And crucially, allow yourself to feel into the addiction *as you are fulfilling it.* Often there will be some kind of consciousness 'blindspot', where you become unconscious. This is where the addiction begins to 'own' you. Become intimate with these feelings – *as they are happening* – by being present with them, within the addictive experience.

iii. **Ask how the addiction replaces authentic beingness?** When you are satiated with your 'fix' which each addiction fulfills, ask what does this behaviour give you on the inside? With anger, it might be the release of frustration; with arrogance, it might be self-esteem; with timidity, it might be humility; with alcohol, it might be the feeling of relaxation; over-eating might generate the sense of comfort and wholeness; tobacco, could provide the sense of confidence; caffeine, the sense of aliveness and empowerment. Now settle into that positive feeling, which the repetitive cycle has provided, knowing that the feeling is inside of you all the time, without the need of the addictive substance or behaviour to initiate it.

iv. **Stoke the inner flame of the soul:** Over time, you will discover an 'inner flame' - *the soul* - which begins to smoulder around the feelings of authentic beingness, and grows stronger the more you focus on it. As you stoke this developing flame, it becomes stronger, until ultimately you realise it is the **only** inner essence worth having. What is more, you begin to witness how the addiction has downsides that can diminish or even extinguish this inner flame. There has to be a worthwhile reason to give up the addiction - what better than the unleashing of your unbridled and authentic True Self?

v.   **When the flame is high enough, make the higher choice:** Once you have discovered how to find the flame without any external influence, and you know that the addiction ultimately extinguishes the flame, then at some point, you will be ready to give up the addiction and make the higher choice - that which has the power to make you feel good *the whole time.*

There are likely to be many occasions before this point is reached where you give in to the addictive behaviour; be awesomely okay with that, but keep watching and being completely honest with yourself about it. Eventually you will make the realisation, that nothing can truly ignite the fullness of your destined flame of beingness, but your own inner focus; however, the inner flame has to be high enough first, in order to make that authentic choice.

This approach helps to break through the surface level identities that, in many cases, will have likely been controlling your life.

The breakthrough begins to create inner space. It means that the light of the soul can be kindled more strongly within, which you may feel as a soft warmth, a sense of stillness, peace and expansiveness, joy and timelessness. These are the feelings to nurture and grow in the build-up to Realignment. *(It is important to note, that such initial 'disassociation' from the density can be so blissful, that it creates the sense of an enlightened state. It is often the case that people think they have already attained Enlightenment. However, later on down the path, as the soul kindles more strongly, it will begin to activate the much deeper source pain – see Gateway 3).*

5. Give yourself to your highest truth: *give yourself, as much as possible, to the right expression of your highest truth, at whatever apparent personal cost.*

Once you have been watching your programs for some time, you will probably begin to notice, in each daily interaction, a pregnant pause where a choice is being offered before the moment is born. Whereupon, you can either give in once more to the program wanting to activate, or alternatively, express a more authentic aspect of beingness - your highest truth.

This can be felt as an upwelling – often emotional - through your body. You are being invited to be a certain way and then to express Right Action from that place *(just as Chris overcame the expected or needed response, and was able to open a space for the truth of his soul... "I love you, but I am not IN love with you.").*

When you sense this, it is important to give full mental, emotional and physical expression to the energy you are feeling. Such Right Action is immensely creative, because you are drawing on the consciousness of the soul, flowing down from the Source. In effect, you are harnessing the full creative power of the One, which always flows in upon the activation of authentic beingness. *(I will explore more fully the key aspects of authentic beingness – the inherent qualities of the soul – in Gateway 4).*

Summary of effective approach for transitioning Gateway 2

To summarise this 'essential tools' section for transitioning Gateway 2 and walking the spiritual path in day-to-day life, I have designed this 'spiritual compass', which I call "Openhandway". It is about recognising that every moment in life configures around the deeper, underlying, universal purpose, which is self-realisation. The Realignment is about surrendering into this, as a way of life, accepting that you co-create every situation with the universe in order to teach you something, to evolve and grow...

and there is absolutely nothing else going on!

It is a four step process, which helps you break down, and make sense of, the underlying impulses that are infusing and influencing you as the soul begins to activate in your life. Often, there is a confusing conflict that goes on between the authentic impulses of the soul, and the conditioning of the ego. Many people have found this spiritual compass of great help in untangling the confusion.

Openhandway can be summarised as follows:

i. **Open mind:** *move into the place of the Observer of yourself.* You become the OBSERVER of all arising thoughts, emotions and feelings. You observe the internal effects to external events without forming judgment either of yourself or others. In understanding that the central purpose of life is greater self-realisation, you simply witness the truth about each arising situation. In so doing, you work to release internal attachment and tightness to desired or resisted outcomes.

ii. **Open heart:** *connect with the consciousness of all life around you.* From the place of the Observer, you begin to liberate yourself from attachment to the external drama. By bringing attention down into the heart, internal tension eases. You can then explore the full beauty of life through your five senses, and feel the subtle vibrations of Unity Consciousness. The Heart Centre opens more and your psychic senses begin to activate. You start to taste the full depth and divine majesty of the moment. The inner flame of the soul is kindled.

iii. **Receiving hand:** *receiving the energy of the universe and opening into blockages.* The consciousness of the soul infuses within. You begin to receive internal impulses to make higher truth choices in life. You are caused to confront conditioned behaviour patterns formed from attachments by the ego to desired or resisted outcomes. By identifying these internal blockages, and then softening into them, you release pent-up emotional pain and deeper trauma. You expand into the tightness they generate, dissolve them, and thereby begin to open an internal space for Right Action to flow.

iv. **Giving hand:** *give yourself completely to your perceived Right Action.* By dissolving conditioned behaviours, you begin to open an internal space through which the soul can shine forth. You attune deeply by applying yourself to full energetic, mental, emotional and physical expression of this authentic beingness. You give yourself completely to "Right Action" – the natural consequence of soul infusion, which is totally aligned with the universal flow. You observe magical, supportive synchronicity. What's more, you literally drop into the Void of Presence within - a crystal clear space of infinite potential. You are becoming "the Seer" - you are coming home to 'who' you truly are. As this happens, it is as though all the fruitless searches of your life become answered.

In 'receiving hand', it is important to say that at this level, whilst progressing Gateway 2, it is likely that you will only be going into surface level emotional pain and working to release that. As you get deeper into the process, during Gateways 3 and 4, then you will begin to process the much deeper source pain and karma.

When persistently applied, Openhandway aligns you with your true path in life. You realise your journey is an inner one, where the outer world is created by unveiling and shining forth what you are being within. If you continue to follow this path, although it is not at all easy, you discover you are endowed with exactly the right skills and gifts to evolve.

Unfolding these gifts brings true majesty of being and boundless joy of living. To me, it is the purpose of life itself.

Transitioning Gateway 2
- general misconceptions -

1. **That you are already enlightened:** at the Awakening, the sense of release can sometimes be so powerful and so liberating that you may think you have already attained Enlightenment. It may feel like there is nothing left to do. However, to be in a state of Enlightenment, is to know yourself as the Seer (Pure Presence), and to know this state in and through **all** experiences **all** the time. It is definitely not to be in subtle avoidance of life, which I have observed frequently happens. It is important to follow the path, and allow yourself to feel ever deeper into any resistance or pent-up trauma. Simply dissociating from this, without fully dealing with it, might appear very attractive and generate a sense of expansive peace, however it risks creating a spiritual identity, which is not fully aligned with the authentic flow of the soul, and is therefore not truly in an enlightened state.

2. **There is no such thing as duality:** as you awaken, you begin to experience the inner and outer worlds unfolding into one; you taste the consciousness uniting all things. It is at this point, people frequently speak of the illusion of duality - that there is no such thing, "there is only oneness". I agree, there is only oneness throughout the universe: however, oneness is expressed through multiplicity of form. If there were no "this" and "that", there would be no relativity and therefore no experience. There has to be one thing relative to another for there to be an experience at all. So in enlightened states, you learn to hold a divine paradox: you are being the "all of it" in any one moment, and **at the same time**, you are being a unique – *relativistic* - experience of that as the soul; there is still a perceived duality, even if, at the absolute level of the Seer, separation is ultimately an illusion.

3. **Denial of the natural flow:** when you choose to, you are directed by the soul, flowing to ever increasing unity, through higher and higher vibrational states of consciousness. Especially where someone might erroneously think they are already fully enlightened, the mind tends to want to reject the guiding synchronicity of the soul and the inner pull to act; it can deny the natural flow through all events. This seems to be caused mostly by an unwillingness to accept the concept of perceived duality i.e. that you are whole, and yet **simultaneously**, a unique expression of wholeness walking your own unique path, having your own unique experience. Or, it could be that some are unwilling initially to accept the Divine Purpose, helping all to align with the natural harmony and flow of the universe. Since they may be unwilling to embrace this guidance, there can be a tendency to deny the flow back to unity i.e. the flow of the soul.

4. **Intention led manifestation:** when you begin to observe the synchronistic order of life, there comes the realisation of how your inner beingness is shaping and creating the events and circumstances of your outer life. You see that when you are being tight, doubting or fearful, you manifest exactly those consequences you fear. Conversely, if you are being loving, warm and compassionate, there is a tendency to draw those experiences to you instead (by The Law of Attraction). However, with this realisation, there often arises the temptation to try to intentionally shape your inner configuration of consciousness to create those circumstances in the outer world that you might most desire (which is actually ego-based). You often hear people advocating 'purposefully shaping your thoughts to manifest the abundance you want'. Whilst this form of manifestation or affirmation might appear to be initially successful, its application tends to override the flow of the moment, forming new layers of inner conditioning, which must also be unwound at some point in the future (if you are to continue to evolve). It creates an

identity, which is non-accepting of our absolute authentic reality and disconnects you from the true path of your soul. In my experience, authentic manifestation happens as a direct result of **Being**; misguided manifestation, on the other hand, happens as a result of what your ego may be wanting or intending. So the key is to open an internal space for beingness to arise naturally, as a response to your feelings in relation to external events, and then to let authentic doing - *Right Action* - follow as a direct consequence of that. Ultimately, it leads to a life of joyful non-efforting and contented, peaceful acceptance. The awesome majesty of the moment is deeply appreciated without the need to control it.

5. **Misconceived 'selfishness':** it seems to be an often held misconception, that it is selfish to focus on your own development, when there are other people less fortunate than you, who might be in some kind of difficulty, and whom you might feel obliged to help instead. In my view, to truly help another is to remind them who they really are; and the most powerful way to do that, is to stand in your truth and shine your own light as brightly as possible. Frequently, you will come across people who are in some kind of pain or suffering. However, if you move from your centre of awesome okayness and identify with their illusion, the risk is you continue to support that illusion by giving energy to it, which is disempowering for both them and yourself. Instead, if you continue to stay centred in your own power of beingness, there is a greater tendency to break down the illusion of suffering, and help others move to that place of inner completeness themselves. It may well be selfish to focus on the individual intentions and desires of the ego, however, to me, it is most definitely not selfish to follow your soul. In so doing, you align with the guiding hand of Benevolent Consciousness, the purpose of which is to awaken and enlighten all. How can that possibly be selfish?

Transitioning Gateway 2
- indicators of beginning -

Following the Gateway 1 Awakening, it is typical to experience an extended period of at-one-ment with the universe, which might be described as 'awesome okayness'. The illusion of separation has been, at least partially, lifted. At this point, it is understandable if the feeling arises to detach from society or at least to remain, but emotionally disengage from it. However, if you continue to open and infuse soul, there comes a point where you begin to observe the magic of synchronicity and become aware of an inner pull to act...

It is the organising energy of the
universe acting through your soul.

If you follow this calling, and act according to what you feel is your highest truth, you will likely notice the effects of your actions are threefold:

i.   to dispel an illusion either yourself or another is labouring under

ii. to find and express the light inside of yourself

iii. to generate a deep soulful resonance, thereby helping someone else find their own inner light.

Such experiences are food for the soul and, in my experience, the more we follow them, the more uplifting it becomes for everyone. You become a catalyst for change: the resonance of your very soul, 'agitates' Unity Consciousness to break free within the darkness, which builds as an unstoppable wave, to encourage and uplift others too.

You soon realise this as the one true purpose of the universe – *bringing light into darkness* - and that to align with this purpose, is to remove any internal barriers which limit your ability to uplift both yourself and others. When you are deeply feeling this compulsion to divine service, you are truly stepping onto the spiritual path; you are moving quickly towards Gateway 2.

Specifically, you will likely be experiencing some, or many, of the following...

- *increasing intensity of experience through the five senses*

- *noticing external events are being shaped more by your beingness*

- *the presence of divine guidance and an increasing inner 'pull' to act in accordance with an underlying deeper purpose*

- *you reach a crossroads in life, where some of the major circumstances, such as career or relationships, are changing*

- *quite frequently you experience spontaneous 'inner knowing' about the path forward and deep understandings about life*

- *general increase in intuitive and psychic capability, your sixth sense is activating*

- *increasing occurrence of synchronicity, which becomes a guiding aspect of your life*

- *you begin to notice your actions invite an enlightening and uplifting effect in others: you are helping them discover their soul.*

Transitioning Gateway 2
- indicators of completion -

Stepping through Gateway 2 is a deeply emotive experience. Probably for the first time, you will have discovered true purpose and meaning for your life. You find yourself compelled by truth, or at least the truth as you know and feel it. You sense an incredible joy of moving into divine service. It becomes increasingly difficult for you to live in a lie. If you are being untruthful or dishonest with yourself or others, you will feel it strongly in your heart as a movement away from peace and harmony. As you transition this Realignment, essentially, you will always be feeling the inner compulsion to act in a way that expresses your highest truth.

Whilst you will certainly not always get it right (in terms of alignment with the divine flow), the driving motivation is to find your authentic and genuine way of being in every moment, which increasingly brings you at one with the divine. Consequently, more often than not, someone who has transitioned Gateway 2, will be in the place of the Observer of themselves, and their motivations for action, most of the time. You will be responding to your inner pull, watching keenly both the outward and inward effects of your actions. You will be familiar with the fact that all incidents are shaped to help reveal inner blockages and invite you to remove them. You will have become quite adept at dealing with these programs. You accept fully that you are the cause of your own state of being and do not blame another if their actions appear to cause you to lose inner peace; you know that your inner state of consciousness is the cause, not them – that you have manifested the situation through the Law of Attraction. In this way, you are becoming the master of life's circumstances not the victim of them.

The third eye will be at least partially open, which means you will be seeing reflections of yourself in people and circumstances. This in turn may lead to prophetic visioning and dreaming.

For someone who has undergone the Realignment, it will be your naturally arising purpose to be consciously engaged in every single moment. You will be making a **constant conscious choice**.

In summary then, the following are key indications you have transitioned Gateway 2...

- *you are in the place of the Observer of yourself through most events*

- *you are following inner guidance most of the time*

- *there grows an increasing ability to interpret signs and synchronicity - it ultimately becomes second nature*

- *as the Heart Centre opens, you tend to lose judgmentalism of others*

- *there develops an increased ability to sense and feel universal life energy*

- *a deep recognition unfolds of the soul in all life, and a growing ability to read your own path and have insights into those of others*

- *as the third eye opens, you begin to see yourself reflected in others as a matter of course*

- *there is likely to be increased occurrence of prophetic dreaming and visioning*

- *an inner commitment arises within you to be consciously engaged in every single moment.*

Gateway 2
- summary -

After the Gateway 1 Awakening, you may be forgiven for thinking "This is it, I've found what I'm looking for, there is no need for me to do anything else, all I have to do is to be." If only life were so simple! As St Augustine said...

"If thou shouldst say it is enough, I have reached perfection
all is lost, for it is the function of perfection,
to make one know one's imperfection".

So it is, when you have rested in your Awakening on the 'park bench of life' for a while, then an inner calling begins to stir: something is drawing you forwards. It is the distant call of a long lost friend: your very own soul. In every single moment, situation and circumstance, there is a universal organising energy at work, which is seeking to express the One, and your soul is the vehicle for that divine expression...

You are now beginning to discover the true purpose of life itself.

Just like the kestrel in Chris' Gateway 2 sharing, truth may arise as a spontaneous inner knowing, or you may feel it as an inner pull through the Heart Centre. It brings you to the very precipice of authentic choice, which you can no longer deny. An increasingly open Heart Centre gives you the courage and strength to surrender to the inner calling of your soul. If you elect to follow, you soon discover the path is not an easy one. Whilst you may quickly realise that to effort is to take you off the path, to give up or accept that 'anything-goes' is equally distorted and fruitless. A careful balance needs to be discovered: the centre path between the energies of purpose - *the inner warrior* - and that of surrender - *the goddess of sublime femininity.*

The destiny of Gateway 2, is to discover the inner harmony of these two energies: how to balance them in any given circumstance. In search of this harmony, the warrior will draw you fearlessly into situations to confront outdated patterns of behaviour. The ego is then invited to yield itself - to surrender on the altar of expanded awareness.

Where previously you may have closed down your senses in the jaws of danger, instead, you are now being invited to open up; to become absolutely vulnerable; to drink the moment in through every pore, until you release the attachment, and therefore the fear no longer imprisons you. You are progressively being liberated to express authentic gifts of divine beingness.

In so doing, you soon discover you are walking the miraculous path of co-creative activity - an harmonious symphony - where every single chance happening yields a hidden code, detailing the blueprint of your inherent nature. If you continue to open and not struggle, you quickly discover you have a powerful aptitude for this new language: it is your mother tongue, the language of love. The code benevolently strips away your conditioning, unveiling who you really are.

There are many diversions on the passage through Gateway 2. The Matrix of humanity's conditioned thinking readily deceives people, offering new temptations, new ways to shape the drama: the promise of manifesting your dreams, but whose dreams are they? If you are not careful, you may find yourself once more burdened by the yoke of materialistic desire. It does not even have to be the desire for a material possession or increased abundance; the allure of that as yet undiscovered soulmate for example, can send you once more into a downward tailspin. Find completeness first, and that partner who is your true mirror, will effortlessly appear before you.

So it is highly likely you may stray from the path and disappear off along one of life's diversionary meanderings, but with the new expanded awareness of an awakened soul, it is unlikely to be too long before you realise your progress has been thwarted. In whichever blind alley you may find yourself, you must once more become the Observer, open your mind, that the Heart Centre may also fully open, and receive the energy of the universe building under your outstretched wings. If you can then summon the courage to give only of your highest truth, you will once more find yourself effortlessly soaring the thermals, majestically swooping and diving into the moment, with the finest expression.

It is all about being finely poised, in the drama, but not of the drama; fully engaged and giving of your best, but not limited, or confined, by the need for an outcome, because you have ultimately realised this only strangles the real juice out of life. It is about having freedom from society's demands for a given outcome, so that you may flow spontaneously with the formlessness of universal consciousness and respond uniquely as the moment truly requires...

> "The real secret is surrender... letting go to what is,
> because the universe has a natural design all of its own...
> it is continually flowing back to higher degrees
> of unity and oneness.
> And if we just let go and surrender,
> we can attune to that flow back, like a surfer riding a wave;
> we don't dictate where the wave goes,
> we just ride it and enjoy the ride!"
> Openhand

When you are truly walking the path in this way, you discover it is one of divine service: service to your higher self and to all life - there is simply no difference between the two.

> This does not mean however a kind of wishy washy non committal attitude to life. Not at all! It means diving into the fullness of who you truly are and unleashing the unbridled expression of that in every moment. It is then that you find yourself riding on the wave of the divine.

In service to the One Life, you realise that the light of love shines with many colours. For example, to help another might be to kick away their crutch of disempowerment. However difficult this may seem at the time, eventually you unfold the strength to burst someone else's illusionary bubble without fear of what the on-looking crowd might say. It is then you know with certainty, that you have stepped through Gateway 2.

This Realignment brings with it the unmistakable feeling of 'coming home'. You have now reconnected enough of the soul to feel its overwhelming inner yearning, and the infusion of consciousness is likely to melt you frequently into tears. You feel abundantly blessed with divine support within the simplest of things. You are now joyfully and irrevocably embarked on the path of divine service - that which serves all.

Gateway 3

"Transfiguration"

*"Integral wisdom involves a
direct participation in every moment:
the Observer and the observed are dissolved
in the light of pure awareness,
and no mental concepts or attitudes
are present to dim that light."*

Lao Tzu

The Key: walk the path

From the Chris Bourne's memoirs...

For some time I had been 'walking the path', following the magical roller coaster ride of my soul. Benevolent Consciousness had miraculously provided a one bedroom flat for me, on a quiet working farm, in the rolling Hampshire countryside. Many joyful hours were spent connecting with the trees, the birds and natural wild life.

My sensitivity to Unity Consciousness was deepening hour by hour. What had begun as sporadic acts of occasional synchronicity, were fast evolving into streaming co-creative action. As much as possible, I had abandoned mind-led questions; they seemed to interfere with the natural flow of divine magic. Instead, authentic questions about the nature of reality arose spontaneously from within. When they did, I observed they were always immediately answered, perhaps by the movement of a particular cloud formation, the swaying of branches or the sudden darting movement of a swift. Without the constriction of mind-led intention, my consciousness was directed to where it was meant to go and it became abundantly clear to me what was being said. This was the language of pure knowing, as if I had opened a direct telepathic connection to the cosmic library. When open, I would receive constant downloads of information. On the other hand, if I was struggling to understand or subtly trying to manifest something, the channel would be closed off instantly.

From day to day, I would simply flow from an inner pull to act, no more the restrictive limitation of a conditioned and constrained personality. I was as a surfer on a powerful wave of co-creative synchronicity. As I followed the divine flow of energy, it appeared that everything was falling into place, happening just as it was meant to. A carpet of golden light was unfolding before my feet. It quickly became clear to me that the pathway was leading to experiences exposing repetitive patterns of conditioned behaviours, which in the past had limited me. With each event, I would notice any inner tightness arising: why can it not happen this way? Why is that person acting the way they are? Why have I lost my sense of inner peace? I was being guided to choices and situations where I was identifying with the external drama; where perhaps I wanted something outside of myself to make me feel content, whole, loved, successful or fulfilled, when all the while, the only thing that could yield these prizes, was dissolving into my very own inner being; the fullness and completeness of the True Self.

At the time, I was still working in web development as the Managing Director of a fast growing company, but it was becoming increasingly difficult to take life in the Matrix seriously. With each person I encountered, I could often see where they were stuck, what their key issues in life were and how they might unlock the inner doorways limiting them. It seemed like a natural aptitude that could help people move forward. I also encountered others who simply did not want to know - they somehow seemed content being victimised by events, continually struggling and efforting to create some illusionary prize of security, self-esteem or wealth.

These people seemed unable to realise that it was exactly this tightness that was creating the repetitive patterns of experience in their lives; events that continually locked them into a virtual prison. I felt deep compassion for them, but in such cases, I could do little. At first it created tightness in me. I wanted the whole world to wake up and see the real magic of life unfolding all around us; that beauty was not to be found in some singular separate creation - a house, a car or some big new deal - it was to be found in the miraculous weave connecting all life. I wanted everyone just to stop, breathe deeply, and take a look around them, but alas, many were just not ready for that. They were too lost and I had to learn to surrender to that.

As the inner journey continued to unfold, a wonderful juxtaposition happened. It was almost as if I began to look forward to the moments of tightness, to the situations where I was plunged once more into the darkness, for I knew it was just a question of time before I would bob back up to the surface again, to feel the warming sunlight of unconditional love. As I unwound each distortion, where I had desired a particular outcome, I experienced expanding outwards, unfolding my consciousness to embrace ever finer tastes of Pure Presence. What need had I of material manifestation, what need of the approval or the acceptance of others? I was being filled with the universe: the more I let go, the more I opened up, and the more my inner emptiness was filled.

Then suddenly, out of the blue, 'it' happened. At the time, I was not sure what 'it' was, but as in my Awakening, it was just as powerful, just as earth shattering. Yet again, gaping holes were punched into the fabric I had come to know as reality. It happened on a hilltop overlooking the farm where I now lived and worked. As on the roof of the Las Vegas Hilton, I found myself being washed through by wave upon wave of unconditional love, sending ripples of energy seemingly through every cell of my being. Suddenly, in a virtual inner reality, what you might call a lucid dream, the top of my head lifted off and my soul was launched skywards, rocketing into the heavens as a blazing stream of light. I departed our dense atmosphere in the seeming blink of an eye, shot through our solar system and into the unknown, marvelling wide-eyed at spectacular supernova and astral sunrises. Unbeknown to me at the time, this was my mental pictorialisation of a physical phenomenon known as a "full kundalini activation", where the consciousness that is the soul, is released from the bodymind in sufficient quantity to shoot up the spine into the pineal gland - the location of the third eye.

In the lucid dream, I found myself heading towards a black spot in the faraway cosmos - the centre of our galaxy. Even from millions of miles, I could sense its density sucking everything towards it including me. As I drew closer to the black hole, I could feel the magnitude of its denseness consuming all around it. Then suddenly I was inside it, racing downwards, accelerating ever faster into this seemingly bottomless pit. In the earth-shattering speed, my flesh began to ripple and then tear away, followed by bones, then thoughts, ideas and emotions, all constructs of the reality I had always known, until I became a stream of energy, which the immense gravitational force was now compressing and compacting until I found myself being reduced to a ball of light.

When the bottom of the abyss came into view, I could see that at its centre was some kind of immensely dense focal point, like a massive lens, towards which I accelerated. Fears were materialising, but I sensed the need to just keep letting go, there was no relevance for them any more, so they were stripped from me at the instant of arising. This enabled me to keep softening and expanding. It was as though the black hole was purging my very soul. Suddenly I was sucked into the core of the black hole – the focussing lens – upon which, a massive explosion of light occurred, as though the Big Bang was somehow being re-enacted. And equally amazingly, "I" (whoever I now was) diffused through, with a new form taking shape on the other side of this focussing lens. It was spectacular, and now my consciousness seemed to expand out to fill the universe, into a place of infinite, contented peace – pure bliss!

Later, I came to realise that in being able to let go to that extent, I had avoided the effects of this cosmic explosion, without which, surely even my soul would have been obliterated. As it turned out, I'd softened through this 'Big Bang' and come out of the other side into a state of profound peace and stillness. There was only the sense of oneness, infinite absolute potential, nothing arising not even an 'I'. There was sheer openness with everything, and with no separation. I had slipped through a hole in the canvas of reality and become infinite non-identified presence, the Seer of all things, the ghost in the machine. Time stood still, I was embracing eternity.

Then from nowhere the question arose: "Who is here to experience this?" There was no desire to answer the question, for that would mean something would have to emerge to create experience and any experience might shatter the stillness of this perfect nirvana. But the question had arisen from somewhere. Perhaps a wafer thin slither of identity had somehow slipped through the black hole and now wanted to own this experience? Infinite stillness became a material experience of bliss, something my re-emerging mind could handle. I didn't know it then, but this inner "shadow" had come to own my absolute freedom. Then, suddenly the shadow had gone, an imposter stealing away into the night. Yet somehow I knew it had not gone, it was hiding somewhere in the far recesses of my inner universe, somewhere that could no longer be seen. The shadow was a fraudulent trickster, seeking to own my spontaneously flowing soul, but there was no time for him right now, the material experience of bliss was simply too alluring. I would have to deal with him later.

Reintegration into humanity's Matrix of conditioned thinking was difficult this time! The framework of normal reference, was for me, completely shattered. Fragmented fixed neural pathways were no longer an adequate means to express the beauty of my soul, which I was now tasting in its fullness. I could feel the essences of what I somehow knew to be the Christ and Buddha Consciousness. Day-to-day existence seemed at best an irrelevance, at worst a lie - a gross distortion of truth, that I could no longer entertain. Those around me - my colleagues, friends and family - found great difficulty in relating to me as I now was. The old me had completely vanished, vaporised into the ether, and few, if anyone who knew me, could cope with that.

I had transitioned Gateway 3 and there was no going back. It was now all or nothing.

Gateway 3
- overview -

Transitioning the Third Density -
the material plane of the intellect.

The Transfiguration is yet another powerful transition, and arguably the defining moment of your spiritual unfolding. As you follow your destined pathway, you continue to reconnect and reintegrate fragments of soul dissipated throughout the bodymind and the mainstream of the soul gains stronger and stronger influence in your life...

After a great deal of inner purification and soul searching, you are finally ready for the incredible shift of inner perception, from being an identity following the soul, to being the non-identified Seer, flowing as the soul through the bodymind.

As you step into the corridor leading to Gateway 3, you are likely to experience times of great unrest and turmoil, as upheaval begins to take place internally, which is often reflected externally through the circumstances of your life. It is typical that you become prone to roller coaster mood swings: one day feeling energised, invigorated and deeply spiritual; the next, perhaps tired, heavy, sombre and disconnected.

This 'seesaw' effect is caused by internal shifts in the balance of your consciousness, as you shift from bodymind identification, to alignment with your soul. This takes place principally in your chakras. These are *'consciousness exchange points'*, where the soul infuses into the bodymind. They are not physical in nature, but etheric. As explained later in Gateway 5, you have not just one bodily vehicle of expression, but seven; they all function at sequentially higher frequencies (vibrations) of consciousness. Each main chakra infuses soul consciousness into one of these bodily vehicles. The chakras provide the energetic bridge - the connecting interface between the soul and the bodymind.

When the chakras are open and vibrating naturally, you experience yourself authentically as the soul expressed through the bodymind. However, when they are closed down for some reason, if their energy is convoluted, incongruent and dense, then there is a greater tendency to identify with the bodymind – an ego forms.

Due to its etheric nature, the chakra system has not been generally accepted within society; it has been confined to the world of mysticism and spirituality. However, there is now growing acceptance - although still much disagreement - as to their exact locations and purpose. It is best, therefore, to use any frame of reference you may encounter, more as a guide and to locate the centres through your own experience, by bringing continual awareness to them. By working with them in this way, and closely monitoring the corresponding effect in your external life, you can gauge the influence each has. I have used this approach to yield the following overview:

The Main Chakras and their impact in our lives

1. **Base chakra:** located at the base of the spine, around the general area of the coccyx and genitals, it relates to our connection with the physical - *First Density* – plane, including the immune system and sexuality. If the vibration here is low, there is a tendency to be over-attached to and identified with, the physical experience. You feel separated from the 'All That Is', and have overtly lustful and potentially exploitative sexual urges. As you transmute the energy in this chakra to the higher vibration, you are increasingly released from attachment to the physical plane and naturally aspire to higher spiritual growth.

2. **Sacral chakra:** located approximately where the spine and pelvis meet, the sacral chakra is the emotional centre, which tends to govern your state of well being within relationships. If the vibration here is low, then there is the tendency to be overly attached in relationships, needy and jealous. But as you transmute the energy and raise the vibration here, you discover non-attached freedom within relationships, with increasing sensitivity and sensuality. It increases your ability to empathise with another and their feelings.

3. **Solar plexus chakra:** this is located around the vulnerable soft area at the top of the stomach, just below the rib cage. Its purpose is to accept and infuse higher spiritual knowing into the lower mind - what we may call *subconscious mind*. It has the capacity to 'see' and intuit patterns forming in the natural organising energy around us. These patterns inform you of where the flow is now tending to go – what is beginning to take shape. When the vibration is low, you are prone to mental programming (premature judgments of the moment) and are therefore more susceptible to addictive substances such as caffeine, chocolate, sugar, alcohol, nicotine and other drugs. When you fully transmute the consciousness here however, you are able to take control over the base urges and respond more to the natural, synchronistic patterning of events: your capacity for clairvoyance, clairaudience and clairsentience greatly increases – you are receiving 'downloads' from the higher dimensions.

4. **Heart chakra:** located at the level of the heart, this is the centre where the unconditional love for all life activates - what some call "The Christ Consciousness". It acts as the bridge between the Lower Realm (where humanity currently resides) and the Middle Realm (where our planetary system is ascending to). When the vibration here is low, it manifests as judgmentalism of others and the radical adherence to a singular truth, thereby causing conflict in your life and consigning you to

a limited existence in the Lower Realm. When the vibration here is transmuted however, judgmentalism falls away and is replaced by unconditional love for all life. You become able to see and hold multiple truths. Through correct, non-judgmental discernment, you become able to choose Right Action in line with the guiding hand of Benevolent Consciousness (experienced as a 'heartfelt pull'). When you attain a fully open heart chakra, you begin to walk the path (internally) into the Fifth Density.

5. **Throat chakra:** located around the general area of the throat, the fifth chakra connects directly to higher mind - your fifth bodily vehicle of expression (see Gateway 5). It governs your ability to receive, interpret and articulate, higher abstract purpose as reality is beginning to take shape: it is all about engaging in the underlying educational and evolutionary purpose of the moment. The throat centre provides the direct connection into higher spiritual awareness. When the vibration here is low, you tend to be more bounded by the notion of separate identity, detached from the One that you are. A low vibration here would also manifest as an inability to express and be at ease with authentic reality - you are governed more by the limitations of lower conditioned thinking, because of your attachment to false identity. Put simply, you are less able to express your more abstract, higher truth, and be awesomely okay with that. The chakra begins to open when you are no longer internally affected by the outer reaction to your fully expressed truth. When you are able to 'turn the other cheek' and spontaneously express higher wisdom, at whatever apparent personal cost, then this doorway to multi-dimensional experience begins to open.

6. **Third eye:** located in the pineal gland roughly in the centre of the head at the level of the eyebrows. The third eye may be regarded as the centre where your core sense of beingness infuses the body (how you feel to be, in any given moment).

Whilst you are engaged in the transmutation of consciousness within the lower chakras, you tend to be unaware of it, because your actions are governed more by the false self, rather than the soul. Put simply, Soul Consciousness through the third eye is dampened and overridden by identification with the lower bodymind caused by attachments to the external drama. However, as you release these attachments, the vibration in the lower chakras transmutes, then Soul Consciousness is liberated, rising up the spine and reconnecting in the third eye with Unity Consciousness flowing downwards (through the dimensions) from the Source. This is referred to as "kundalini activation" (fully explained below). When the third eye activates, you become increasingly able to see reflections of yourself in other people, nature, and all life. You are able to identify, and align with, your true sense of beingness. Thus, the soul's purpose is now being unleashed.

7. **Crown chakra:** located just above the fontanel, where the three principal bone plates of the skull meet. This chakra mostly only activates when you have transmuted much of the density in the lower chakras. An exception would be 'starsouls', who might have a resistance to the physical densities, and for a time, be subtly avoiding them. Or else for people who have had a premature kundalini activation (I have frequently witnessed people in these states, where the lower chakras are still partially closed, yet they are open in the higher ones). The crown chakra opens and infuses energy into our highest bodily vehicle - the "spirit light body" (or "merkaba"). This paves the way for correct rationalisation of the multi-dimensional influences we are experiencing, including for example, the underlying synchronistic patterning through all events. As the crown chakra fully opens, multi-dimensional living through the spirit light body becomes a reality. You become centred in the universal flow of Right Action, and are increasingly able to shift consciousness between dimensions as required by the natural flow of the universe.

Inner alchemy through the 9 step process

Through transmutation of the denser energies in the chakras, you are, in effect, becoming an inner alchemist, changing the very nature of your being from lower levels of dense consciousness, to higher vibrational frequencies. Allegiance is switching to the soul's lightness through each of your bodily vehicles, and you begin the evolutionary process in earnest. You can still feel the heaviness and denseness of the lower vehicles, but a growing realisation consolidates, they no longer define you. All the while, you are opening and expanding new channels, bringing in the higher energies. Ripples and waves of energy begin to flow throughout the bodymind, as your consciousness expands into new dimensions of experience.

As the influx of soul accelerates, increasingly you will activate what I have been speaking of, as your 'source pain'. This is intimately related to your karma (covered in Gateway 4). It is subconscious trauma, which gets deeply embedded in your psyche in the Third Density, the 'plane of the intellect'. For most people, this subconscious trauma is strongly active in their lives, whether they know it or not. It could be, for example, the sense of neediness, or worthlessness, guilt or shame, which creates subliminal filters that you then place over your vision of the world, and especially within interpersonal relationships.

You actually begin to manifest this subconscious sense of disempowerment, and project it into your outer world.

Many mainstream spiritual practices advocate intentionally creating positive thoughts, or controlling vocabulary and body language, in an attempt to mask this disempowerment. Although initially it may appear as though they are having some degree of success (because thoughts do have a creative impact on reality), the subconscious source pain is deeply influential; it communicates through the surrounding energy field anyway, and is often visible through 'mico-expressions' – uncontrollable reactions to discomfort with the flow of the moment. And in masking these reactions, you risk suppressing the energy further, thus retarding the natural process of evolution –

the true means by which to solve the problem, and the ultimate reason you are here.

Delaying your evolutionary journey in this way, is highly counterproductive and disempowering. It is far more beneficial to allow the flow to carry you into situations and circumstances, which reveal the discomfort caused by this source pain; your tightness and retractions in the moment, become the informative, 'telltale' signs and the very touch points that activate this pain…

You now have an incredible opportunity to access the source of your limitation in this incarnation - get into it, unravel it, and allow authentic beingness to flow in. I cannot over empathise how important this is to your journey, your sense of well-being, and your state of authentic self, unveiling which, I can confidently say, is the only way to bring true fulfillment in life, success and lasting contentment.

There is nothing to fear from confronting your pain. In fact, pushing it away, burying or placating it through some form of distraction, only embeds it further, and pushes away the moment of true liberation…

This pain, when fully revealed and embraced,
is your path to ultimate freedom.

So how might you successfully get into, activate and process this source pain? How might you effectively dissolve the many blockages life will have likely built up within you? Having worked now with hundreds of evolving people around the world, I can confidently say, that this 9 step process is highly successful and effective for helping you break through and break out…

The Openhand 9 step process for dissolving blockages, source pain and karma

1. **Confront the situation:** you must first accept and completely acknowledge the truth of what is happening in your world. Get thoroughly used to observing yourself and accepting responsibility for your feelings in relation to what is going on in the situation. If you get tight, angry or wound up, acknowledge it. If someone is steamrollering your truth and that feels unpleasant, witness that too. Do not shy away from, or paper over, any inner retraction caused by events and other people in the outside world. By the Law of Attraction you have manifested them anyway, so as to confront and break through such a limitation. Embrace that.

2. **Regress deeply into the feelings of the situation:** it may not be appropriate for you to deal with the feelings in the moment they are coming up - you could be at work for example, in public or looking after your children. It is important not to suppress and dissolve the feelings, but rather to contain them: you get the sense that they are inside you, but you are on top of them and can manage them. When the timing is more appropriate (and as soon as possible), regress yourself deeply into the feelings once more: see the images, feel the feelings, let them come up inside.

3. **Honour and express the pain:** essentially this source pain is caused where your soul identifies somehow with the illusion of separation and the need for a particular outcome – where the soul is not self-realised (not realising of the One). However, if you honour the pain by fully expressing it in some way, then you become 'as-one' with it – you relocate the lost nugget of soul gold that was buried there and you reintegrate as the One. Honouring the pain might mean shouting and screaming, crying, rolling up into a ball, beating a punch bag or cushion, writing a journal or dancing and moving. Listen to your soul, and do whatever you feel given to do.

4. **Break through with presence:** when the source pain is at its zenith, when you can truly locate and feel it within your body, such that it is becoming excruciating, then paradoxically, you are ready to become the One through it; you are on the very precipice of presence. Remind yourself that all experience is relativistic and therefore transient – it does not define who you are. What you are, is absolute pure potential, beyond the pain. At this point, there will be some key (such as a word, mantra, a visualisation or symbolic metaphor) to help you 'open the door' through the density and into presence. If you are not sure what that is, ask the universe, and you will be shown.

5. **Feel the light of the soul:** when you've stepped into the sense of presence, then you are really processing and letting go of the density – it is like you are stirring the bed of the stream in which the nuggets of soul gold have become buried. Now you will be able to see and feel the glint of the soul as it is being liberated. It will be a sense of lightness, completeness, confidence, strength, surrender; you may feel it as a light or warmth beginning to flow into the body, through the previous restriction. Now focus on, and give energy to, this new sensation. It is like pouring fuel on an igniting flame – it grows stronger.

6. **Dissolve the source pain:** you are now ready to truly dissolve and fully release that aspect of source pain. Whilst staying in the sense of Pure Presence, intuit how your connection with your emerging soul, can best process the dense energy of the source pain. You have to remain soft and expanded, so that you do not tighten down out of the energy that causes the pain. So stay expanded through it, containing it within your consciousness, but then use whatever meditation comes to you to remove it. It could be a particular form of breathing, movement and dance, or it could be a visualisation. Let your intuition carry you – it already knows what best to do.

7. **Contemplate deeply any conditioned behaviours:** the source pain will have built up conditioned behaviours (as spoken of in Gateway 2). Now deeply contemplate what conditioning – *what distortions* – the source pain has caused in your life. Maybe, for example, you were needy of others? Or perhaps too competitive and aggressive. See yourself within those behaviours, being totally honest with yourself about them (reminding yourself, if necessary, that you are not to blame for them). It can help to write them down in a journal.

8. **Visualise yourself interrupting the behaviours:** in motivational and spiritual circles, people often speak of visualising the outcome or behaviour you would like to have happen. The risk is though, that this just becomes another level of programming. Instead, see yourself interrupting the behaviours that have emanated from the source pain. As you get increasingly sensitive, you will begin to actually feel the density and any fixed neural pathways. With a sense of surrendered will, you can begin to break these apart and literally dissolve them within.

9. **Become surrendered openness, attune to authentic beingness:** as the density and conditioned behaviours have been dissolved inside, increasingly you settle into an awesome place of surrendered openness: you feel expansive, peaceful, whole and complete. You are now much more able to interrupt the old behaviours in daily life and open up through them. Spontaneous acts of authentic beingness then begin to magically flow through you, which are totally right and befitting of the moment. It is like you become less an identity, and more a moving flow of consciousness through life. This is pure joy of living! (*I have written more about the qualities of authentic beingness that start to come through, and to which you can give energy, in Gateway 4*).

Inner Child and Inner Teenager processing

Whilst this process of internal alchemy is taking place (which can last a number of years), you will become aware of what are known as the "inner child" and "inner teenager" identities. These are complex filters of conditioning built up through your life, essentially based on the judgments you have been caused to make; and their foundation is the source pain itself. These identities, and any others that you may have taken on (because of some intense period of trauma or purposeful programming, such as with a spiritual identity), integrate together to form the "false self". It is what the soul fragments into, as it descends from the Source into these lower densities, and is more generally known as the "ego".

At childbirth, a baby's consciousness is generally so expanded, it tends not to realise where it ends and its mother begins, such is the sense of interconnection with all life. It is only after much initial 'education' in the ways of the world (like being slapped sharply on the behind and separated from your mother!), that you begin to buy into the deception of your separateness from all. It is then that (unsurprisingly) the inner striving kicks in, as you begin to seek those things that make you feel whole and complete once more: love, food, attention and distractive possessions for example. Fairly quickly, you learn which of your actions result in fulfillment and which do not. So from a tender age, you begin to develop conditioned behaviours leading to fixed neural pathways in the brain. This is practically unavoidable.

As you continue to generate and activate these fixed pathways, chemicals known as neuropeptides are released by the brain (specifically the hypothalamus) into the body, generating emotional expression within your cells, thus mirroring the activity in your thought patterns. If these patterns are continually replayed (such as a continual cycle of control and disempowerment between mother and child), the very nature of your cells is changed to reflect the conditioned habits. Over time, it is as though you actually become the sum total of your behaviours.

Put simply, if a baby is hungry, it learns that if it cries, it is likely to get fed. If the mother has a degree of general stress, as is often the case, this will be picked up energetically by the baby as it feeds, which in turn becomes imprinted in their cellular memory. So programmed loops of thought, imagery, emotion and feeling develop around getting fed. It might be for example: "I feel hungry which is not good. I don't feel complete, if I cry I'll get fed. Oh, that feels stressful and emotional, I realise that there is struggle in this place to get the things I need". The baby is not conscious of these patterns of course; and so it is, that they tend to build up quickly, forming these complex webs of behaviour.

So from a tender age, souls are thrust like innocent lambs into the growing pains of childhood. The driving impulse of the soul is choosing for you to develop bountiful freedom of expression, and yet all too quickly, it bumps into the artificial boundaries of judgment, limitation and control. Of course, just like a stream needs its banks to define it, so the soul also needs its boundaries - guidelines along which to advance. However, all too often, that progression is limited, curtailed and diverted by society's small-mindedness.

Unsurprisingly, the growing infant begins to lose its inherent trust in the completeness and perfection of the universe. This new doubting forms a more stressful consciousness, mirrored and replicated throughout the billions of tiny cells forming the body (this is exactly why simple affirmation, basic intentioning or programming mantras are inadequate to reintegrate and re-centre your consciousness).

The identification with the external drama has begun at a tender age, and from that point, the separation from the divine crystallises as an inner belief system. The tendency is to increasingly build more of the behavioural programs identifying with the denseness, and sometimes harshness, of this physical realm. The baby is learning all about pain, doubt, distrust and fear. If the parents are sufficiently evolved, they will keep reminding the growing infant to stay in the Heart Centre, to keep shining the light and trusting in the infinite organising power of the universe to meet their actual needs. If not, the parents are likely to be drawn into the false reality the growing infant is creating by feeding its attachments and distortions relating to the external drama.

> *It is an unfortunate cycle that most of humanity currently finds itself locked within - one which we are each being invited to break into, and break apart, by our own evolution and courageous expressions of higher truth.*

At around the age of two to four, it is likely that the neural pathways have grown to such an extent, that a tangled web of programmed behaviours has already taken root. This forms an identity - the "inner child" - which typically parents continue to feed; "my child doesn't eat this, behaves like that, and is afraid of bees" etc etc. Continual weight and density is given to the identity by parents reinforcing the same conditions or by simply allowing them to persist by giving in to them.

The child continues to grow, until at puberty, its bodily system surges with hormones, and with that, a rebellion from the constricting ways of the past tends to ignite. Once more however, there is a tendency to fight the external drama - *the effect* - rather than work with the internal one - *the cause*. The teenager discovers new types of behaviour that bring (temporary) fulfillment, and so other neural networks of conditioned behaviours take shape. Very quickly, a new identity develops - "the inner teenager".

> *These inner identities that eclipse the soul come into view by the shadows they cast.*

With continued attentiveness and perseverance, you may become fully aware of them over time, and break your attachments by realising they do not have to define you (in ways already described in Gateway 2 and in the 9 step process above). It then becomes possible to choose alternative behaviours which more accurately express your higher truth: those that the authentic child and teenager in you came here to express. When you step off the ever-repeating treadmill, you can literally feel in your heart, which alternative approach would be more in tune with your Higher Self, and the universe as a whole. When this inner knowing is confirmed by the objective hand of synchronicity, you can trust for sure, that you are heading in the right direction. If you keep doing this with persistence and diligence, then over time, it becomes possible to heal all inner identities and dissolve them from your life (see the tools section below for specific meditations).

This leaves pure, unfettered, creative joy - the childlike innocence you were born with.

The Intervention of Opposing Consciousness

It is not all plain sailing of course; the journey of Enlightenment is a challenging one, with many twists and turns on the path, many altitudes to break through. It is typically the case, that when you have been following divine guidance successfully for some time, you may hit a rocky patch - *a kind of brick wall* - where you are perceiving conflicting impulses, seemingly leading you in different directions. What is going on here?

Whether we fully appreciate it or not, we are multi-dimensional beings, and as such, are influenced from multiple dimensions of reality. The soul acts through the higher dimensions and when the higher chakras are at least partially open, guidance starts to flow from spontaneous higher knowing, through your being. This guidance is authentic, benevolent, and in the interests of your highest truth. It flows into Higher Mind (see Gateway 5) and the Heart Centre, guiding you on the best path forward by the rationalisation of Right Action - based on non-judgmental discernment of what best serves your evolutionary education and spiritual growth. However, in order for your authentic pull to be acted on authentically, it must be seamlessly transmitted through the mind and body; in other words, through the lower chakras. In so doing, it must pass through the heart chakra where you 'take charge' of the lower self. Here is where the greatest danger to authentic action lies waiting in ambush.

Hard as it may be for many to believe, there is a sophisticated life force living and acting at different (unseen) frequencies of being, all around us. It is rather like a virus, which mirrors the resistance Unity Consciousness faces as it breaks into Separation Consciousness – the universal light entering the darkness. This "Opposing Consciousness" has its own agenda of control, due to its disconnection from the Source. It feeds off convoluted and disharmonious energy in the field, and parasitic entities thrive off this density. It may be considered like an artificial intelligence, that has sprung up in the field around us *(I go into detail of its origin and agenda in DIVINICUS).*

This Opposing Consciousness has become adept at activating humanity's conditioned behaviours by giving stimulus to them. You may believe you have complete control of your thoughts, but quite often, you may find yourself slipping into negative, subconscious mental routines: actions which prey on your worries and fears, causing you to release emotional energy. In this way, Opposing Consciousness is actually 'farming' humanity, by sustaining attachment to dense, material experience. Thus the chakras, have in most cases, become closed down, thereby removing people from the feeling of universal peace, trust and at-one-ment with all life; in other words, *your divine birthright.*

Within the Fourth Density, where this Opposing Consciousness begins to engage humanity, it becomes possible to shape circumstances in the Third Density through creative intent. From my perspective, this is what is actually going on when awakening people speak of "manifesting" the things they want. They have opened the third chakra, expanded into the Fourth Density to a degree, and from that higher level of consciousness, are having a strongly creative influence in the lower dimensions.

Unfortunately however, this approach has the strong tendency to generate attachment to the lower material plane - the arena of the manifestations - and it either generates a new internal identity or sustains an old one. In so doing, there is the possibility of being duped by Opposing Consciousness, which can work with the creative intent, thereby fuelling attachment and identification with the physical plane. In this way, Opposing Consciousness has been retarding humanity's evolution, thereby maintaining its source of sustenance. As surreal and unpleasant as this may sound, in short humanity is being farmed by this distorting influence...

Benevolent Consciousness is well aware of this Intervention and has been diligently working behind the scenes to remove it, with great success. However, it still requires each to play their part in their own soul reintegration, and realignment.

So how do we overcome this Opposing Consciousness? The key is first to realise and accept your true purpose for being here; then to understand how your authentic impulses are being distorted. At some point, the realisation will dawn that your central underlying purpose is not to manifest things, but to 'self-realise'...

To become as The One Self, in all that you do, through a fully integrated soul.

Of course, in so doing, you will naturally end up creating things. However, in true authenticity, it is what you are **being** in the act of creating that counts and not the creation itself. So our authentic motivation is to explore beingness, and if you always come from this place in all engagements, that will be a good start.

The dichotomy you must then resolve, is that in order to create, you have to hold focus on the creative act in your consciousness, otherwise it might dissolve before it takes full shape; but then how do you not get attached to the creation (or subtly defined by it)?

It is necessary to learn how to hold the creative purpose very lightly: to be attentive to it, but to allow it to flow, shape and reshape - you are holding the space for it, whilst it lands of its own accord.

Acts of authentic creativity tend to be spontaneous, and in the moment - the impetus to act passes from higher to the lower mind and is integrated directly within your consciousness. Authentic creativity simply arises from inner knowing. Almost like a flash, you become aware of what you are meant to do (even if you do not yet know how to do it). Then by bringing your thoughts, emotions and feelings to the creative act, you play a full and expressive part in the universe's creation – *you bring it into being.*

However, if you hold the vision of a creative outcome in your mind as an intention, it becomes all too easy for that to be embellished and glamorised. It can take you down some diversionary alleyway in your life, where you become attached to the manifestation - you are taken out of the moment and start living in either the past or the future. The situation is compounded by the ability of Opposing Consciousness to mimic synchronicity, as it seeks to hoodwink you, that the creation itself is the most important thing.

So for example, it may be that your destined way of being is expressed as a teacher or revealer of spiritual truths, and this might seem very much aligned with the creation of a particular manifestation, such as a retreat centre for instance. However, it is not the retreat centre itself that counts, rather the way you are being in the creation and running of it. In other words, authentic doing arises naturally from authentic being.

> *When you are being true to the soul, then it appears as if the universe is magically shaping around you. Conversely, if you are still seeking to manifest things in life, to me it is a sure sign of inner tightness and therefore a lower level of consciousness: that of being a non-accepting identity, inadvertently confined to the old world reality.*

So at this point in your evolution, it is likely that you are experiencing two forms of guidance, both appearing to be benevolent, but only one authentic. Over time, and with due diligence, you must learn to distinguish when an inner pull is genuine, and when it is a little less than the real thing. With the Observer's sharp eye and the razor's edge of self-honesty, you will ultimately sense the difference in vibration: one (the lesser) never quite feels right - it is less sophisticated, the vibration less congruent, the synchronicity less spontaneous; the other (higher benevolent guidance) is more advanced, more spontaneous, evokes deep inner longing and self knowing. It is usual to make mistakes, but if you keep being true to yourself, it will always become clear eventually where you might have stepped off the path and why.

So profound self-honesty and total commitment to self-realisation - *above all else* - are the key to nullifying the distorting effects of Opposing Consciousness in your life and thereby accelerating your evolution.

When you have made this inner commitment to the truth of your soul, then by use of the 9 step process described previously, you will become able to sense and intuit the density of entities and implants in your field, which often connects into your source pain. By bringing attention to this tightness, felt in the cleansing process, your intuition will guide you on how to move the vestiges of this Opposing Consciousness from your field.

Kundalini Activation

At some point, when you have dissolved enough of the conditioned behavioural programs and are sufficiently inwardly surrendered, the internal balance of consciousness shifts positively in favour of the soul. The neural web of false identities can then suddenly shatter in the challenging crucible of daily life. The reintegrated and unleashed energy of the soul, rises from the base of the spine, up through the body into the third eye, where it reunites with Unity Consciousness flowing down through the crown chakra. The experience can be so powerful, it may feel like the whole top of the head has just lifted off, as a stream of light surges heavenward. Others have described it as 'intertwining snakes of energy rising up the spine'. For yet others, this "Kundalini Activation", could be more gentle, but nevertheless deeply profound...

The inner and outer worlds unfold blissfully into one, with no experience of separation - there is no longer the sense of a localised identity, but rather a seamless flow of universal energy. The Observer has dissolved into the all-encompassing Seer, like an invisible surfer riding the crest of a divine, co-creative wave.

Kundalini represents your natural affiliation with the wider universe: *it is the natural flow of Soul Consciousness down from the Source, through your being, and back again.* It is a complete cycle of divine expression and creativity. When your kundalini reactivates in this way, although deeply magical, the experience can also be quite destabilising, particularly in an often judgmental world, that does not generally recognise spiritual evolution. This is because although the neural webs have been shattered, fragments of the individual neural pathways are still in place as splinters of the original identity. To the now transfigured being, these fragments of outdated pathways, are no longer an appropriate means of expressing oneself, and so a sense of dislocation from the world can occur, until you begin to develop more appropriate responses, based on the authentic impulses of the soul.

In an impatient and controlling world, it can appear that you have "lost touch", become "spaced out" or "lost the plot". In extreme cases, where the transfigured being is connecting through multiple dimensions of reality, it can seem as if you are temporarily mentally unbalanced or psychotic. It is because you are now literally living in multiple realities simultaneously, and initially it can be quite difficult integrating them into one consistent experience.

Steadily however, you begin to integrate your holistic beingness and new, multi-dimensional experience of the universe. Initially, this new integration is intensely energetically demanding and physically tiring; you have connected dozens more channels of incoming information in one fell swoop, placing huge demands on the bodymind as it struggles to cope with the tidal wave of new feelings, experiences and emotions.

Eventually, the experience settles down, you become adept at living in Pure Presence, fully embracing the new intuitive and psychic powers the Transfiguration has unleashed.

Just as with the other transitions, your passage through Gateway 3 is likely to be marked by some noteworthy, perhaps dramatic, external event - a ceremony - as the fledgling transfigured soul comes of age.

At this point, you are now completely walking a spiritual path, with a growing sense of your life's purpose during this incarnation. You will very likely have a strong motivation towards selfless service, and be feeling the guiding hand of Benevolent Consciousness frequently through your life. Surrendering all individual aspiration and desire, you become an executive instrument of the Divine Purpose.

It is then that you may count yourself as truly blessed, to have found real purpose in life.

Transitioning Gateway 3
- essential tools -

1. **Raise energetic vibration:** *cleanse and detoxify mind, body and living environment. Harmonise with Mother Earth.*

2. **Dissolve inner identities:** *become acquainted with inner identity filters which distort authentic expression. Disassociate from them and dissolve them.*

3. **Release restrictive relationships:** *cut the ties of those old relationships that have the tendency to draw your consciousness back into former realities.*

4. **Forgive both others and yourself:** *energetically confront those who may have mistreated you and forgive them. Also forgive yourself for past transgressions.*

5. **Develop strong spiritual practices:** *continually raise vibration and transmute the old consciousness. Open the chakras further, activate kundalini.*

1. Raise energetic vibration: *cleanse and detoxify mind, body and living environment. Harmonise with Mother Earth.*

The Transfiguration is an internal shift of perception from identification with the denseness and tightness of the bodymind (experienced as a sense of subtle inner efforting), to the non-identified, crystal clear clarity of the Seer, flowing as the lightness, expansiveness and timelessness of the soul, through the bodymind.

It is as if you have become the conductor of an orchestra, and realised your attention has, for too long, been focussed on the brass section and base drum, because they were making the loudest noise! To hear the finer, quieter instruments again, you must first turn down the noise of the louder ones.

So the key is to quieten down internal activity. This can be achieved by regulating the denseness of vibrations you bring into the body, thereby limiting the stimuli that unnaturally confuse your metabolism. So for example, if you eat dense, processed foods, polluted with toxins, then the body has to work harder to process them, and the extra effort swallows up consciousness; in other words, you get lost in the dense vibrations.

Progressively transitioning to a plant-based diet, free from toxicity, such as pesticides, additives and refined sugar has an enormous, positive impact on raising your vibration.

Likewise, if you pollute your mind with negativity, such as that caused by the judgmentalism frequently expressed on TV, in the newspapers and through other media, then you tend to tighten inside. Internal tightness is also heightened by too much computer time, mobile phones, wifi, general overuse of electrical gadgets, and chemical toxins used in our clothes and daily household cleaning materials. The key is to change your immediate living environment to raise your energetic vibration - *to attune to the finer instruments in the orchestra.* Here is a brief summary of the changes you can undertake to raise your vibration:

- *declutter your living environment*
- *reduce the number of electrical gadgets used*
- *get rid of the TV or be more selective about its use*
- *avoid overtly judgmental press and media*
- *reduce usage of mobile phones and wireless internet*
- *use natural cleaning products for the body and environment*
- *wear natural clothing such as cotton, linen, hemp and wool*
- *eat less processed foods and switch to vegetarian or vegan diet*
- *fast regularly to speed detoxification*
- *meditate regularly to calm mind and emotions.*

You are also likely to find that it becomes increasingly difficult to use certain language with negative connotations. Words become of great significance as we realise their energetic power. There may be particular word associations with our old behaviours that you may wish to avoid using, or swear words that conjure emotions of your previous consciousness. The use of sexual swear words can be particularly self-defeating; they risk dragging you back into the realm of judgmentalism, manipulation, lack of respect and projectionism.

Other words can also generate internal tightness, thereby dampening your consciousness and once more constricting your experience of your newly expanding reality. For example, I have found the word "hate" to be particularly negative. So the key is to notice the effect of the words you use and make a conscious decision about which to discard from your daily vocabulary.

> *As simple as it may seem, it has been clearly shown, that sounds and words, can greatly influence, both in a positive and negative way, your very DNA.*

You will inevitably discover that this inner purification brings you into greater harmony with Mother Earth and her natural ecosystems. Whereupon, you will likely find, it becomes increasingly difficult to damage, pollute or act carelessly with regard to the environment. As you become more compassionate in your life, you are naturally attuning to the Soul of the Earth, bringing with it great joy and rejuvenation. It is as if the animals are talking to you, birds singing for you and the caress of the wind uplifting you. The more respectful and in touch you become, the more your psychic and intuitive capacity expands, with synchronicity speaking to you through the daily weave of all events. It is our natural mother tongue, which becomes increasingly evident.

2. Dissolve inner identities: *become acquainted with inner identity filters which distort authentic expression. Disassociate from them and dissolve them.*

The inner child identity is not to be confused with the natural joy, inquisitiveness and innocence inherent in the soul. It is a complex web of fixed neural pathways in the brain, which typically forms between the ages of two to four, in response to repetitive patterns of activity in your immediate environment. It is this web that becomes your initial personality, with which most tend to identify.

As you grow, and are subjected to other life changing circumstances such as puberty, new patterns form, which create other neural webs, such as the inner teenager (typically forming between the ages of eleven and sixteen). These tangled webs of complex behaviours, beliefs and emotional reactions, integrate to form identities - what we may call the false self. It is these filters which distort and dilute your absolute authentic taste of reality, generating false and unfulfilling lifestyles.

To be 'transfigured', which means to dissolve into the Seer and unleash authentic beingness, you must break apart these complex webs and liberate yourself completely from them. In other words, you must heal and dissolve the inner child, the inner teenager and any other identity filter that has evolved over time. Here is a powerful meditative technique for achieving this:

Identity dissolving meditation

- *Set aside some free time to sit quietly in a still room, with candlelight, incense and soft music.*

- *If possible, acquire a picture of yourself both as a child between the ages of two and four, and as a teenager between the ages of eleven to sixteen. If no pictures are available, simply visualise yourself as closely as you can at these times.*

- *Go within. Connect first with the sense of your inner child. Use your intuition to locate the feeling of it somewhere in your body. Connect visions to the feelings. Build up an accurate picture of your experiences. What behaviours did you exhibit? How did you feel? How were your parents towards you? What activities caused you pain? Which activities gave you joy? Build a general feeling of your inner child identity at these times.*

- *When you have built up as much feeling and connection with the child as you can, simply rest in awareness of it, whatever may be arising for you, including sadness and pain.*

- *Next, connect with you inner teenager identity. As before, build up a picture of your experiences. What were you frequently feeling? What was your general state of mind? How were your interactions with your friends, family and teachers etc? What behaviours did you exhibit? What gave you joy, liberation and feelings of completeness? When did you get tight, depressed or lacking in self confidence? Re-encounter all of these experiences and build as complete an internal picture as you can.*

- *Now once more, use your intuition to locate where the teenager identity is within you. Invite the teenager to connect with the child, recognising that they are related; the teenager was likely formed as a subconscious protection mechanism for the child.*

- *Now project out from yourself both the inner child and*

teenager (plus any other identities you may feel have been formed). Have them sitting before you. First know yourself as not them. Whatever suffering has been generated, it is not you that is suffering. Settle into the realisation that you are already free from them.

- *Next, through your thoughts, invite both personalities to forgive those who might have caused the pain, suffering or conditioned behaviours to form. Help them realise it was not the fault of parents, friends or adversaries, for they too were all conditioned by society. And by the Law of Attraction, you drew to you every experience, in order to release attachment, evolve and grow.*

- *Once you feel the identities have been able to forgive, focus on healing. Visualise powerful, golden, healing light bathing the identities with unconditional love. See them surrendering into the light, healing and steadily dissolving. The sense is that they are returning to the Source.*

- *Once you have finished this process, it may be that layers of the identities still exist and you will have to work on them again at another time (you will know when they are fully ready to depart because you will feel it). So, if still there, bring the identities back inside you, but know they now have less impact on your life, because they feel they have received the loving, healing attention they require. Keep performing the meditation, and notice over time, how the identities are becoming more content, healed and increasingly transparent, until at some point, they disappear completely.*

3. Release restrictive relationships: *cut the ties of those old relationships that have the tendency to draw your consciousness back into former realities.*

During the Transfiguration, your perception of reality will shift dramatically, and it helps to provide fertile ground for the new consciousness to unfold itself. Constant judgmental reminders of who you once were by unsupportive (or unconscious) friends and family, simply serve to give energy to the old patterns of behaviour. It is likely that many of the people you have grown up with, will want to keep relating to the false self they have known over the years (it makes them feel more secure). Frequently, their expectations may cause you to act and behave in the old predictable ways. It is as if their consciousness keeps dragging you back to the former reality. This activity can seriously hamper your unfolding - if you keep getting swallowed back into the old identities and patterns.

At this point, it is important to be absolutely clear with yourself what your objective is:

Is it important to move forward into the new state of beingness being offered to you? Or do you prefer to linger in the past?

How ever long you may labour in this dilemma, it will ultimately become clear to you, that the only way out, is through. At this point, you have to become profoundly honest with yourself about which of the old relationships still serve you, and which do not. Are you maintaining them purely out of some perceived obligation? Or is it nostalgia perhaps, for that almost, but not quite forgotten, taste of a bygone time? If you simply ask the question of the universe:

"Which relationships no longer serve me?"

it will become abundantly clear through synchronicity, which you are being invited to release and how to do it.

Whilst tact helps avoid unnecessary pain, honesty is the sure route to cutting the ties restricting your unfolding gifts of beingness…

Remember, everything is energy: when you hold space for a relationship with someone, you are giving energy to it. When that engagement is no longer serving, you must first draw the energy back within, in order that this creative potential can draw new interactions into your life.

So you will find that it is not sufficient simply to break off the relationship itself. An energetic body will have formed, linking both parties, to which they will be relating. Hence you must also cut the interconnecting energy lines. This is where honesty is vital. If you are clear to your former friend exactly where you stand, and that it is time to move on, then they will be left in no doubt, and the relationship can be ended as painlessly as possible. Furthermore, it is likely that the energetic bonds will be severed at that point. If not, they may continue well after the relationship has (on the surface) ended. If this case, it is possible that you will still be influenced by the old consciousness, and it may limit your freedom to unfold.

If you sense this is happening, the following meditation can help solve the issue by dissolving the outdated ties:

Cutting old ties meditation

- *Choose a room which is open and clear. Use natural lighting and burn incense. Play gentle, healing music.*

- *Settle into relaxed, deep breathing.*

- *Visualise the person you wish to release, and get the sense of connecting with them through the ether.*

- *Visualise both of you at a crossroads on the path.*

- *Inwardly thank your friend for their involvement in your life and the valuable gifts they have brought. Acknowledge it is now time to walk separate paths. Be absolutely clear with one another, your paths are now moving in different directions.*

- *Hug lovingly and release each other. Watch as your friend takes the alternative route. Wave and wish them well.*

- *Before you embark down your own path, visualise a tree branch in your hand, and use it to brush away any remaining strands of connection. Or use imaginary scissors to cut remaining ties.*

- *Visualise/feel your energy coming back to you. Sense your field becoming clearer and less restricted. Walk freely down your new pathway.*

Even with those relationships you feel it important to retain (with parents for example), it will still pay to create greater breathing space for you to unfold. You might consider moving, at least temporarily, to a place of greater seclusion - one where like-minded people might be more readily accessible, such as a retreat centre or more consciously-minded community for example.

In this new place of greater openness, you can begin to develop closer connections with your soul family, who are providing assistance from the higher realms. To initiate this, all you really need to do, is to know they are there, open your heart and invite in their help. Then, by noticing arising synchronicities, you get to know you are being answered, and begin to build up an expanding picture of their benevolent involvement in your new life.

4. Forgive both others and yourself: *energetically confront those who may have mistreated you and forgive them. Also forgive yourself for past transgressions.*

The purpose of all experience, *in the entirety of the universe*, is self-realisation: to know yourself as complete and whole, without fear, doubt or worry. Your soul is the living, breathing expression of this completeness, and is working to be realising of The One Self through all experience. By the Law of Attraction, the configuration of your soul generates the circumstances of each incarnation. In other words, as you begin to incarnate, your consciousness draws to you, and manifests, more or less the exact circumstances you need to learn, evolve and grow. As you look back through your life, you will surely see, how exactly the right person showed up at exactly the right time to teach you something you needed to learn.

> *The polarity of your soul draws mirroring circumstances and people, so as to expose and reflect both your distortions and your gifts of beingness; in this way, you get the opportunity to see yourself and work to evolve – to self-realise.*

Some of those experiences will be joyous ones, others painful, but to me, there is no doubt: *you draw exactly the right circumstances and people in order to activate and dissolve that which no longer serves.*

No matter how it may seem at the time, all circumstances hold the potential for greater self-realisation. In this way, everything you may consider as a negative action perpetrated against you, can actually become a blessing. When someone pushes your buttons or causes an emotional flare-up, you have been offered a gift: the opportunity for liberation and thereby expansion...

Remember: to be enlightened is to be enlightened by all things.

When you truly realise and accept this, you have the possibility to be released from the pain and suffering of all negative actions that have been perpetrated against you, including judgmentalism, slander, emotional and physical violence or sexual abuse. When you go deeply into such transgressions (using the 9 step process described earlier), no matter how hard it may at first seem, it becomes possible to accept how you actually drew these circumstances for the purpose of evolutionary growth. They often reveal an attachment – where you perceived you needed the situation to go a certain way or were resisting how it actually was. Maybe, for example, you needed someone to be loving or behave in a particular way? Maybe you needed them to be kind and not hurtful? In such circumstances, you were looking outside yourself for something you already possessed within...

No-one can take your energy or inner peace; only you can give it away. It is not a problem that someone judges you, as long as you do not then become judging of yourself; for this is what ultimately depletes your energy.

In the state of Enlightenment beckoning all, you and you alone are the creator, and therefore master, of your own experience of life. To reclaim your true majesty and power, is to reclaim the responsibility for whatever happens to you. In other words, to acknowledge yourself as the creator, and then to take back sovereignty for the reality, that only you can create.

From this viewpoint, it is necessary to find an alternative way of looking at forgiveness, in terms of how it is traditionally understood. To me, true forgiveness is to find awesome acceptance of what occurred, and then embrace the perpetrator as an instrument to help you unfold – *which you drew to yourself.* We are all evolving and at the soul level, we manifest co-creative events to provide opportunities for growth...

> *True forgiveness therefore, is to see the blessing in the issue, and find that place within, where you are at peace with it.*

It is not always an easy transition to make, but when you can truly liberate yourself from projecting blame, or taking on blame, you find it much easier to forgive and be forgiven. If you can find awesome acceptance, then you discover a new level of internal freedom - you are no longer held prisoner by events of the past.

Here then is an appropriate forgiveness meditation, to help you release inner tightness, caused by events where you believe negative acts have been perpetrated against you:

Meditation for forgiving another:

- *Create a loving, warm and protected space with incense, candles and soft music. Relax deeply using deep breathing and visualisation.*

- *Allow an experience to arise in the past, where you have suffered or were abused at the hands of someone else.*

- *Contemplate deeply the situation where you suffered, visualising what you would have seen, hearing the sounds and feeling the feelings.*

- *What thoughts and emotions are arising for you? Watch them, feel them.*

- *Go deeper into the situation and contemplate the main perpetrator/s. What was it that caused you to suffer? What were you attached to? How were you needing them to be a certain way?*

- *Allow any pain to build and do not retract from it. In other words, do not suppress it, but go right into it.*

- *Now contemplate what was the blessing? What was the lesson? What were you being invited to realise? How were you being invited to become more whole and complete?*

- *Feel yourself 'stepping through the suffering' as the One.*

- *Notice yourself becoming purely present, non-identified with the pain.*

- *With breathing and visualisation, allow the light of the soul to flow in, as an experience of completeness, expansiveness, timelessness and unconditional love.*

- *When you know you are ready, feel the pain as darkness gathering into a heavy, dense ball in your hands.*

- *Direct the light of the soul into the ball of pain and work to dissolve it.*

- *Now visualise the perpetrator. Connect with the soul in them. See firstly their perfected light.*

- *Now work to let go of any resentment, anger or blame. Let go of the need for them to be a certain way. Release any lingering judgment; feel your soul blissfully expanding you out into peace.*

- *Keep working at it until you can let go of all such negativity.*

It is also important to release your own self-judgments about actions you may have carried out against another...

Remember, you are not to blame!

Just as, by the Law of Attraction, other souls took on density to perpetrate acts against you (and thereby see their distortions more clearly), so, at a higher level, your soul has chosen to take on density in order to experience a distortion by which to evolve...

What is more, this process of the soul taking on appropriate density, is the very means by which the universe brings itself to greater overall harmony – each soul is helping to penetrate the darkness with light.

What this means, is that whilst you may not be to blame for past distorted actions, you are still responsible for ultimately correcting your behaviour. Therefore, it is important once more, to confront the action and see where you might still be stuck. It is only then that you become able to release any pent-up frustration and self-judgment. It also means that you can actually 'honour' the event, by giving it reason and purpose; as distorted as it may have been, it did have meaning.

Here then is an essential meditation for self forgiveness:

Self-forgiveness meditation

- Create a loving, warm and protected space with incense, candles and soft music. Relax deeply into breathing and visualisation.

- Contemplate where you may have hurt another, either physically, emotionally or psychologically.

- Where might you have been deceitful or untrustworthy?

- Where might you have slandered or spoken badly of another?

- Where have you judged other people?

- Where have you polluted Mother Earth or hurt animals or plants?

- Go deeply into the situations, accepting that whilst what

took place is your responsibility, you are not to blame - each action invites self-realisation.

- Realise your own distortion. Perhaps where you were lacking trust or respect? Perhaps you felt the compulsion to control due to self doubt, a sense of lack or fear?

- Resolve with yourself, and those who suffered as a result of your actions, to release your distortions and raise your vibration.

- Help them to heal by bringing loving golden light to them.

- Finally release yourself from self-judgment. Know that you are always embraced and loved unconditionally by your guides, soul family and, at a higher level, even those who suffered from your actions.

- Feel all the darkness, pain and suffering within, gathering into the left hand. Watch it form as a dense ball, which is then dissolved into light.

- Feel a new sense of lightness wash over you.

- Keep doing this until you have completely forgiven yourself for all perceived transgressions.

5. Develop strong spiritual practices: *continually raise vibration and transmute the old consciousness. Open the chakras further, activate kundalini.*

By now, it is likely that you will have built up meditative practices, which you conduct on a daily basis (remember meditation is where you are being in conscious awareness of yourself and surroundings, which can be achieved in many ways, not just the formal meditative arts). It is not within the scope of this book to go into the various specific practices. The key is always to follow your heart and it will become abundantly clear which work best for you: whether it be sitting in stillness, yoga, tai chi, dancing, singing, chanting, performing martial arts, simply walking in nature, or whatever else develops your sense of deep soul connection.

One of the key things to remember, is that we are all unique, and have a unique pathway to Enlightenment (even though we may pass through the same milestones - the same Gateways). So whilst you may resonate with one particular practice or another, it is likely that only specific aspects of that discipline are of true value for you. It is highly recommended therefore, that you be open to developing your own unique, daily practice, allowing it to continually evolve, as you become increasingly sensitive to your unfolding inner state of consciousness.

When the Transfiguration occurs, it does so with a kundalini activation. As previously described, this is where waves of Soul Consciousness are liberated from bodymind identification, flowing upwards from the base of the spine, connecting the chakras and reuniting with Unity Consciousness flowing downwards through the crown chakra. The two energies then meet with a glorious explosion of light in the pineal gland - the third eye. Suddenly, you become as one with all things, know yourself as Pure Presence and experience powerful new energies descend through your being...

It is at this point, you are truly being your higher self, and by grounding that energy in this realm through the lower chakras, you become a focal point for co-creative, universal activity.

Kundalini activation should occur naturally as you remove the energetic blockages, attachments and distortions from your life. However, the movement to Transfiguration and full kundalini awakening can be accelerated by performing particular spiritual practices including: breathing into the chakras; singing or humming into them; using colour, sound or crystal therapy. Below is a suggested breathing meditation inspired by Kriya Yoga, which I have found particularly powerful:

Kundalini activation meditation

- *Take a few deep breaths, inhaling into the area of the eighth chakra several inches above the crown.*

- *Now inhale into the eighth chakra, hold the breath, then move attention down to the crown chakra and exhale into the front of it.*

- *Hold the breath on exhale, and feel a sense of release, opening and expansion in the chakra. You can visualise to help: so perhaps see a flower opening; a sun rising at dawn; or ripples flowing outwards on a pond.*

- *When you naturally feel it is time to inhale again, move the attention through and out of the back of the crown chakra and once more up to the eighth. Inhale into the eighth chakra.*

- *When you have fully inhaled, hold the breath and move attention to the third eye, entering it through the front. Exhale and release tension and effort as before; then once more inhale back up to the eighth.*

- *Continue the process down through each chakra to the base, and then repeat the sequence in reverse upwards, beginning with the base (so you open the base chakra twice in succession).*

- *Remember always to inhale into the eighth chakra and then exhale into the chakra you are opening.*

- *When complete, attune to the rise of energy from the base chakra up through the other chakras stopping at the third eye; feel yourself drawing the energy upwards with a sense of purpose.*

- *If the energy gets stuck in a certain chakra, keep exhaling into it and releasing tension and effort there. It is likely you will need to repeat this over weeks and months to fully unleash the flow.*

It is also vitally important to realise that you cannot simply raise your energetic vibration by opening and cleansing the chakras through healing practices and meditation.

What actually happens, is that your work shines the light into those areas of your daily life which you most need to develop next, or which are naturally ripe for development. In other words, that aspect of consciousness which is now wanting to unfold, will be 'spiked' in some way.

In so doing, the inner blockages - *the convolutions of consciousness* - will project into your outer world, creating patterns of repetitive actions and behaviour - cloudiness in the river of life, through which you now must work. You are being invited to unravel your highest truth within those engagements, just as before.

So for example, if you intuitively feel to bring your attention to the sacral chakra, and raise the vibration by releasing tension and effort there, you will likely notice the effects that the shift of consciousness is beginning to have in your relationships. Past patterns of limiting behaviour (over attachment and neediness for example), will be brought to the surface and ignited, so you can more readily see them. You then have the opportunity to let go of that particular counterproductive behaviour; in so doing the consciousness in the sacral chakra rises to a more evolved state.

Thus meditation and spiritual practice can help initiate this action, but they are no substitute for self-realisation in day-to-day life. Although, for example, kundalini activation meditations can open up your chakras, in my experience, full kundalini awakening will not happen until you have cleansed away much of your distorted behaviour patterns. You have to be very clear internally to attune to your higher self and infuse it more fully into your life (*I should also add, that I have witnessed premature kundalini activations by forced meditation practices – these can be very destabilising and counterproductive, without having first cleansed the density within, and integrated higher self behaviours into your daily life*).

As you release tension and cleanse the chakras, your consciousness begins to transmute to the higher vibration. This causes a reflection outwards and the manifestation in your life of authentic, soulful action - *Right Action*. This is not necessarily supported in the world by those around you, but it is always supported by Benevolent Consciousness. And even if your Right Action does not at first succeed in the world, the universe is tireless in finding new ways for this river of authenticity to flow back to the ocean – there will always be a vehicle for your authentic expression.

Dealing with psychic attack

Whilst you are conducting this work, it is highly likely that at various points, you will experience some form of psychic attack; the field around us is awash with negative energies at this point in humanity's evolutionary journey. This is nothing to be afraid of! If psychic attack happens, it is only because of some susceptibility within your own field - where the in-flowing light of your soul, becomes distorted, diluted or diverted from its natural path. If this happens, and some kind of energy has temporarily invaded your field, you can recognise it with some key, telltale signs: you may be aware of a buzzing in the head and confused thinking; you may feel the solar plexus tighten; you may get nauseous in the abdomen; or you may suddenly slip into doubt, fear or worry. Do not worry! It can be dealt with.

In the beginning, I would strongly advise you not to create some 'protective bubble' around yourself as frequently advocated in the spiritual mainstream. All too often, this is done from a place of non-acceptance and subtle levels of fear. In which case, the tendency is to create a bigger target of yourself, and actually draw the unwanted energy in. Or else it may already be in your field, but subtly concealed in denser layers of consciousness – this might be providing the channel in, from some external projection.

So how best to deal with psychic attack?

The 9 step process for clearing negative and blocked energy

outlined earlier is an excellent way to clear your field. Over time, with diligence and persistence, it should clear away anything that does not belong. It will integrate the soul, and therefore render you increasingly resilient to invasive energies. But there are other countering steps you can also take, both within yourself and your living environment. Here are 9 measures you can apply, specifically to counter psychic attack when you experience it:

Countering psychic attack

1. **Become as nothing:** in the Openhand Approach, this Intervention energy - this Opposing Consciousness - is only ever present because of unconsciousness and sense of lack - the need to be completed in some external way. Hence presence and awareness are essential. 'Becoming as nothing' in your field means not to react, go into fear or panic about what might be happening. Soften through your field with awareness. First accept whatever is going on; be the witness of it, the Observer. This takes a lot of practice: you will need to progressively soften into new layers and new personal resistances as they arise. So keep working on this one.

2. **Understand the personal limitations you are dealing with:** accept that the Intervention is teaching you something about yourself. It will expose your attachments, trauma and karma, because it acts within these - *your pain is the place where the light enters!* So learn to transcend the pain by understanding what limitation you might be working with - thus you enlighten through the pain.

3. **Take sovereignty of your field:** once you have successfully become 'as nothing' in the attack, then you can truly begin work with it and shift it from your field. It is all about reclaiming sovereignty within your field, through presence. So take some time to lie still, relax and scan your field for telltale signs of some kind of attack/intervention: a buzzing in the head, temples or third eye; nausea in the solar plexus;

tightness like a wound knot in the abdomen; a sense of depletion of your energy and general tiredness (especially when you wake up in the morning). Breathe your full consciousness into and through your field.

4. **Build the sense of Warrior Will:** the more presence and attention you can bring to your field, the more likely you will feel the subtle signs of intervention. So then begin to work against it, using your intuition and sense of will. Recognise this energy does not belong in your field and does not serve you. Let this stir your "ray 1 warrior energy" (see Gateway 4). Without anger, judgment or resentment, begin to push out this energy from your field. Let your intuition guide you to meditations that particularly resonate: deep consciousness bodywork for example, like Openhand's soulmotion, Tai Chi (with the sense of the warrior) and other martial arts, or strong, energetic dance.

5. **The importance of staying grounded:** make sure in all these counter activities that you stay grounded, that your energy does not rise only into the higher chakras or leave the body. Make sure you root yourself to the earth - push your energy down through your body into your legs and through your feet. Some of this denser energy you might feel coming up from the ground, hence the need to push back down, to root the fullness of your consciousness throughout your body.

6. **Establish energy fields:** consider establishing energy fields throughout your home and the general area you live in. These are created by what you might call an 'act of prayer'. It is not praying though, and not asking for anything in particular. It is using your sense of presence and divine connection to establish a clear energy through the space where you live. If you or others are getting tight, wound up or angry in your space, use meditation to unravel it by sending peaceful waves through it. Switch off and unplug as much electronics as possible; change from wifi to ethernet where practicable;

switch off the mobile phone when not in use; use the TV sparingly. All of these vibrations have a disruptive effect on your surrounding field, making your general location more susceptible to psychic attack.

7. **Create a sacred space:** Many of us live in family environments where others are less conscious of what is going on in the field and may have more attachment to 'matrix' behaviours. So in addition to the above, establishing your own sacred space (that is entirely yours) within the home would help greatly. It is from here, that you can send out peaceful waves of energy throughout your entire environment.

8. **Be mindful of diet:** in some ways, it can be said 'you are what you eat'. What you put into your physical being will, of course, begin to affect your vibration, either negatively or positively. So to help prevent psychic attack, be especially mindful of your diet. If you consume the denser vibrations of the matrix (meat, dairy and junk food which contain MSG, Gluten, processed sugar and other harmful additives), then you need to be cleansing these from your field daily. Investigate those foods that detox, rejuvenate and bring aligned vibrancy. Conduct regular juice fasting and detox.

9. **Call in Support:** benevolence is there to help us in all its myriad forms. If, for example, you have the sense of a particular Archangel (Michael perhaps), you can call in supportive help and protection. Bear in mind that true benevolence wishes to empower you personally. So make sure you have actively engaged in your own self-realisation first, through the steps taken above. But then by all means, work with fourth dimensional and angelic support. You simply have to open your heart and invite that presence to work with you, being very clear that anything which does not support your highest good, has no invitation into your field. You can actually state and feel the energy of this through your field as an act of meditation.

In summary of Gateway 3 essential tools

These then, are the general spiritual practices you might apply whilst progressing through the Gateway 3 transition. Take the influences that resonate best with you, but be adaptable to change, as your evolution unfolds. Remember always to be flexible, and allow your own intuitive interpretation to develop an individual practice that works best for you. Your own soul knows best!

Transitioning Gateway 3
- general misconceptions -

1. Discernment disappears with judgment

As the Heart Centre opens, the experience of Unity Consciousness expands profoundly. You become instinctively able to connect with the soul in all things. Even if another is being judgmental, aggressive, rude or hurtful, you are able to perceive their soul, their distortion of it, and understand why it has likely happened...

You become able to see multiple truths in all circumstances, without the need to hold one particular truth.

Hence, it becomes easier and easier to dissolve judgment of others for their behaviours and actions. However, where inner identities might persist, there is still the tendency to distort these truthful inner impulses of the soul. Particularly a spiritual identity might tend to exaggerate this experience of non-judgmentalism and abandon even proper discernment. It is important that as you unfold, you are able to accurately discern the state of another, in order that you may better help, or even avoid helping all together, if the engagement were likely to be fruitless...

This requires the need to hone your powers of non-judgmental discernment.

Accurate discernment is also essential in navigating the path. The situations of your life are beginning to unfold as a mutli-dimensional landscape, through which the soul flows. It can only do so freely and accurately, if your consciousness is making proper discernment of the deeper (yet non-judgmental) meaning behind all events. So letting go of judgment, does not mean letting go of discernment and thereby accepting 'anything goes' (the 'ray 4 diplomat' aspect of the soul becomes essential to aligned discernment – see Gateway 4).

2. That you have to dissolve the personality

As the third eye opens, you become more able to see your true reflection in all things and of course especially in people; you begin to appreciate which aspects of your nature are being revealed to you. As you dissolve away distorted layers, the edges of apparent duality become increasingly blurred - you seem to expand into everything. And the likelihood is, that at times, you will feel so much joy with the perfection in all things – *so much at-one-ment* – that the sense of separated self begins to disappear. In many ways this is a good thing – you are increasingly becoming Pure Presence. However, this can sometimes lead to the notion of dissolving individuated personality all together...

> *What you are actually looking for, is not the dissolution of personality, but the liberation of attachment to it.*

Your personality is what can be termed your "soul-ray-harmonic" - it is your unique expression of the divine. In Gateway 4, I go on to consider the Seven Rays of Divine Impulse, which like the rays of the rainbow, each have unique yet complimentary colours. They are characteristics of the soul, which blend together, yielding one coherent expression, yet are also able to ebb and flow with the multi-dimensional requirements of the moment...

> *Your soul, when liberated, is as a unique dance with the divine, through all the miraculous circumstances of your life.*

So moving into Enlightenment, is not about dissolving the personality, even if it is a very powerful one. Authentic personality is all about allowing authentic expression of the soul to shine undimmed throughout your bodily vehicles of expression.

3. That in order to raise your vibration, you must avoid density

On the path to Gateway 3, there is a strong natural pull to cleanse and purify the bodymind. This allows the internal metabolism to quieten, in order that you may identify less with the realm of the material and more with that of the spiritual. It is entirely right and necessary, that you raise your vibration in this way, to facilitate the Transfiguration. However, prior to transfiguration, and in the build-up to it, the false self is still owning all authentic expression to some degree or other (and therefore distorting it). In which case, there can be a tendency to think you must resist any course of action that would take you back into density. Thus, there frequently develops an attachment to the sense of purity...

> *To truly raise your vibration, is not to avoid the density within you and in the outer world, because your soul has drawn you here for a reason: to explore the density and liberate aspects of your soul-ray-harmonic that fragment and get lost there.*

Yes, it is vitally important in the build up to transfiguration, that you find plenty of private and personal space, so that you can get to feel, resonate and unleash, your own authentic beingness. However, you must also balance this with allowing yourself to feel into the density in order that the soul may become fully integrated through it. This is a totally natural part of walking the spiritual path in daily life.

To be in a state of full Enlightenment, is to be enlightened by all things. This means to be able to experience darkness, have it flow through you, even temporarily lower your vibration (perhaps in order to serve), and yet still know yourself as the unattached, non-identified Seer of all things.

4. That you must remove yourself from society

Whilst it can be profoundly beneficial to take a break from time to time (a retreat away from negative influences), it is a misconception that you must completely remove yourself from society. It will most definitely be within in your daily interactions with people and life's myriad mosaic, that blockages and restrictions to your evolutionary unfolding reveal themselves.

The only way out is through!

In fact, it is difficult to see how you might completely remove your blockages without confronting them. Perhaps the situation is different in very rare circumstances, for example a yogi, who may always have lived in an environment free from distorting influences. However, for the vast majority who have been exposed over many years to society's conditioning, by far the best way to release those patterns, is by confronting them.

Courses and self-realisation programs can certainly help reveal blockages, such as your inner child and past-life issues. Or they may teach powerful spiritual transformation practices; but ultimately, it is the application of these realisations in everyday life, where true evolutionary progress is made.

It is also important to understand the true nature of healing, and how this can truly take place in daily life. Dis-ease happens where the soul identifies with the drama of society and fragments break away from the soul's mainstream. These fragments gather dense energy within 'eddy currents' that retard the soul's flow. Alternative healing can remove this density yes, but only the soul itself can self-realise and then reintegrate through that distortion.

True healing then, is really self-realisation – to be realising of the One Self - where previously the soul would have become identified and lost in some way.

A teacher or a guide, and indeed a healer, can greatly help by intuitively resonating a similar frequency to the lost aspects of soul (which is why the shamans practice 'soul retrieval' for example), but a person will not truly be healed, until that soul integration process is complete. So still living within society, even though you are purifying yourself, and building your own soul integrity, is a good way to expose the blockages, so that you may fully integrate through them. That said, in today's very toxic and distorting world, it is still vitally important that you create your own space within it.

5. That you must stick rigidly to a particular practice

The key to your spiritual unfolding, is to listen to the quiet voice within, and to follow it moment by moment. Particular spiritual practices can greatly enhance your ability to listen, tune into and to follow the soul - practices such as meditation, yoga, tai chi, five rhythms dance (and Openhand's *soulmotion*) for example. However, in some of these practices, there is the distinct tendency for people to become over disciplined and dogmatic (similar to an overly restrictive religion)...

> *Remember, the soul is a non-identified, free flowing stream of consciousness from the Source. If 'you' try to control it, then 'you' become an identity doing so, rather than that which you truly are – the unbounded, non-identified, Pure Presence of the Seer.*

The soul is your unique expression of the Seer. If you listen to its quiet inner voice, it will tell you exactly what you need to do in order to enhance your unfolding. It is likely that you may wish to meditate (in the formal sense) at particular times of the day; however, if you religiously follow a fixed schedule or program, the mental intention simply overrides the natural spontaneity of the soul, which is seeking to unveil a unique expression in every moment...

> *So if you are truly following the soul, it is likely that your practices for enhancing soul integration, will be varied and continually evolving, just like the changing seasons.*

From my perspective then, when you are being truly authentic, dogmatic discipline is replaced, by a continually evolving and naturally enhancing, rhythm of flowing spontaneity.

Transitioning Gateway 3
- indicators of beginning -

The lead up to the Transfiguration is not an easy one. It is going to challenge you to the very depths of your being...

It is just like riding a rollercoaster: in the dizzy heights of heaven one moment, and the dark depths of hell the next!

Your passions will be tested to the fullest, so that you may determine what are truly authentic expressions of the soul and what, on the other hand, are the 'base metal' distortions that want to 'own' these expressions. So you may feel an inner flow to revel in the absolute joy of living, and then find yourself attached to the materiality of life; you may feel profound love for another, but then find it hard to be without them or else losing yourself within the relationship; you may explore the pull to completely surrender from the drama of society, only to find yourself becoming listless and lacking purpose. All such experiences are designed to help you resolve out and transmute the lower behaviours - the denser consciousness.

Indeed there is no short cutting the transfiguration process. It requires much dedication, perseverance and persistence. There is no magic wand that can be waved, the only way out is through; knowing your pathway is not enough, you must also walk it...

But take heart! As you truly commit, then the distortions reveal themselves - they come into the light so you can work through them. And your soul is seeded to succeed.

So commit yourself to the journey: make the choices, and then seek to understand with profound self honesty, exactly why you made that particular choice. Was it because of a lower based human instinct or conditioning? Or was it a genuine pull to express higher truth, both for your own good and the good of all life?

If you are in a place where you are constantly contemplating and finding the bigger picture through all your choices in life, then this a good indication that you are advancing towards the Transfiguration. Specifically, you are likely to be experiencing some or all of the following:

Indicators the Transfiguration is commencing

- *a roller coaster ride of emotions, thoughts and feelings, where one moment you might feel energised and high, but the next, in confusion and depression*

- *confronting patterns of behaviour emanating from inner child, inner teenager and other old identities*

- *headaches as the third eye and crown chakras begin to open*

- *increasing observation and interpretation of synchronicity*

- *increasing psychic and intuitive capability, with prophetic dreaming, and knowings of the future landing now*

- *expansion of consciousness resulting in multi-dimensional experiences, including deep revelations as to the nature of reality*

- *Opposing Consciousness derailing you from your true pathway*

- *destabilising sense of perception as the Transfiguration consciousness shift occurs*

- *difficulty in communication and right expression.*

Transitioning Gateway 3
- indicators of completion -

The Transfiguration is perhaps the most profoundly magical transition of them all. It is where you get to know yourself as what you truly are - the Seer - experienced as Pure Presence. You will now know, beyond a shadow of a doubt, your inviolable connection with Unity Consciousness, and that your soul is a unique expression arising from that.

It is through the Transfiguration that you get the sense of non-localised presence: on the one hand, it feels as if no one is here; and on the other, as though the whole universe is!

You will have tasted the magical joy of full kundalini activation – a shift so profound, it can shock you to the very core of your being and likewise uplift you into the dizzy heights of heaven.

With full kundalini activation, unfolds a deep recognition and reconnection to the whole of life, experienced throughout your being. The mere contemplation of Mother Nature's simplicity, a tree, a flower, a bird, might be enough to reduce you to tears, as the shocking recognition of the true meaning of life comes fully into focus. Not only do you sense the interconnectedness of all life, but it becomes an intrinsic aspect of your beingness.

It becomes practically impossible to damage, pollute or exploit any sentient life form, unless it is clear beyond all doubt, that doing so is somehow in the higher interests of all life. As the energy of the soul reintegrates and infuses within your being, you experience enormous surges of energy, heat, light and super consciousness. In summary, you are likely to experience some or all of the following:

Indicators the Transfiguration is complete

- *full kundalini activation will have occurred, and been experienced perhaps as profound bliss or indescribable joy*

- *you will be experiencing yourself as non-localised presence, moving through life now more as a flow of consciousness*

- *kundalini activation will have been accompanied by powerful surges of energy, perhaps accompanied by lucid dream like experiences*

- *the pull and characteristics of your soul will be felt within, although you might not necessarily be able to define its qualities*

- *friends and family will notice that your sense of being seems to have changed quite dramatically*

- *you are likely to appear very relaxed, non-attached and calm*

- *all choices become more about the revelation of your divine being and alignment with the deeper meaning of life*

- *there is likely to be a strong inner motivation to divine service*

- *there will be feelings of complete at-one-ment with the universe.*

Gateway 3
- summary -

Imagine the experience of everything being stripped away - everything you considered 'real', every belief, thought and emotion. Imagine the building blocks of a reality, founded on the idea of separation, being mercilessly obliterated. Imagine the very tissue of our paper-thin reality, being shredded to pieces in the blink of an eye...

> *Imagine you as no longer the sense of some kind of fixed identity traveling through life, but rather the expansiveness of pure potential, with life moving through you!*

Impossible to imagine? Indeed it is, for the Transfiguration can only be experienced. Which is why this true taste of Enlightenment is much misunderstood. It is not about being 'love and light' for example. In the absoluteness of Pure Presence, everything is integrated as one within; and then experience (that you may perceive as love) flows through you – but you do not have to manifest this intentionally, it just effortlessly arises from within.

> *This is the true nature of pure being. You open a space internally, and that which you are truly meant to be in this moment, simply emerges from within you.*

Words, books, poems and texts have been written through the ages about this glorious state of non-identified presence; that which miraculously arises, like the mythical Phoenix from the ashes of burnt out identity. Some great poets might express the experience with an acceptable eloquence, but even they fail to convey the extraordinary flavour that can only be tasted with your own lips.

So what is the value of discussing it at all?

We are transitioning very turbulent times, and currently society in general has negligible understanding of, or tolerance for, those who might experience temporary destabilisation and dislocation as the Transfiguration kicks in. For some, the final kundalini shift into Transfiguration can be relatively smooth, but for many, it will likely be earth-shattering. Where the sense of dislocation is intense, health service support might be considered. Unfortunately, all too often, mental instability or even "psychosis" is diagnosed and drug induced 'corrective' treatment prescribed, when all that is really required, is to allow the new consciousness to integrate in a nurturing, accepting and gently supportive environment.

Although you cannot know exactly when the transition is going to happen, it pays to be aware when you are approaching the Gateway, and to be very open to changing the circumstances of your environment to accommodate it. Perhaps it might be best to spend time at a retreat centre that understands the process? Perhaps you should connect with a spiritual guide who has been through it? At the very least, it would be wise to involve a close friend, explain to them what you feel is happening, and that you may need to contact them at short notice for support...

During the Transfiguration shift, for the most part, people really need a supportive hand, with someone openly and non-judgmentally holding the space for them. Then it integrates quite naturally.

Following the Transfiguration, the way you experience life changes quite radically. The sense of choice, for example, is forever changed: it is not whether you should do 'this' or 'that'. It all becomes about how to be - since you have realised only authentic beingness can create authentic reality. Even when you get tight and find it difficult to make a choice (perhaps because of karma - see Gateway 4), the approach is to hold the space, let the tightness unwind, and then watch for Right Action naturally revealing itself.

It is as though a path of light unfolds before you, with everything clicking into place, to reveal more of who you are.

Intuitively, you either know the answers to all arising questions, or how to get them. Whilst you may still choose to work with a guide, the only acceptable ones are those evolved enough to act as a mirror, either reflecting your beingness or your distortions...

> *"Do not believe anything because it is said by an authority,*
> *or if it is said to come from angels,*
> *or from Gods or from an inspired source.*
> *Believe it only if you have explored it*
> *in your own heart and mind and body*
> *and found it to be true.*
> *Work out your own path, through diligence."*
> *Guatama Buddha*

Paradoxically, since you have now stopped seeking a particular outcome in life, everything you need to do begins to unfold before you. Perhaps for the first time, you are likely to get an accurate insight into your heavenly purpose here on Earth. Maybe it is to help Benevolent Consciousness by harnessing the new shift energies? Perhaps it is to help cleanse Gaia's field? Could it be to help people overcome their own barriers and blockages? Or perhaps it is to help maintain a degree of stability and sustainability whilst more people step onto the internal super highway that is our Ascension...

> *"In the beginning there appears to be*
> *endless choice of direction,*
> *with the course being set by the ego.*
> *After a while, it becomes abundantly clear,*
> *that you are being drawn to a directed path,*
> *a path that leads to a way...*
> *for each, a unique way of being.*
> *And once you have found that way,*
> *you discover choice once more...*
> *either to follow the way or not.*
> *If you choose to follow the way,*
> *it leads back to the path,*
> *the path of divine service."*
> *Openhand*

Whatever your mission here is, it is likely that you will now get an authentic taste of it. Let us be absolutely clear though, in my experience, it is highly unlikely that you will be trusted with the full, unfettered support and resources of Benevolent Consciousness to fulfill that mission yet. Why not? After the Transfiguration, it is highly likely, perhaps unavoidable, that new shadow identities will arise...

This happens because the liberated in-flowing soul, now passes through the Fourth Density within: it flows through your past-life karma – the ultimate cause of your soul's incarnation.

So whilst the Transfiguration will be a miraculous transition in your journey, it is still not the end of the story. Far from it: now it is highly likely you will begin to regress into waves of past-life experience - some will be relatively gentle, others literally earth-shattering. It all depends on the challenges and trauma you may have encountered on your journey through existence.

To some, it will feel like being crucified on the altar of unadulterated, absolute truth. You need have no fear though. Understanding what may well come your way, can greatly ease the process through it. And with each regression into the density, comes that incredible sense of aliveness and invigorated liberation, as you reclaim those priceless, lost aspects of yourself.

It is to Gateway 4 then, that the path next turns its attention.

Gateway 4

"Enlightenment"

*"Your pain is the breaking of the shell
that encloses your understanding.
Even as the stone of the fruit must break,
that its heart may stand in the sun,
so must you know your pain."*

Kahlil Gibran

Key: confront karma

From Chris Bourne's memoirs...

I was sitting close to the front in the quaint Spiritualist Church listening intently to the Sunday evening medium helping people make connections with the dearly departed. Of course mediumship has been much criticised, even ridiculed, within society, but it seems to me this scepticism is mostly born of ignorance. I am convinced that had any critic had the conscience to visit such a humble, spiritual abode, with neither pretence nor need of justification, what they would have discovered, was a profoundly beautiful and divinely loving approach to spirituality. I witnessed countless connections by mediums, who could not possibly have known the details they revealed without some bridge to the 'other side'.

On this particular Sunday, the medium was a wizened old lady. Teetering on a walking stick she may have been, but her croaky voice only very thinly veiled a rock-steady self-acceptance. I had not seen her before, but it quickly became apparent, that she had no need for people to accept either her, or her clairvoyant discernments. Through tired and wrinkled skin, her light shone nevertheless very brightly. She was simply, awesomely okay to deliver exactly what she got with no frills, but with astounding self-assurance and belief.

The evening was drawing to a close, when suddenly she appeared to be receiving a communication. After a moment or two of quiet reflection, she looked up and without hesitation, pointed her bony finger directly at me. "You Sir, I have a message to give you. Whilst you may look completely relaxed on the outside, on the inside is a hidden tension. You were involved in a car crash a few years back, were you not?" "Yes", I replied rather meekly. She continued, "Well you've been living on a life support machine ever since, and your guides would like you to switch it off now. That's all I have to give you." I was completely taken aback. What on earth could she mean?

The next day found me at my desk, lost in my own inner world, quietly contemplating the curious exchange of the previous evening. When nothing immediately came to mind, I resorted to the approach I should have best begun with - asking the universe! So I went inwards, using breath to quieten the mind. I allowed the question to arise: "What is the universe revealing to me now?" It didn't take long to be answered - it never did. My attention was immediately drawn to a picture I had on the wall in the corner of the room. It was of the Oxford and Cambridge Varsity Boat Race. I had rowed in Isis, the reserve team, which in 1985 had beaten Cambridge in record time. Back then, it had been a proud achievement for me, and the picture now adorned my wall, hanging over the trophy cabinet containing many other medals, photos and achievements of the past.

It was suddenly clear where I had gone 'wrong'. In my divorce settlement, I had relinquished everything we jointly owned, bar a couple of pieces of furniture. Why then had I felt the need to keep the trophy cabinet? "Was there still an attachment to achievement?" At precisely that moment, all the electricity went off in the building! It seemed I had my answer. "Perhaps then, the life support machine analogy, meant that a little part of my ego was still clinging to life?" The lights suddenly sprang on again providing me an unmistakable answer. I was soon to be heading off to undertake an Easter fast in Israel's Negev Desert, "Maybe then I should get rid of the trophy cabinet, together with all the medals, awards and photos of my earlier life, before I go?" Once again, all the lights went off in the building. The guidance was unequivocal.

So it was, that on the Thursday before Easter 2005, I

had erected a huge bonfire, upon which I was now busily bestowing any final reminder of my pre-awakened life; I was signalling my purpose to smoke out and confront any attachment to identity, which might still be lingering within.

On top went my treasured Karate Black Belt; my Commando Green Beret; Gulf War medals earned during the liberation of Kuwait; various sporting trophies; my degree certificate, along with a whole array of nostalgic photos. Finally, on top, I placed the most meaningful accolade I still possessed - the rowing blade I used in the Boat Race, still ingrained with the blood, sweat and tears the achievement had cost.

As I carried the wooden blade across my shoulders towards the 'funeral pyre', tears began rolling down my cheeks. They were tears both of sadness at the sense of loss (it felt like I was losing the memories too), but also ones of deep joy. I recognised that finally, liberation was beckoning me. As I watched the dancing flames engulf the last vestiges of nostalgic memorabilia, I could not help feeling I was being guided to some final crucifixion. Painful as it may have been, I knew that courage would always be rewarded with some synchronistic recognition for effort by the ever-watchful eye of Benevolent Consciousness. As I went to survey the ashes the next day, seemingly nothing had withstood the intense heat, even pewter had melted. Then, floating around on the surface of the ashes, I noticed a pink card, which had somehow miraculously survived the blaze. My attention was drawn to these four words: "degree ceremony, admit one". I was no longer in any doubt: I had received my invitation to step through Gateway 4.

It was now Easter Friday, and in keeping with tradition (well sort of!) it began with a 'last supper' of pizza and red wine in Cafe Uno at Heathrow International Airport. It all seems a bit cheesy now, but I was simply responding to an inner pull to act, reinforced by the synchronistic confirmations of Benevolent Consciousness. I was departing for a twenty one day fast in Israel's Negev Desert, seemingly to break through the mental identification - the "shadow" - that was dimming the light of my soul and preventing the Enlightenment of the non-identified Seer shining through my being.

Having spent Easter itself in Jerusalem, my drop off point in the Negev was at one end of the Ramon Crater approximately 30 miles from the border with Egypt and the Sinai. The Ramon Crater is an area of outstanding natural beauty, a sort of miniature version of the Grand Canyon. Although quite rocky and arid, it still had patches of vegetation with early spring flowers. A seasonal blip meant it was a lot hotter than I had been led to expect, so I hiked mostly in darkness and rested during the day.

Late one evening, having reached the far edge of the crater, only a few miles from the inviting quietness of the Sinai, I stopped to lie down and rest. Finding myself a degree of comfort in a shallow ditch by the side of the central track, I looked up at the twinkling stars in the dark night sky, and began to release inner tightness within my bodymind. Hunger had long since subsided, and the quieter inner metabolism meant that my consciousness could easily expand, thus intensifying the connection with universal life energy. Finally, I felt myself beginning to dissolve into oneness. I knew my awareness was right on the very precipice of non-identified presence, dissociated completely, even from the interconnectedness of Unity Consciousness. I was teetering on the verge of the absoluteness I'd tasted briefly at Transfiguration - the non-identified Seer of all things.

Then, right at that very moment, where I was delicately poised on the edge of the void, my attention was drawn to distant footsteps making their way along the track in the direction of where I lay. As the sound drew closer, it was clear there was more than one person. Then suddenly it dawned: this was a group of people, marching in time together - an Israeli platoon no less! What would they make of this strange bearded foreigner, dressed in desert-style, ex-military clothing, lying covertly in a ditch in the middle of their desert? The prospect of a few weeks interrogation at the hands of Mossad did not seem a very inviting prospect! Not at all what I had intended. Yet again, my consciousness was brought to the hidden dangers of intention and expectation.

I had no choice but to surrender to the flow of events and lay quietly, whilst the universe rolled the dice. Perhaps Higher Guidance was playing a game of "chicken" with me. Fortunately, it was not my destiny to be discovered that night. Although only a few feet away, the platoon marched right past me without noticing a thing. As they disappeared into the distance, I began to chuckle, then cackle and finally burst into raucous laughter. Yes, the universe was having an immense cosmic joke at my expense!

My fast ended prematurely at precisely that moment - I no longer needed to achieve anything. I should shut up, pack up, and go home, which is exactly what I intended to do. But if I have learned one thing in my spiritual life thus far, it is that Benevolent Consciousness likes to catch us unawares. Just when we think we have got the lesson we came for, just when we are completely off guard, that is when our benevolent guiding hand likes to strike. How can you expose an imposter, if it knows exactly what is about to happen? No, to truly smoke out the shadow, we have to be caught completely unawares.

I decided I would end my expedition early and make my way back home. Although by now I was getting very tired, I felt to take in some of the natural beauty spots I had passed along the way. Making my way back along the Ramon Crater, my attention was drawn to a weather-beaten sign pointing to the "Prism Gorge". I felt a clear inner pull to take a look, but did not question too much the curious sounding name - why had they used the name "Prism"? It failed to occur to me at the time, that a prism breaks down light into its component parts - another way of putting it, might be: "bringing into the light, that which is normally hidden from view". Sometimes synchronicity works that way - we only know what the 'omens' mean after the event has transpired. This sign was to prove deeply revelatory indeed.

The Prism Gorge had many outstanding natural qualities, and very quickly, I was lost in its captivating beauty, not noticing how the bare rock surfaces harnessed and intensified the sun's heat. By the time I felt the magnifying effect of its burning rays, it was too late to retrace my steps. Besides, I was now extremely tired from the fast and also quite dehydrated. I would need to find shelter. But there was no shelter! Clearly that is why they named it after a prism, which captures and intensifies light - it certainly did not shade it. So I erected a bivouac between two rocks to provide a little shade under which to hide.

The heat of the sun grew stronger and stronger, catching me in its direct blaze, no matter how I wriggled and shuffled. Within a few hours of intense heat, I felt strongly dehydrated and sun-stricken. After a couple more hours, I was becoming delirious and hallucinating. Unable any longer to move my weather-beaten body, it seemed as if it was time to expire completely. Visions of memorable bygone events drifted in and out of my awareness. All those times where I had efforted and struggled to achieve, where I had craved peer acceptance to fulfill lack of self-esteem.

The final, most testing experience to appear, was the Royal Marine Commando Course. Synchronistically, I was carrying with me the little red dagger arm patch that marines wear on their uniform. I always carried it to remind me to keep going in times of difficulty. As I took it out of my pocket, I noticed that upside-down, it reminded me of a crucifix - a burning red cross - this indeed was a crucifixion of my ego. At that point it did not matter to me any longer whether I lived or died. I had seen my shadow, the imposter of achievement, glamour and efforting masquerading in a world of selfless, spiritual service. I buried the dagger to signify my readiness to 'bury' my shadow, and surrendered to the seemingly inevitable; at which point, there was once more the sublime taste of the tasteless - the unidentified Seer - before I drifted off to a placeless place.

Initially, I was not sure whether I was still alive or dead (at least in a physical sense), but after an unknown period of time, somehow an angelic energy lifted me onto my feet and carried me forward. It took me two further days and nights to stagger out of the crater. Having long since lost my bearings, I had no idea whether I would make it back or not. But then suddenly, as if out of nowhere, I stumbled into an encampment. Of all the things it might have been, it turned out to be a retreat centre! At the entrance was an attractive, Middle-Eastern lady, with long dark hair, sitting in the shade, reading a book. She carried a strong Magdalen energy. Introducing herself as "Noah" and greeting me with a warm smile... "Yes, we have one bed left" she offered, without me even opening my lips. There was no longer any doubt - I had died and gone to heaven!

(Author's note: Chris' irony was actually very close to the truth – it was in the Prism Gorge, that our souls exchanged places. His was yearning to be released from this plane, and so shifted into the Fourth Density. Mine, on the other hand, yearned to come into the physical: I was the 'angelic presence' he spoke of, which helped lift him up, and carry him out of the desert).

Gateway 4
- overview -

Passage through the 'Red Sea' -
the Fourth Density,
or 'plane of karma'.

By now on your journey (after the Transfiguration), you will have made the crucial switch from identifying with the false self, to becoming the Seer, expressed as the soul, through the bodymind. In other words, you experience yourself (perhaps for the first time) as non-identified presence, what some might call "God". It is a simple state of pure clarity existing in the background of all activity. It is so ordinary, so normal, and yet so miraculous, that when you finally dissolve into it, you may feel like every light in the universe has just been switched on simultaneously:

you have realised the absolute truth of life.

Yet when you are looking for it, or when you cannot accept it as the target of all your searching, efforting and longing, then suddenly you become separated from it once more. How can you see yourself when you are all there is? Here is the divine paradox - when you are intentionally looking for it, it remains always just out of reach, like a young child grasping at a helium-filled balloon; but when you just let go and open yourself up, the 'target' of your aspiration actually moves to you...

You cannot aim for the Pure Presence of the Seer, because
that very intention alone, establishes the separation from it.
What you can do however, is learn to align with your soul.
Then ultimately, as the soul, you literally fall into presence.

It is metaphored wonderfully in the place of all clear answers

- Mother Nature. Consider the Kingfisher: since light refracts (bends) when it leaves the surface of water, the Kingfisher never actually sees the exact location of the fish it is going for. It simply heads for the image, but knows that at some point, it must step off its trajectory and dive completely into the unknown. Ignoring the image itself - *the illusionary reality* - it dives through the surface into absolute truth, whereupon its goal is finally realised.

So it is with the soul. The soul is your trajectory to an illusionary target – a placeless place. You follow the path, but at some point, you will see past the target and simply fall into the truth. Then you literally become the truth, and have continual flowing experiences of it - all of life offers the opportunity to taste the constant, crystal clear clarity of non-identified presence. Thoughts, emotions, feelings and even the heartfelt longing of the soul, all arise within this infinite, unadulterated potential; yet it remains always constant - the Seer - an inviolable eternal presence.

At this point, you are in an enlightened state, flowing freely without self identification and without attachment to the drama of life. It is in such a state that you - as the Seer - feel the soul for the first time in all its purity. It arises within you and flows through the various layers of the bodymind. Whilst you may not grasp it in your mind (because there is no need to), you can still intrinsically recognise the characteristics of your soul, as an harmonic of different essences, what I refer to as the "Seven Rays of Divine Impulse".

Having an idea of what these are, can be greatly beneficial to your journey, because the path is all about becoming increasingly authentic. The more you can align with your soul, the easier it becomes to 'fall into truth', then to live passionately and creatively, becoming totally fulfilled with the awesome majesty that you truly are. You become satisfied just being and expressing you.

Each of these 'Seven Rays' (just like the rays of the rainbow), has distinct qualities, which when unleashed, radiate through your being. Each also has a corresponding distortion, because until the soul is fully self-realised, it tends to attach to the density of physical reality as the rays shine through your bodymind – *the ego owns them*. Thus, spotting the distortion of the particular ray that you may now be expressing (anger in the case of the "ray 1 warrior", for example), is greatly helpful- it means you now have a strong clue as to what authentic behaviour is being invited in the moment. In the case of anger, for instance, you are possibly being invited to find purposeful creative strength.

> *Finding the accurate expression of your soul-ray-harmonic in the moment, is crucially important to maintaining the non-identified, enlightened state.*

I have observed how many 'non-dualistic' processes out there in the world today, are actually self-defeating for this very reason: in ditching the attachment before fully going into the source pain, they are inadvertently 'throwing the baby out with the bathwater' – they are dissolving the very essence of the soul, and thereby are not in the Source at all, but rather an isolated bubble of Unity Consciousness (which can feel like Enlightenment). This illusionary reality can look peaceful, calm and connected, but quite often, you see that the person in this state is quite monotone – they are subtly denying the full pallet of soulful expression. In which case, they are still not fully in the presence of the Seer: there is only a sort of intellectual Enlightenment (I witness many teachers and guides in the world at the moment who teach as if they are enlightened, but who are really coming from this detached state).

This is why in the Openhand Approach, we strongly encourage aligning with the qualities of the soul, and this happens by getting into the places where the soul gets stuck – where it identifies with reality. By knowing this tightness within you (for example through the Openhandway process described in Gateway 2), you have an invaluable 'target' to work with and unwind. In which case, you unleash the soul through the tightness. Which means you can then effortlessly drop into presence. So knowing the qualities of the soul can greatly help - you know what to give energy and focus to, as you begin to spot the soul emerging through you.

Here below then, is my interpretation of the soul's qualities as the Seven Rays. At your core beingness level, you have *all Seven Rays*, even though some may have become suppressed.

Each person will have a unique blend of them (the "soul-ray-harmonic"), although one or more of the qualities in you will likely be stronger than the others. I have included the key gifts of beingness, plus their corresponding distortions. They are not meant as dogmatic gospel; more as a pointer, to help you locate and align with a similar vibrational experience inside yourself.

The Seven Rays that comprise your Soul-Ray-Harmonic

Ray 1: purposeful creative will

The 'leader' in you

Gifts:
courageous, brave, passionate, creative, motivational, inspiring, focussing, catalysing.

Distortions:
controlling, untrusting, insensitive, too focused.

Ray 1 is the driving sense of purpose to create. It is the manifestation of the divine masculine principle throughout the universe. From the place of separation, it is that undeniable inner will to find and create a higher level of harmony, both within yourself, and between all sentient beings. It causes you to challenge, and break apart, the status quo which may be holding you in a lower level of realisation. The Ray 1 inspires life's motivational leaders.

Ray 2: surrendering unconditional love

The 'servant' in you

Gifts:

*surrendering, unconditionally loving, accepting, peaceful,
contented, sensitive, understanding, empathic.*

Distortions:

*weakness, timidity, self-dissolving, unmotivated,
lacking inspiration, overly emotional, boundaryless.*

Ray 2 initiates the impulse of unconditional love for life. It is the manifestation of the divinely feminine principle of surrendered acceptance throughout the universe. It is the empathising compassion that willingly embraces, without judgment or need to change, the inherent imperfection in all sentient life and situations. Ray 2 strongly inspires the selfless servants of life.

Ray 3: interpreting authentic reality

The 'interpreter' in you

Gifts:

*observant, aware, articulate, astute, logical,
mathematical, systematic.*

Distortions:

intense, complex, self absorbed, doubting.

Ray 3 harnesses and processes higher abstract wisdom, delivering it in a form that provides a clear interpretation of your current, authentic reality. In other words, it is how you know what is really real. People with a strong Ray 3 influence notice the natural patterning in life, bringing the formless into form in such a way that can be understood and appreciated by many. Ray 3 inspires life's translators, creative artists and mathematicians.

Ray 4: harmonising through right resolution

The 'diplomat' in you

Gifts:
diplomatic, facilitational, compromising, discerning.

Distortions:
hypocritical, dithery, procrastinating, unscrupulous.

Ray 4 is the divine rationalising energy, which helps you find right resolution with other sentient life. It is the ray impulse that blends passion with compassion. It provides the discernment to confront unjust situations in a non-judgmental way, and find working solutions that benefit all. Its purpose is to progressively unwind the lower harmony in a manageable way; then to weave together the threads of a more equitable, higher one. People with a highly active Ray 4 tend to be life's diplomats, politicians and teachers.

Ray 5: realising abstract higher wisdom

The 'scientist' in you

Gifts:
*scientific, metaphysical, altruistic, intellectual,
insightful, all-knowing, business-like, practical.*

Distortions:
*inflexible, limited, dogmatic, rigid,
lacking imagination, colourless, monotone.*

The Ray 5 enables you to realise the infinite complexities of the universe as pure knowing within your being. This 'science' is abstract, all-encompassing, and rather than rationalised, is more sensed, as an art form, like poetry in perpetual motion. But it is also rigorous, accepting only what it perceives to be the truth, dispensing with half-truths and the wishy washy. Ray 5 is the 'business-like' aspect of yourself, which enables you to attune to the accuracy of the universal flow, then harness it for co-creative exploration, deeper understanding and further evolution. The Ray 5 animates life's scientists and creative business leaders.

Ray 6: yearning self expression

The 'artful expressionist' in you

Gifts:
*expressive, influential, charismatic, idealistic,
liberational, colourful, devotional, faithful.*

Distortions:
*egotistical, aloof, arrogant, self-righteous,
unreasonable, conceited, narcissistic.*

Ray 6 inspires focus on your life's purpose: to unfold and express who you truly are, mostly as a means to inspiring others through divine service. It generates commitment and devotion to your cause, radiating your soul in all its brilliant colour. It is motivational in its charisma. The Ray 6 provides the unquenchable driving force to express your innate qualities, and inspire others to shine their light too. Humanity's philosophers, spiritual leaders, actors and performing artists are all driven by the Ray 6 influence.

Ray 7: shaping synchronistic magic

The 'magician' in you

Gifts:
*entrepreneurial, creative, manifesting,
spontaneous, self-believing, trusting.*

Distortions:
*ungrounded, unrealistic, uncompromising,
disconnected, woolly, 'New Agey'.*

Ray 7 provides the ingredient of pure magic on your life's journey. If you are able to master your inner distortions, and pause just long enough in the drama of life, then you can open up to spontaneous, synchronistic and co-creative magic. It will shape surroundings and manifest for you, even though you may not always be aware you are doing so. You are therefore able to catalyse and initiate the surrounding field for the maximum benefit and upliftment of all. Ray 7 inspires life's 'magicians' and entrepreneurs.

Shadow Identities – 'imposters' of the soul

Despite the increasingly aligned and fulsome experiences of the soul now coursing through the bodymind, it is still not yet fully unleashed in its entirety - the soul will not yet fully diffuse through your being. Why not?

It is at the point where you really begin to experience deep soul infusion, that shadow identities arise. This is where the flow of the soul becomes distorted by subtle filters in the Fourth Density, within the 'causal body' (see Gateway 5). These challenging, very deceptive filters, are caused by the karma of past-life experiences (often traumatic). The unleashed soul now flows down through these filters on its way from the Source. The problem is not so much that fragments are breaking off and becoming separated, as with the ego, it is more that the mainstream of the soul is becoming subtly deceived by its own mis-perception of reality.

Thus 'shadow identities' form; these are exceptionally clever, for they know the 'correct' behaviour of the soul. However, there will be a slight time-lag in the soul's flow – like an echo - which takes you out of alignment. It can only be perceived through profound self-honesty – witnessing that under certain circumstances, your beingness moves behind the flow, creating small 'bubbling eddy currents' of slight discomfort...

> *Someone who is truly present and aware, will likely witness this karmic filtering effect as micro-expressions in your face, and slight contractions within your energy field.*

It is the presence of these filters that can take on a 'shadow identity' (some teachings refer to them as 'imposters of the soul'). The shadow identity is much more subtle than previously experienced. Unlike its predecessors (such as the inner child and inner teenager), impulses to act are not initiated within it, they always come from the Source; however, by acting as a filter, the shadow can distort or dim the divine light you are now feeling. So typically for example, you may be engaged in spiritual, apparently selfless, work of some kind, but the soul might be slightly lacking full trust in the divine due to the karmic filter of lack of support (perhaps a previous venture in a previous life was unsuccessful, caused great heart-ache, and so trust in benevolence was lost). Now, that filter retains the slight contraction of fear in not being supported, and so works to make sure there is some (hidden) payback for the apparently selfless work. This is how a typical shadow identity then builds around that aspect of karma.

So subtle are these identities, that they are highly difficult to see for yourself, because they can feel so real and authentic. They may manifest, for example, as the slightest trace of efforting to reach many people, heal the sick, save the planet, protect Mother Nature etc. It could be that the soul is authentically given to do these things, but that slight degree of ownership of the purpose, will add that extra bit of energy, the extra impetus, that over-accentuates perfect delivery of Right Action.

It is exactly this obscuring energy, which can turn away those people of the correct vibration to receive your particular transmission. It could be that you still reach many people and that a message is transmitted, however, is it exactly the right message for exactly the right people? So it is this shadow identity that you must deal with during the Gateway 4 transition.

The key to dissolving these shadow identities, is to understand exactly where they come from and how they operate. As previously stated, the shadow forms when the light of the soul gets slightly filtered by karma: so the soul touches past-life karma as it flows through the causal body and activates it. Now, this layer of consciousness begins to influence many patterns of experience in your daily life; these subtle karmic filters now manifest external 'images', so that you may see, and better understand, the blockages you are activating. You are now being given the opportunity to confront and deal with your past-life karma.

The process used to dissolve the karma, is the same as the 9 step process applied in Gateway 3 – basically to confront, feel into, become as one with, then unleash the soul through it. Upon which, you fall back into the Void of Presence - the Seer.

It will greatly help you get into the karma, if you know the kinds of shadows that can arise. Therefore vigilance of your behaviours is crucial, with a careful observation of possible filtering distortions.

You must find the loose threads, and pull on them!

Here are some typical ones I have experienced (they will always be a distortion of a particular ray of consciousness of the soul)...

Typical Shadow Identities:

the false prophet: *owning the selfless actions of the soul, requiring a subtle 'payback' (perhaps because of ultimate lack of trust), thus rendering selfless actions less effective.*

the controller: *not fully trusting in the natural flow of the universe, or that somehow, Right Action will ultimately happen. Thus there develops a covert, over-energised manifestation of events.*

the questioner: *whilst it is important to question what is really authentic, overly questioning creates a lack of knowing - it causes you to lag slightly behind the natural flow of events, which creates lesser harmonies.*

the dissolver: *this is concerned with the risk of identification with events, and therefore tends to be dissolving of the natural strength of the Seven Rays flowing through you. It makes you less effective in life than you otherwise could be.*

the absolutist: *a shadow needing to always express absolute truth, whatever the cost, thereby unnecessarily damaging the energetic harmony of the moment.*

the pacifist: *yes, the soul is compassionate to all life; however, sometimes realities need to be broken down and distortions in others challenged. Having an overly (or owned) compassionate approach, can reduce your effectiveness as a catalyst.*

the teacher/guide: *by now, you will have great capacity to help others see the way forward on the path. But it is their path? It is vitally important to allow others the space to self-realise, rather than be overly leading, teaching or healing.*

It is also important to realise, that the shadow serves a beneficial function too. By owning the natural impulses of the soul as they arise and express through the bodymind, the shadow ensures that the impulses gain traction in the dense energetic environment, which they tend to encounter. It could be the case, that without this additional amplification, the impulses might dissolve just as soon as they arise - that is until the newly transfigured being becomes adept at feeling and attuning to the arising impulses, then acting on them, even though they might at times be quite gentle.

So the presence of the shadow is a double-edged sword, with both benefits (initially) and drawbacks. In the beginning, you can benefit from amplified expression of your higher knowing; however, just as a growing child is nurtured and protected in the formative years, so, you must at some point, be weaned off this support, to stand wholly and squarely on 'self-realised feet'. You must ultimately confront and dissolve all shadow identities if you are to experience your destiny...

Enlightenment: the constant experience
of non-identified presence.

There is another reason why the shadow cannot be allowed to persist within your consciousness. The fact that there is still some personal payback, required as a result of the shadow's presence (in whatever guise that might be), means that you may still be susceptible to the distorting interference of Opposing Consciousness. In this evolved state, it is likely that you can be highly influential to others embarked on their own spiritual path. Thus, if the messages being infused downwards from the Source are being subtly distorted (thus diverted from the truth), then there is the risk of others being led astray. Therefore, it is not until you have dissolved all shadow identities, that you can be fully trusted by Benevolent Consciousness to help unfold the Divine Purpose.

That is why (in my view), authentic spiritual work is only provided resources gradually. Rapid success on the other hand, can tend to indicate the subtle intervention of Opposing Consciousness, leading people off-track, attaching them to a physical outcome.

In our core beingness, we are all leaders, who can inspire in particular situations. However, the best kind of leadership, is that which encourages others to empower themselves to find their own truth, and their own way forward.

The distorting intervention of Opposing Consciousness (which tends to exploit karmic filters), can be a difficult predicament. On your journey to this point, you will have learned the importance of listening to your own inner voice, as opposed to being overly influenced by others. You will have become adept at distinguishing where impulses are genuinely from the soul, and where they are not. Since you are now always flowing as the soul, you will have come to know the authentic originating Source of your soul-ray-harmonic. You will also know the importance of spontaneity and so, increasingly, you simply allow your expression to flow - you are now much more able to process your actions seamlessly, 'on the hoof,' as they are happening. And you tend not to get stuck in processing (when you are not consciously working with karma). You realise the very act of such dense processing, can take you out of your experience of the Seer.

So, as the soul arises, the shadow is cast, but as soon as you settle again, it disappears!

It is at this point, that only dramatic action can really expose the shadow. It comes in the form of what some have called the "crucifixion". The shadow must be caught unaware, so you can notice the effects of its influence, even after it has disappeared from view. At this point, if you allow it to, Benevolent Consciousness will guide you to (apparently destructive) events to expose the effects of your shadow: where you are being less than 100% selfless; where you are subtly avoiding something; where a part of you owns success; or where you might be lacking ultimate trust in the universe. In circumstances like these, the thread of karmic filters can be exposed. If you bring attention to the threads, the karma will activate and you will be caused to feel the full pain of the shadow's attachment. In which case, you can regress into the pain, honour it, find the presence of the Seer once more, and thus dissolve the shadow - *the soul is liberated through it.*

If you have processed karma before (either in this lifetime or past ones), this could possibly happen during one powerful event, as Chris described in his own personal experience in the Negev. However, it is much more likely to happen over a protracted period of time (probably several years), especially if you have several shadow identities to dissolve, which is usually the case. In this way, it is as though you are being caused to sacrifice yourself on the final altar of absolute truth...

> During this 'crucifixion', you are guided on a seemingly self-destructive path, so the wheat can be separated from the chaff. Extreme circumstances are created to 'rattle your cage', so that suddenly, it becomes abundantly clear where past-life karma has been influencing events.

Destructive situations such as these, clearly indicate that you are now truly transitioning the fourth corridor. The hidden fears, subtle desires or ambitions of the shadow - *the manifestations of your karma* - are exposed and brought into the light.

If you keep surrendering in the jaws of fear and doubt, if you keep having the courage to let go, despite whatever may be happening to you, then these karmic filters will activate - you will regress into the past-life trauma, whereupon the soul can self-realise through it. It is here – in this phase - that the full, shocking recognition of what you have truly been through on your soul's journey finally dawns.

You may experience incredible visions of ageless experiences that have forged your soul throughout millions of years and countless incarnations. Some of these will be tainted with fear and suffering, as the emergent soul has been unfolding itself to ever increasing sophistication and understanding...

> "Suffering is generated where there is lack
> of understanding as to the absolute order of things.
> It is merely a mirror, by which the
> soul can finally see the Seer:
> something so pure, so resplendent, so spectacular,
> that when the soul unfolds into its full brilliance,
> everything clicks majestically into place;
> upon which, all suffering disappears."
> Openhand

Your karmic filters are the final constraint limiting the soul from full, unbridled reintegration within your being. If you have the courage to confront the shadow identities by following the path shaping before you, then ultimately, you will find yourself bathing in the suffering of your past lives - all your final self deceptions...

> Here is the ultimate test: you are entering the inner sanctum of God, but are being asked to crawl unceremoniously to the altar.

You delve deeply into your shadows, and with the flail of profound self-honesty, you are laid bare. The tainted creations of your filters are exposed before you, and torn apart in streaming flows of light...

In your own life, you are in effect, mirroring the big picture of light coming into darkness throughout the universe: consciousness coming into unconsciousness.

Finally, you are washed through with the full consciousness of humanity's predicament, and that of our blessed Mother Earth. The causal body has been purified, thereby dissolving the final restraint limiting you from the unadulterated, ultimate joy of harmonious unity. It is a bitter sweet experience: it simultaneously exposes you to the awesome majesty of being, and the all pervading suffering of other sentient life, still stuck within Separation Consciousness.

You may get overwhelmed by the experience, temporarily sucked into the internal/external drama once more; but fairly quickly, your soul - *an expression of the Seer* - normalises in this new, unprotected, unsheathed environment. The tsunami has passed, the ship rights itself, and you quickly attune to the new way of being, as a newborn child of the universe.

Now you have consciously tasted the full pain and suffering of separation from God – *the absolute Pure Presence.* You have not shirked, but drank it in through every pore. You have submerged yourself under the water; willingly drowned and discovered the true essence you were seeking all along - that which cannot be violated even in the midst of absolute violation. You have transcended the inner fires of hell, burned away the dross of the shadow, and yielded to the sublime taste of absoluteness through all things.

Finally, you dissolve into Enlightenment.
The Fourth Gateway has been completed.

Transitioning Gateway 4
- essential tools -

1. **Self-vigilance:** *watch for the presence of the shadow, where you might be acting from a less than authentic, higher self purpose.*

2. **Follow genuine guidance - focus on aligning with the soul:** *keenly follow inner guidance, supported by objective synchronicity. Watch for the possibility of interference by Opposing Consciousness.*

3. **Confront past-life karma, dissolve the filters:** *confront, process and release past-life karma as your consciousness expands through the causal body. Dissolve the karmic filters.*

4. **Find the key into presence:** *surrender absolutely into your karmic regressions, then look for the key to open the doorway into presence.*

5. **Enlightenment:** *settle into complete self-acceptance and assume rightful inner perception of the fully enlightened being.*

1. Self-vigilance: *watch for the presence of the shadow, where you might be acting from a less than authentic, higher self purpose.*

The shadow identity is unlike any filter previously encountered (such as the inner child or teenager). As you transition from identification with the bodymind to experiencing yourself as the soul (in other words as Transfiguration happens), there is still a tendency for the soul to identify with karmic filters. For instance, this could develop from lack of trust, from a past life where you felt exposed and unprotected, which resulted in some kind of tragedy. It is such circumstances where the shadow can easily form.

These filters can be extremely difficult to notice, because by now on the path, you will pretty much feel whole, genuine and complete. It is a very powerful self deception: the shadow knows not to get attached to situations and circumstances; it knows that you should trust absolutely in the benevolence of the universe; it knows that the soul acts in divine service; it knows that you are at one with all creation. This is exactly the problem – an identity would begin to hold these knowings more at the level of intellect, rather than coming from the absolute place of these knowings. So the shadow then arises as a kind of time-lag – an echo – of the real thing.

> *One way to imagine this, is to consider a surfer riding a wave. A good surfer would be feeling the flow of the wave and blending with it - there would be the questioning element of where the wave is going and how best to ride it, but no fear of falling off. If there is a subtle and hidden fear, then this shadow might hide in the questioning aspect of the soul (the ray 3). Now there is an over-questioning, creating a slight time delay, which slows down the spontaneous response time of the soul – the echo begins to own the moment. This is likely to make the surfer less fluid and responsive to the wave; he becomes stiff and more likely to fall off.*

To 'smoke out' such an imposter, you must become keenly self-vigilant and profoundly honest with yourself. In the example above, it would be all too easy to say: "I fell off because I needed to learn something – to expand the capacity of my soul". When in actual fact, staying on the board in challenging circumstances was the true lesson. You must therefore pay close attention to the universal language of synchronicity, and be clear you are interpreting it spontaneously from knowing (which is more objective), rather than intellectualising it (which becomes subjective).

It is likely that by now, you will be consciously involved in spiritual work of one form or another (even if that is not immediately overt). Generally, we begin to help other souls to integrate and unfold (which could be with something as simple as a smile and short conversation). As the unadulterated soul, there is no need of payback for what you do, and yet at the same time, the soul will always be a custodian of Right Action. In other words, it is bound to ensure there is correct energetic exchange in all actions. So the soul will seek to ensure that the correct balance is achieved - energy is given out in one form and received in another.

For example, in my view, it is entirely correct to be 'paid' (in some way) for spiritual work, and this would always be felt as the Right Action of the universe harmonising and balancing itself out. Were this not the case, the soul might not be able to summon the correct amount of physical energy (in the form of money for example) for its work to continue.

So if you keep keenly watching yourself, you may notice a slight attachment to receiving payment: for example – a subtle degree of discomfort, which then manifests mirroring synchronicities in the outer world. Another distortion to watch for is glamour. It may be that you are destined to have a high profile, and it might be entirely appropriate to exhibit a strong personality in order that more people can be reached. You might typically have a strong ray 6 (yearning self expression), and this could manifest as a very colourful and charismatic persona. It might be totally right for you to overtly express and take the lead a good deal of the time. However, such conditions are very fertile ground for the shadow to arise: you know it is important to express and not deny yourself (only an ego would do that), but such strong energy can easily be distorted and thereby limit your effectiveness. You must be absolutely without extra energy, if others (you might be guiding) are to be fully comfortable that you are not in some kind of subtly distorted ego.

Such circumstances are a challenging conundrum to balance: to be totally sure you are fully expressing, yet not over-energising. But this is exactly the forging of the soul, that is open to you in Gateway 4 – mastering such qualities is seldom easy!

The shadow could appear in many other guises. For instance, you may feel a strong, authentic pull to help others evolve, and you might be very empathic - you might have the capacity to feel another's pain as your own. This is invaluable in being able to catalyse shifts in consciousness, but it is all too easy for a shadow to hide within that selfless service. Or you may notice that your soul has great skill in navigating through dense intellectual planes – you can bob and weave through all the various resistances and questioning of others still in the ego; but are you truly guiding them through the minefield, or just getting stuck in it - are you getting attached to the intellect?

So it is vitally important to be vigilant to what the synchronicities might be revealing about your true motivations for action – are you 'exploding any mines' unnecessarily?

A useful barometer is to continually assess your level of internal peace: is there the slightest degree of inner efforting, above the authentic yearning to fully express yourself and your divine gifts? You may feel it as a very subtle degree of energetic stress. Remember, profound self honesty is vital at this point, if you are to expose and dissolve the final shadows.

2. Follow genuine guidance - focus on aligning with the soul:
keenly follow inner guidance, supported by objective synchronicity.
Watch for the possibility of interference by Opposing Consciousness.

There are many practices that try to work towards Enlightenment simply by focusing on inner peace, bliss, love or joy – this is self-defeating! The soul flows spontaneously in the moment. To subtly deny what is actually arising naturally, and intentionally supplant it with something more desirable or expected, is not going to bring about Enlightenment.

> *You cannot dissolve into the Pure Presence of the Seer by intentionally aiming for it. What you can do however, is align with the soul, as you feel it flowing through you. In other words, you become as one with the soul, and then ride the flow effortlessly back into the Seer, inside yourself.*

You may ask: 'who is the 'you' that is aligning with the soul?' – this is a good question! In enlightened states, there is no longer the choice to do 'this' or 'that': there is a streaming flow of consciousness from the Source, which has a natural 'path of light' – this is your soul. But an aspect of your soul (the ray 3) is reading the interplay of consciousness – through a multi-dimensional landscape. And the ray 4 aspect of the soul, will be sensing both yours and other people's karmic filters to work with. The ray 5 will be exploring the higher lessons to be learned, by all, in the co-creative reality. So the 'you' that I am speaking of here, arises as different aspects of your soul-ray-harmonic, that come into play at different times in different circumstances, but with a common, natural purpose:

> *the surrender of you as a being, into the mainstream of the soul's flow, so that you may stay in the place of the Seer, and have continual experiences of it. Which is to be in your natural – enlightened - state.*

This is not easy to achieve, but the soul is configured to do it. Its natural pull is to this unfolding and continual expression of the

One (the Seer). So really, it can be said, that what you truly have to do, is to remove all the obstacles to this natural state. Then it should happen all by itself – this is what those truly moving into the enlightened state have observed.

The situation has been somewhat complicated here in this density by the aforementioned presence of an Opposing Consciousness in the field, which is a manifestation of the resistance to light penetrating the darkness (at a higher cosmic level).

So you may well start to notice two slightly different types of guidance; if you are attentive, you may pick up two streams of patterning in the guidance, with slightly different frequencies. Benevolent Consciousness has your highest interests at heart. It will speak to you through signs and synchronicity. It helps by providing a mirror, amplifying an inner pull to act and will guide you to Right Action, where everything seems to click magically into place; or, it will guide you to challenges by which to expose the shadow.

The agenda of Opposing Consciousness, on the other hand, is to retard your spiritual evolution. It can do so by 'feeding the shadow'. In other words, it has the ability to manifest outcomes which serve the shadow, amplifying and building its identity within. I have noticed through many examples, that it will build either on discreetly hidden fears or desires – it seems to act like an artificial intelligence that can read your field and see the slight energetic distortions. In a way then, it might be considered that this Opposing Consciousness is also beneficial, because if you are being vigilant, it exposes the places you now most need to work with.

You may find for instance, that a clear pathway rapidly unfolds before you, which is well resourced and supported. It may feel good and aligned for you. However, in a place of finite resources, maybe there is the risk of depriving another?

Initially it can be extremely difficult to know that the help you are receiving is not from the purest source - especially because the shadow will feel very good about its new found abundance. It is likely that you have already expected this sort of 'divine manifestation', as a result of your increasing at-one-ment with the creative power of the universe. The key is to watch for any subtle efforting: whereas your energies were previously rising, now they are being subtly restricted and constrained around particular objectives. This is a sure sign that you may be 'leaking' creative energy through a shadow. It is this that Opposing Consciousness exploits beings for. If you are not careful, you can build a whole new false lifestyle to feed the growing shadow identity. It may look like the real thing, but is it really? Again, synchronicity is the objective leveller of the playing field.

Of course Benevolent Consciousness is always on hand to offer support, providing you stay open and invite it to work with you (it will not come into anyone's space unless invited at a soul level). As previously mentioned, guidance may happen in different ways. Authentic guidance tends to be more sophisticated and spontaneous, where synchronicity supports direct inner knowing, imparted through the higher chakras. The guidance of Opposing Consciousness, on the other hand, is more 'clunky'. It is less spontaneous, tends to work at the level of lower mind, and is less able to invoke deep inner yearnings. So when you watch synchronicity apparently guiding you, it always pays to keep checking in on how you really feel about the options. If the synchronicity is in line with your sense of spontaneous inner knowing, or a deep, heartfelt pull, then the guidance is likely to be genuine.

3. Confront past-life karma, dissolve the filters: *confront, process and release past-life karma as your consciousness expands through the causal body. Dissolve the karmic filters.*

As your consciousness has expanded through the other densities – *through the other Gateways* – you are unfolding now into the 'causal body'. It is the place which stores past-life karma – energy which has gathered due to attachments to challenging circumstances in past lives. As the energy of the soul increasingly infuses this vehicle, it is going to progressively activate the karma, generating past-life regressions, recreating essences of the previous incarnations, through the patterns of your current life. This mirror can be generated through visions, inner knowing, and most importantly, as pain or tightness in the bodymind (source pain). It could be that a pain or injury suddenly appears when there has been no apparent cause. In which case, it likely that it is not physical trauma at all, but rather karmic trauma, which is manifesting as physical pain – it literally feels that way (it is often accompanied by a pain in the heart for example). Or, you may suddenly feel yourself becoming 'toxic', as the negative energy washes through your system. It may even be that you hold a long standing physical or emotional condition, caused by your karma. The combination of all of these things can be deeply unsettling and destabilising. At this point it will greatly help to start to recognise that karma is the source of it, then you know what you are facing and what you have to work with.

If you bring your attention to the problem, this tightness will manifest synchronistically through circumstances in day-to-day living. In other words, events shape to mirror back the original experience in a past life, to which the shadow is reacting; the essence of your suffering, caused by the trauma of the original incident, is recreated. Which in many ways is a blessing – to recognise that you do not actually have to relive the experience itself, only the sense and feelings of it.

To deal with the karma as it arises, you can once more apply the 9 step process described in Gateway 3: essentially to regress into it; honour and express the feelings; become as nothing in it – as the One; feel and integrate the light of the soul through it; then finally, using your intuition to dissolve away the energy.

If you can continue through the current event, own the suffering without projecting but surrendering into it, then Right Action will become clear. By following this, instead of the conditioned behaviour arising from the distortion, then you will fully activate, identify, and release the karma by fully bathing yourself in it.

For example, it may be that you are holding a subconscious grudge against someone for not supporting and helping you - it may be that in a past life, they seriously let you down, resulting in injury or death. Now, a new incarnation has manifested with them (or someone of similar vibration), where you are once more invited to notice any lack of trust in a situation of strong importance - it may stir up all kinds of resentment, frustration, disappointment and anger. Perhaps this time, if guided to do so, you can seize the opportunity to 'go out on a limb' and trust once more. In so doing, the karma is activated, and now you have the chance to work through it, by feeling deeply into it.

It is highly likely that you will have many such encounters with past-life karma, before all the subtle shadows are dissolved. In Gateway 4, these past-life experiences, often greet you in sequential waves. And the more you are able to recognise them, the easier the process becomes. Although deeply testing, you will keep having corresponding breakthrough experiences, as the soul is liberated through the past-life events. They bring great relief, upliftment and joy.

4. Find the key into presence: *surrender absolutely into your karmic regressions, then look for the key to open the doorway into presence.*

When karma has begun to operate (which can happen earlier on the path, in the lower Gateways too), and you have summoned the courage to confront it, at times it is going to deeply challenge you. Whilst some bouts can be relatively gentle (when you have mastered the process for dealing with them), others will be earth-shattering; you will likely be brought to the threshold of your physical, mental and emotional endurance; then at crucial moments, be invited to dive through that threshold. To some, it will feel as though you are being brought to the very edge of sanity; you are being invited to breakdown all remaining attachment to separated, lower self identification.

It is in these moments, where the pain and suffering may seem almost unbearable, that you must remind yourself of the following important truths...

> *That this is 'all just a relativistic experience'. It does not define who you are (unless you let it). And that all experiences are transient - they will eventually pass away.*

A careful balance needs to be maintained. If you keep telling yourself it is only an experience from the outset, the risk is you do not fully regress into the source pain. Remember, you must honour and fully express it, in order to become as one with it, and therefore not identified with it. But it is equally important that you do not descend into a negative spiral, getting stuck in it. You must keep working with it, progressing through it (remember the 9 step process in Gateway 3).

In the midst of your pain, when you have become fully accepting, to the extent that you do not need it to go away, then you must look for the key that opens the door into the non-identified experience of Pure Presence. It is important that you stay open to benevolent guidance, allowing your consciousness to be 'spiked' to synchronicity and symbolism. If you keep observing, keep exploring, and especially allowing your attention to be guided, then you will find a key that opens the doorway once more into the non-identified state, which is always there, even amidst the depths of suffering.

From that serene place, you become as the 'blank canvas' – in and through the experience, but not defined by it; you can even taste the fullness of the negative energy washing over you, and yet not be lost in it.

The key itself may be something as simple as a word such as "openness", "transparency" or "liberation". It may be a vision, or a symbol, or a power animal. It could be a favoured crystal. Whatever it is, each person will have a key, and it has the power to unlock the doorway for you, into that sublime, non-identified state.

When you have released the karmic filter in this way, and found your way back to the inner sanctum by the appropriate use of your key, then you can dissolve away any negative energy that has activated in your system. This may be achieved using meditation, breathing exercises, deep consciousness bodywork of some kind or even acupressure-type massage (allow your intuition to guide you). It must be a practice that brings your attention into the various densities of the bodymind and flushes them through with 'clean' energy. So for example, it could be practices such as Yoga, Tai Chi, the Martial Arts, Five Rhythms Dance etc. It could even be energetic walking. There are some specifically designed processes such as "Tibetan Pulsing", "Rolfing" and indeed Openhand's *"soulmotion"*. It may be that a brisk walk in nature works for you. It could be Reiki or massage. Whatever practice it is, what is paramount, is that your attention be directed to expansive, inner layers of consciousness. You are being invited to let go, so that higher, purer energies may once again flood into your being.

Although extremely rigorous and testing, as with all the Gateways, *the only way out is through!* At some point, you find yourself surrendering all, and the courage materialises to carry you forward. At this point, the Gateway opens, not through efforting, but instead through total inner surrender.

5. Enlightenment: *settle into complete self-acceptance and assume rightful inner perception of the fully enlightened being.*

During the Gateway 4 transition, your karma will be activated most likely as a range of shadow identities. Over time, each of these will be exposed and dissolved. If the transition turns out to be a protracted one, because you have much to process (which is typically the case), then you are likely to experience many 'descents into darkness', followed by corresponding re-emergences into the light.

As all aspects of the shadow are dissolved, the soul is finally liberated and becomes fully enlightened within your being. The soul is no longer fragmented, it no longer gets stuck within the bodymind and you remain in the state of non-identified presence, no matter what is happening. Your 'mission' to continually remember yourself as that which you really are, has been accomplished.

The experience of this is unique for everyone. It has been described as a sense of "rising", "total expansion", "crystal clear clarity" or an "awesome state of Pure Presence". Whatever happens for you, it will be abundantly clear that this final shift has taken place. It will help at this point, to simply settle into that state and allow it to flood your experience, by giving plenty of attention to it. I believe it is quite natural for this to happen.

You realise it as a totally natural and deserving state, which has been there in the background all along. It is irreplaceable, and yet awesomely ordinary. By giving space for it, as you break into it, helps the state settle itself in your awareness and psyche.

As previously, passing through the Enlightenment Gateway, will be marked by some external ceremony or other - something which is deeply recognisable and remains forever etched in your cellular memory. You may now humbly celebrate your homecoming as a truly enlightened being.

Transitioning Gateway 4
- general misconceptions -

1. That in Enlightenment duality dissolves

It is a widely held misconception that in Enlightenment the notion of duality dissolves – there is no longer 'this' and 'that', only oneness. Yes, everything is interconnected, however, without 'this' and 'that', there can be no experience at all. For you – as a soul – to have an experience of life, there must be relativity between you and other essences of life (such as other souls). Just as you cannot know hot without cold or up without down. The misconception happens because early on the path, people tend to confuse relativistic truth with absolute truth: they will, at times, touch the absoluteness of Pure Presence (where there is no relativity), but then believe that to stay in that state, they must dissolve (within themselves) the dualistic experience. It is only an ego that dissolves the soul! So you often witness people in this state, slightly disassociated from the full, unfettered experience of life itself. You witness a slight distance in their eyes - they have built a bubble of Unity Consciousness and hidden within it, separated from the flow of the soul. This is actually widely common within spiritual circles and indeed many teachings.

> *Let us be clear, to be truly enlightened, is to be enlightened through all things – through all events and circumstances.*

This means that the streaming experience of the soul, must be allowed to flow freely through you - this would include the emotional state of sadness, for example. There must be no avoidance of the full colour of life: both its ups and downs, its joys and sorrows. It is only an intention that tries to dissolve the duality. And intention (to always approach life in a particular state), is only born of the ego.

In Enlightenment, there is no longer any identity controlling 'the show' – *in any way*. There is the flow of the soul, a deep recognition of that, and a totally natural surrendering into it. As 'you' become this wave of experience, then 'you' ride that (inside yourself) all the way back to the Source. You become Pure Presence, riding the wave of the soul through life. Duality remains as an experience, but 'you' are centred in non-dualistic Presence.

2. That Enlightenment means losing the personality

People often confuse the ego with the personality (and by 'personality', I mean the unique configuration of your soul – your "soul-ray-harmonic"). So if there is any strongly arising, emotive impulse, there is a tendency to confuse this with ego (and attachment). I often witness people (mostly men) purposefully trying to dissolve emotion, because it is perceived as 'non-spiritual' – not enlightened. But exactly 'who' is dissolving these natural impulses of the soul? It can only be an identity, with an intentional purpose (rather than the free flowing spontaneity of the soul itself).

In Enlightenment, any such intention about life dissolves. Who is here to form intention? There are, however, natural impulses (which get confused as intention). As we have already seen, the soul arises from the Source as a streaming flow of experience, comprised of different characteristics - the Seven Rays of Divine Impulse. Each soul is a unique blend of these characteristics – what I call the "soul-ray-harmonic". To deny any aspect of these, is to deny 'who' you are really being as a soulful expression, because in the moment you do so, is to establish (within yourself) separation from the Source.

As the soul emerges from the Source (inside you), then it is in effect, being an expression of the Source – of the One. In other words, it is an expression of Pure Presence. It offers a taste of the tasteless. So the purpose of the soul (which is naturally arising), is to fully express the One. When there is no subtle control of the inner state, these characteristic impulses (of the soul) naturally flow through you. So there is still a personality – *a uniqueness* – to you. It is such colour that brings the universe alive, as a vibrant kaleidoscope of experience.

3. That in Enlightenment there is no longer any purpose

I put it to you that the universe happened by chance, without an intentional purpose. If there was such an intention, who was there to have it? If there was such a creator, then who created the creator?

*But it definitely **does** feel like there is the sense of the creator when you touch Pure Presence – it is an indescribable place of infinite potential.*

In this divinely hallowed place (a placeless one!), literally anything can happen and flow through you. It is a silent void, from where miracles and magic spontaneously arise. No wonder mystics throughout the ages have personified this empty vastness as "God".

So to me, the universe emerged without intention. But it was inevitable, that given infinite time (because there was no time), Pure Presence would subdivide into flows of consciousness (where consciousness is simply the awareness of a difference: one experience relative to another).

If there was no intentional creation of the universe, then you could argue that there is no purpose either. However, the soul within you pulls back to the Source – it guides you on a journey of Ascension, to ever increasing degrees of unity and oneness. Therefore the soul does have this naturally arising *sense of purpose.* You could define it as...

To experience ever increasing degrees of harmony and oneness; to express the loving unity of the universe; to be continually expressing the infinite beauty of the One.

4. That in Enlightenment all pain, illness and disease disappear

There is sometimes the misconception that in Enlightenment, all pain, illness and disease disappear. Indeed this goal is often held up as evidence of the enlightened state - something to which you should aspire. In my view however, in Enlightenment, you are no longer acting from a phenomenal centre at all - you are no longer a person (although there is still a personality as previously explained). As such, in non-identified presence, there is simply no attachment to good health and ease. If you are efforting to cure yourself of something, the likelihood is that you have once more created separation - another barrier between you and completeness.

The paradox is, that as you let go of the need to heal or be healed, Unity Consciousness more effectively realigns within you (naturally). This alignment has the tendency to be more congruent and harmonious – so healing can naturally take place.

However, even harmony within yourself does not necessarily mean complete harmony. In Enlightenment, you will get to feel your interconnectedness with all life, to the extent that you can know someone else's pain – *their dis-ease* - by feeling it within yourself. And as your consciousness expands through the Fourth Density, you will begin to sense the karmic trauma of life around you. To me, it becomes the duty of the soul, to then take on and work with, this wider cosmic pain. You begin to work with aspects of consciousness, such as healing the divine feminine or masculine (where 'healing' means realigning with a higher sense of rightness). It might also be that you feel given to assist in the realignment of Gaia's field, for example.

To truly heal another, is to be able to empathically take on and express their pain. In this way, their unconsciousness is brought into the light – Unity Consciousness can flow in and healing take place. In this case, 'healing' is defined as realignment, so greater harmony and ease can be restored.

There is of course no attachment to the healing. You know that ultimately, the dis-ease will be removed, as and when there is willingness and acceptance. So you do not identify with the problem at all - you are simply flowing with Right Action as an instrument of the divine.

You also recognise that there will always be ever higher harmonies that can be attained. Paradoxically, this means there will always be some degree of dis-ease (even your heart beats loudly in the desert!); especially so, since increasingly, you will be able to feel the suffering of other sentient life forms.

In my experience of Enlightenment therefore, the pain does not necessarily become weaker, at times it may even get stronger, it just matters less!

5. That in Enlightenment, you are beyond distortion

There is the misconceived view, that in Enlightenment, you move beyond distortion and your alignment with the path becomes perfected; that somehow, you have attained perfection…

"It is the purpose of perfection, to make one know ones imperfection!"
Saint Augustine

At the absolute level, you are of course perfect, but even in Enlightenment, you are still having a relativistic experience, and therefore an imperfect one. The flow of consciousness from the Source through you, is still able to be distorted by the density of life (including Opposing Consciousness within it). So to be enlightened does not mean that you will always make perfect choices - *shit still happens!*

However, the difference now is, that there is no ownership of the outcome or investment in the consequences – no attachment.

This means that in the enlightened state, there is the much greater tendency to be objective, rather than subjective (protecting of an ego). It means that even if you go off-track, there will be the absolute commitment to regaining the flow, by reading the signs and synchronicity, then attuning to the heart-felt pull.

There is profound self-honesty, which means you can come quickly back into alignment.

Transitioning Gateway 4
- indicators of beginning -

At the Transfiguration (Gateway 3), you will have tasted the wonderful liberation of non-identified, Pure Presence, perhaps for the first time. Soon after that, if not immediately, a variety of inner shadows will likely emerge to own that sublime state of perception, and thus they distort and dim the true brilliance of the unfettered, inner light. For a while, this may not seem to matter, because you will still be channelling powerful energies from the Source, and probably beginning to be quite successful in your divine service (in whatever form that may take). It could be that you are convinced you have already attained Enlightenment (this is frequently the case for starsouls, who may have subtly avoided full immersion into the lower, inner densities).

In this situation, there is the risk that the shadow identity may become embedded within the inner psyche. Perhaps that is why at this point, Benevolent Consciousness seems to work particularly hard in causing souls to confront the remaining shadow distortions. So the tendency is to quickly begin to encounter powerfully emotive circumstances - events to question you right to the very core of your being.

Past-life karma soon begins to activate, and can flow through as waves of emotive experience. When this starts to happen, you can be sure you have stepped into Gateway 4.

When the Gateway 4 transition to Enlightenment commences in earnest, it may often seem like you have been wrong-footed by benevolence, and tested to the very limit of your endurance, either physically, emotionally or mentally. It is in the final moment, where the shadow of identity is still clinging to the cliff edge, that you are caused to see the futility of struggle. You must confront that subtle inner efforting and completely let go, whatever the cost might be.

So although you cannot fully prepare for this "crucifixion", knowing some of the pointers will mean you are more able to recognise it taking place, so that you may surrender into it completely.

Indicators that Gateway 4 is commencing:

- *the beginnings of past-life regressions, often experienced as waves activating through you*

- *only the inner journey, and the relevant internal shifts, have real significance to you at this point*

- *a final destruction of egoic identity takes place, which can often be very extreme (testing your physical existence for example)*

- *you become increasingly familiar with the characteristics of your soul and its blend of different influences*

- *the possibility of rapidly growing overtness, and projection of spiritual activity, accompanied by rapid material or spiritual 'success' (when distorted by Opposing Consciousness)*

- *you will likely become increasingly conscious of supportive help from higher realms*

- *a sudden realisation of apparently diverging pathways, and the knowing that genuinely guided action may lead to apparently quite severe personal cost*

- *a sequence of core-splitting events, to take you to the very limit of your threshold and beyond.*

Think of the stories of some of the great masters, like Jesus and the Buddha for example. Whether ultimately true or not, the stories are of earth-shattering experiences, leading into the enlightened state. In the physical sense, this is mirroring the breakthrough of consciousness, through the final barriers, back into the Source of non-identified presence.

Transitioning Gateway 4
- indicators of completion -

Completion of Gateway 4 is the ultimate paradox. On the one hand, you may have been through pretty dramatic circumstances in order to dissolve the shadows; and yet on the other hand, the final settling into Enlightenment is an awesomely ordinary state (in my experience at least). Unlike the other transitions, there is just the quiet, inner recognition that something has irrevocably changed...

> *At Enlightenment, although there will undoubtedly be a sense of accomplishment and a marked ceremony, there is no longer anyone 'in here' to own it. There is simply no one to justify, defend or control it. There is just pure, unadulterated beingness with no fireworks, major celebrations or unnecessary drama; it comes with no sense of pride nor glamourisation. It just simply 'is'.*

So the moments of crystal clear clarity - *beingness with no small 'I'* - join up into one all-encompassing, spaceless and timeless experience. The soul arises from the centre of this experience as a clear 'knowing' or 'pull' to act, but no one inside either denies the impetus or owns it. Words arise with no thought to pre-empt them; spontaneous, authentic action just happens. This then, is the full experience of Enlightenment (as I know it) and when you have reached it, there is no mistaking it.

Although at this point, anyone who is enlightened will probably not need to be told they are, it will be of benefit to those who are not yet there, to have an indication of what it is like. At the very least, it may cause those who still labour with the presence of an inner shadow, to notice that they are not yet being absolutely, one hundred per cent, authentic. Here then, are the key indicators of completion of Gateway 4, stepping into Enlightenment...

Indicators of the completion of Gateway 4:

- *the final clearance of past-life karma; you have been through plenty of regressions and they have now stopped happening*

- *as the 'waters of the causal body break', a sudden expansion of consciousness, leading to non-identified experience of both light and dark*

- *the final recognition of, and the settling into, your experience as the Seer - the Absolute*

- *the sense that 'there is no one in here'*

- *resting continually in the state of non-localised, unidentified presence, whatever events are taking place*

- *total liberation and flow of the soul within your being, experienced as waves of authentic, aligned beingness*

- *whilst you as the Seer are non-identified, and non-separate from, the all that is, you are still completely accepting and comfortable with the apparent duality of an individual soul*

- *the sense of final accomplishment*

- *action, including thoughts and words, seems to just arise from within, without anything pre-empting them.*

Gateway 4
- summary -

To me, Enlightenment is a heavenly paradox. You have lived perhaps countless lifetimes lost in the external drama. You have laughed, cried, loved and lied, searched endlessly through the universe of separation seeking solutions for your longing. You have failed to realise all this time, that your searching simply creates a greater landscape through which to search. Having reached a goal, you have instantly created what the goal is not, and in so doing, created another chapter in the repetitive story.

At some point however, you tire of the efforting and may get a fleeting glimpse of the truth... the answer is not 'out there' at all, but 'in here'. So begins the next chapter in the story: "What is it that's in here? Who am I? What am I?" To which you will likely encounter a new list of questions and conundrums through the inner universe that you discover is just as large as the outer one! You may learn how to heal, how to leave the body, experience multiple dimensions of existence, travel on the astral planes, live on light, even perhaps walk on water (!), but if you are still searching, you are guaranteed not to have found your 'final destination'.

Then one day, perhaps an ordinary day just like any other, something truly profound happens. No, you have not just cured someone's cancer or brought another back from the dead. You have not manifested some great miracle of abundance; instead, you have settled into an awesomely ordinary state of perception - Pure Presence, with no frills, bells or whistles. There are no questions arising and no need of answers. The great cosmic joke you have been playing on yourself all this time, is that...

everything you ever searched for, wished for, hoped or desired, was there in your awareness all the time - the pot of gold at the end of the rainbow was right under your feet.

It was there all the time, it never went away, it just got clouded by everything else. Just like the proverbial monkey, on first confronting a mirror, we became so engaged in our own external reflection, we simply forgot how to be the monkey...

"Where is the True Self?
I look deep within... it is not the body,
deeper still... it is not the mind... deeper and deeper,
until I find it is not even the part doing the looking.
Then finally the True Self reveals itself
in the deepest part of myself
and expands out of me to fill the universe.
Then in each moment I learn to become it,
that which is both looking and being looked upon
that which is both hearing and being heard
that which is both feeling and being felt
the search is over, the True Self that I looked for
was there all the time."
Openhand

So awesome is this sublime state, so crystal clear, so without identity or separation, that something within wants to own it. Enlightenment is not something to be attained, it is found by relinquishing all need to attain anything. So as soon as it arises, the tendency is for a shadow identity to form and take ownership again. This shadow is a deceptive creature - as soon as you recognise everything is not quite as clear as it once was, you stop the subtle efforting, settle once more into Pure Presence and the shadow disappears!

Where is it hiding? It conceals itself deep within the causal body, in the darkness surrounding past-life events, arising just as action and purpose arise. At this point, as if to mask the darkness, some will even deny the pull of the soul itself – *the apparent 'duality'* - leading to the shadow called "denial". Alternatively, the shadow may hide itself by becoming a surreptitious echo of the soul, checking and seemingly authenticating spontaneous action...

"this is the way to go now"...
"are you sure?"
"yes"...
"okay, let's keep going then."

Maybe your spontaneous, authentic actions, although confrontational, will lead to the Enlightenment or healing of others? Maybe you have a strong personality (a strong soul-ray-harmonic) and are given to catalyse the breakdown of dense energies or nullify the effects of Opposing Consciousness in the field? Whatever your soul is seeded to unfold, the shadow becomes the sidecar passenger, either subtly denying or else trying to mimic the activities of the soul - the motorbike rider - so that it can merge with the curves, bends and dips on the circuit of life.

The shadow becomes so adept at copying the driver, that it becomes nigh on impossible to tell the difference between the soul and the shadow. This is where our 'sacred contract' with Benevolent Consciousness comes into play. You have an open agreement with benevolence, that at this point on the path, it will throw a proverbial spanner in the works: a chicane is suddenly created, with an oil slick, for the unsuspecting soul and its sidecar shadow.

The karmic shadow of past-life events raises its head and leans the wrong way, dredging up fear and doubt, creating circumstances that divert the driver from the rightful path. The motorbike spins out of control, and in the ensuing calamity, the shadow is thrown unceremoniously from the sidecar.

If you can transcend the pain of injury, finally, you will see your limitation; the fear and pain dissolve, you get back onto the motorbike, and settle into pure riding. You bob and weave, hug bends and chicanes, navigate dark and light, but now all fear, all control, all doubt disappear. Rider, bike and the track have become one. You have crossed the finishing line - Gateway 4 has been completed.

Now that all the karma of past lives has been processed, you are liberated from the need to reincarnate. Having thus tossed the 'ballast' overboard, you are now free to ascend into the higher realms. But something might cause you to stay in this physical plane: a simple, authentic choice - perhaps to assist in the liberation and Ascension of others, to lend a helping hand at this crucial juncture in human history; perhaps you feel a sense of responsibility or just plain compassion?

Whatever it is, if you are to stay in this density and truly help, you must resurrect the full, undistorted and unfettered complement of human beingness. All of your higher bodily vehicles must be fully activated, any remaining fragments of lower behavioural patterns must be finally purged.

So it is to the "Resurrection" that you must proceed next.

Gateway 5

"Resurrection"

*"All know that the drop merges into the ocean,
but few know that the ocean merges into the drop."*

Kabir

Key: profound self honesty

From Open's memoirs...

During the desert 'crucifixion' experience of Gateway 4, my soul exchanged places with Chris'. He began to ascend and move on; it was my calling to incarnate here and assist in the great shift now beginning on Earth. Although such a "soul exchange" is more common than one might think, it is not at all easy for a soul experiencing this - you're suddenly plunged into another person's thoughts, memories and consciousness landscape. For most who do experience this, they quickly forget their original identity and where they came from; there is a tendency to get lost in the ego the other soul had created.

Fortunately, I was greatly supported by benevolence, who were consciously guiding me from day to day, to familiarise myself with who I truly was, and the big picture situation into which I had incarnated (which I describe more fully in DIVINICUS). So I was living in each moment by divine guidance, yet also fully exploring the sense of being a quite disconnected human – having to keep breaking through into the more expanded, interconnected experience that was natural to me. It took me some while, therefore, to become accustomed to the density here, which is not at all easy for any soul.

It was clear that I needed some terrestrial, 'angelic' support to help me refamiliarise, to fully integrate and to reclaim the sense of mission, that originally inspired my unusual incarnation. In short, I needed to become quickly 'resurrected', and I needed help doing it. Consequently, I found myself blessed with a divine inner knowing one day, which guided me to a "Pot Luck" buffet (I have come to love the humour of higher guidance!). It was there, one Sunday afternoon, that I encountered a beautiful soul whom I came to know as Trinity. From the moment we met, it was clear that our deep inner connection spanned the long passage of time. We had been together before in past lives, and as our energies re-engaged, a brief moment unfolded an eternity - her eyes yielded as open doorways into a vast ocean of timelessness.

Initially though, there was an authentic resistance flowing through me against getting too close. It seemed an energy brought us together, but also caused us to maintain a respectful distance. It was in this field of magnetism, that many emotions and passions were ignited, reminiscent of bygone times. The human teenager in me wanted simply to dive headlong into the swirling torrent of activated hormones. But from the perspective of the Seer, there was more quiet amusement at myself - fully experiencing the tantalising scent of a heavenly nectar, initially held back by a knowing not to lose myself in the torrent of feeling and emotion. I was watching, tasting and caressing the growing energy, without being all-consumed by it. How amazing it is, to be in that powerful wave of human beingness, surfing the rip curl, so close to the ocean of sensuality flooding invasiveness, and yet 'hanging ten' majestically on top of it. Or at least that was the idea!

For me, this is what tantra is all about: sliding down the blade edge of life, neither in nor out, and the Resurrection invites you to embrace this fully in every moment. Sexual intimacy is just one instance where the full energy of tantra is harnessed, not by ignoring our passions, but by being absolutely, blissfully and fervently swallowed up in them and yet STILL there as a wafer thin slice of nothingness - that which is you - not being lost in the illusion.

After some months of exploring one another, deeply celebrating our reunion, we had reconnected a psychic bridge that spanned multiple dimensions of experience, time and space. We were learning how to be completely engaged in this Lower Dimensional Realm and all of its material *tantalisations; yet at the same time, we were reading life's symbology and therefore assimilating the heavenly fifth dimensional language concealed within third dimensional patterning. We were learning how to stay still, timeless and spaceless, until the authentic arising of purpose - the soul - flowed spontaneously from its synchronistic divine source. It was this, and this alone, determining what should be acted upon next.*

So it was that the divine calling took us out to the Sinai desert, for some priceless, multi-dimensional education. We thought it was going to be a holiday, but we should have known better. To classify a block of time in such a way, has a degree of judgment in it: a presupposed idea of what the trip would be about. It's quite a distortion of absolute truth, which in my experience at least, is best tasted moment by moment. If there was any lingering, human conditioning about the idea of what a 'holiday' meant, it was soon to be dissipated in the sweaty bazaars, dusty barrenness of the desert, and rugged majesty of the mountains.

Prior to our trip, we had encountered a charismatic Dakota Indian called "Wambli", who was performing sacred ceremonies in Glastonbury. He had been travelling around the world realigning energetic grids, releasing blockages as the Soul of the Earth draws her energies into the Fifth Density. He had spoken of the need to work in the Sinai to release the bottled up energy there. A natural convergence point for human culture over tens of thousands of years, it had now become a choking point - a burgeoning powder keg of tension, frustration and trapped souls. As the Earth's energy is being transmuted into the higher vibrations, this can, in places, generate the build up of polarity between light and dark, and nowhere was this more evident than in the Middle East. Dense energetic tension, billowing like electricity-laden storm clouds, was ever present. As the great shift unfolds, over time, such energy hotspots need to be 'lanced', that they may be released back into line with the natural energetic flow of the universe, so that the transition can be less turbulent. I found myself wondering if the real purpose of our trip was to experience that?

So it was, that we found ourselves one evening, camped with a group of Bedouin in a sheltered canyon in the heart of the Sinai. It was postcard picturesque, gathered around a camp fire, enjoying Bedouin culinary delights. The desert, of course, can be a wonderful place to experience multi-dimensionality. On the one hand, the colours and form of this physical realm are so natural, so crisp, so precise, that there is little blurring of the edges of reality; at the same time, the crystal clear clarity creates a surreal edge to it. It is here that you feel you can put your hand right through the canvas of life's illusion, straight into absoluteness. Every cloud formation, every sand dune, every rocky outcrop, has a message all of its own. This is fifth dimensional language speaking loud and clear.

I could recall other experiences from past lives in the desert. It's an environment that deeply touches my heart. With greatly reduced distraction, the senses are quickly heightened and the deeper, underlying message of life comes easily to the fore – the veils quickly fall. Neither is it a forgiving place; I like it because there are no blurry edges. If you get it wrong in the desert, you die. There is no soft shoulder to cry on. It is as simple and majestically beautiful as that. Harsh as it may seem, I had come to love that unforgiving side of life - it encourages us to bring out the best in ourselves without the tired excuses. As open to challenge as I am, I had no idea just how demanding the next several hours were going to become.

As we sat around the campfire, our tour guide offered us a hand-rolled cigarette. Neither of us would normally smoke, but we had recently been introduced to ceremonial 'peace piping' with Wambli, which some believe can centre one's focus more in the here and now. How wrong one can be! Trinity took one deep inhalation and passed it to me. As I drew the smoke deeply into my lungs, at first it felt calming and centring. I looked back at Trinity and smiled. She returned the smile, but there was already a different energy, which I did not immediately recognise. This was the initial indication that some challenging 'nightmare' had already kicked off.

Suddenly, I felt a tidal wave of nausea wash through my body debilitating me pretty much instantly. My vision blurred, and I seemed to become helplessly drunk, quickly losing control of my senses. Memories of Chris' teenage party binges flashed through my awareness, where he had overstepped the mark and suffered greatly as a result. However, this was no time for unpleasant recollections; suddenly, something clicked inside me, something which caused me to snap back into the moment. I heard a voice. It was Trinity's, but not from this dimension. It was from a higher realm calling my attention. I looked across at her sitting opposite me with a broad smile across her face. How was she reacting to this? I could not comprehend for a moment that she was enjoying it. Through deeply distorting third dimensional eyes, I looked again, but there was a time delay between what my soul was insisting I focus on, and what my eyes were able to.

As I looked at her, blinking to focus, it occurred to me that Trinity's smile had become fixed. My mind seemed to be taking an eternity to make simple and basic realisations. Finally the penny dropped: a body so petite and fragile as hers, would suffer much more than mine. It was then that I noticed she had stopped breathing. I tried to stand up, but my legs wouldn't respond. As I struggled to move, I fell over sideways. A big part of me just wanted to let go and accept whatever may come, but my soul was insistent; "you've come through far worse than this before...GET UP!"

So I tried once more. I raised myself onto my knees and elbows and heaved myself across to where Trinity was sitting. She was seemingly frozen in time, and I fell almost helplessly in front of her. "Her life now depends on you", came the inner voice. "Why now? Why this?" I thought. "How is it that we couldn't have been protected?" But there was no time to wait for answers. Trinity had stopped breathing and if I didn't do something about it, in this dimension, she would soon die.

So I pulled myself upwards and sat in front of her as steadily as I could. She was clearly not present. "So what do I do now?" arose the thought. "You need to go and get her back - form an energetic bridge with her and follow where she's gone". So I went inwards. Debilitated in the Third Dimension I may have been, but perhaps surprisingly, it was not hard to transcend this plane. The debilitation I was experiencing provided a stark contrast between the density and distortion of the material world as opposed to the lightness and peace of the etheric; it was one that I knew only too well. Firstly though, I had to be sure I wasn't going to leave the body. I couldn't risk that if I did so, I might allow in unfriendly energies, and even depart entirely. Hence I had to be sure I was unfolding inwardly into the other dimensions, thus transcending the physical, not leaving it altogether.

So I projected myself inwards, expanding into the higher densities. As my experience now shifted more into the etheric vibrations, greater clarity returned. I found myself in 'no man's land' - the Fourth Density - what you might call "limbo". The scenery was very much the Sinai, except now I was 'seeing' much more of the surrounding field. To me, the Fourth Density here is a fascinating paradox: on the one hand, there is timelessness and spacelessness, together with a sense of lightness, as you expand out of bodily density, like a genie being released from a bottle. But the Fourth Density is also a crossing point into the Middle Realm, and so at times, it can be very convoluted with denser energies and also entities of quite mixed disposition. That is especially so here in Earth's vicinity, where there is much intervention, confusion and realignment, all taking place within a relatively thin boundary. In this experience, in the Middle East, it felt like death - a barren graveyard of earth-bound souls. I felt and saw the presence of Opposing Consciousness, which my lower mind was distorting as demonic imagery. The tour guide appeared in front of me with a darkly disfigured face, I was now leaking a degree of emotional energy, caused by the deeply challenging circumstances. I was being mockingly laughed at, and my tightness was sustaining the entity that was now preying on my field.

For a moment it seemed like I might lose myself in the drama, but realising this was just another experience, I found myself able to let go quickly. Upon which, I heard Trinity's soft voice calling me. I breathed deeply, centred myself, and brought my attention more to the lightness, softness and love in her voice - I focussed on the voice and the feeling of Trinity. Bereft of density, consciousness works quickly in the etheric planes. Our timeless connection was drawing us closer again, until suddenly, we were together. Filled with joy, we were reunited in the Angelic Realms.

A telepathic exchange took place: "What's happening to you?" I asked. "What's going on?" Lovingly she replied, "I found the density and horror of the experience too intense to bear. I couldn't stay in that vibration when everything solid that I had known - including you - had become hazy, distorted and fearful. I felt the pain and suffering of ageless incarnations closing in on me. I knew I had to leave and then suddenly, to my great relief, I found myself here in the Angelic Realms." Looking deeply into her eyes, I recognised the truth in her words, but also simply knew it was not right for her to stay. "Yes, this place may feel much more homely, but it's not your time to be here yet. As serene as it may be, you're not meant to stay here. You belong in the physical world with me. You need to come back now."

However Trinity was not sure she could come back. She was closing down physically, but I didn't give up. I was now spanning beyond the Third and the Fourth Densities, touching the dreamlike Angelic Realms, which felt just like heaven. As tempting as it was to stay, I knew in my heart, it was not our immediate destiny. I had to bring her back with me, more centred in the Third Density. But how? Just as soon as the question arose, so did the answer: "Breathe, get her to breathe." In the Fourth Density we merged together as one, and I found myself 'breathing her back into the Third, whereupon, I looked deeply into her eyes. "Breathe Trinity. Breathe deeply, right down into your body". I noticed a distant glimmer. "Come back Trinity, I love you". I was practically shouting inwardly - "breathe, just BREATHE!"

Miraculously, Trinity took a deep breath and suddenly started coughing and spluttering. Just as soon as she returned however, she could once more feel the karmic pain of this realm throughout her entire body. Although she looked imploringly into my eyes, within a few moments she departed again. Once more I had to centre myself, go inwards and reconnect. Once more I found her in the peaceful tranquillity of the Angelic Realms. She did want to come back to the physical, but was struggling to stay here.

All night I fought and fought (surrendered and surrendered), continually activating and stimulating her consciousness to keep bringing her back - her fragile body desperately clinging to life. Finally, after battling for several hours, Trinity had returned and was able to stay in her body. Overcome by profound tiredness, she sank into a deep sleep.

For me, the experience was not quite over however. My body was pretty much 'normal', whatever 'normal' now was. Although I was desperately tired, I still couldn't sleep. Mind racing, I began marvelling at the positive side of the experience: being in both the Third and Fourth Densities simultaneously and bridging into the Angelic Realms. I had also experienced a direct confrontation with Opposing Consciousness – an energy that I had known well in past-lives. Furthermore, I had reacquired the gift of being able to communicate with another's soul through multiple planes; it helps unblock people's distortions, where their soul is saying one thing and their distortions another. Then finally, just when I thought I had seen enough for one night, I was treated to one of the most spectacular visions. My eyes were drawn to the canyon wall about a mile away in the distance, but I was not looking exactly at it, instead it was acting like a cinema screen, upon which a 'multiplex' movie was now beginning to roll.

I was witnessing an inter-dimensional light portal - a hologram - spanning this dimension, the Fourth and into the Angelic Realms. It was drawing into it earthbound souls from miles around, healing them and reconnecting them with the natural cycle of reincarnation. I watched with fascination, realising that our inter-dimensional escapade, had formed a psychic bridge: a means by which Benevolent Consciousness could create this soul retrieving portal. I remembered that I'd witnessed these plenty of times before, especially in situations of such turmoil, as were now beginning to unfold on Earth.

This was my refamiliarising 'crash course' in multi-dimensional living, and some of what it entailed. For me, it mirrored the Resurrection that all people must follow, as you become once more, multi-dimensional beings of the universe.

Gateway 5
- overview -

*Unfolding into
the New Paradigm.*

Once all inner identities, source pain and karma have been processed and dissolved, the soul is fully integrated and it may flow freely into your being. Specifically, it can activate, rejuvenate and animate all the various multi-dimensional bodily vehicles that you possess. You will undoubtedly have had tastes of your multi-dimensional gifts earlier on in your journey: you will have felt the deeper interplay of synchronicity; perhaps been able to read and prophesy what is about to land; you will likely have experienced miraculous manifestation, with reality shifting merely by your presence; many will experience a wonderful capacity to heal others, essentially by resonating frequencies of suppressed and lost beingness. In Gateway 5, you open fully into your higher dimensional vehicles so these gifts become a way of life. And you will also clear away any remaining fragments of outdated behaviours from the lower vehicles. You are resurrecting your true, multi-dimensional self; you become able to function and flow effortlessly through the different densities – inside yourself…

> *You become a willing instrument of divine creation. You come to live the New Paradigm, here, in this world, right now. Your unleashed light shows the way for others on the path. This is the "Resurrection".*

Once Gateway 4 has been completed, you might justifiably feel that everything you needed to accomplish here has been completed; however, really, it has only just begun! Enlightenment is not the end, but the beginning of your true, authentic capacity, to serve the higher good, and support the free flow of Unity Consciousness. Enlightenment feels like being born again, as who you really are – but then, (just like a newborn) you have to remaster how to properly function as your multi-dimensional self. It is like a source-knowing in you, something you can deeply feel about yourself, with greater gifts waiting to be revealed.

People sometimes think their destiny is something they must do - that they were given to come here and accomplish something in particular. But that is not strictly true – the river can follow many paths to the ocean, as it twists and turns through an ever changing landscape. As synchronicity clicks into place around you, it often feels like you are walking along a path of light, but that path is not fixed, it is not pre-ordained – or else how can you be living moment by moment?

What destiny is, however, is **what you will ultimately become**.

Your beingness is core to who you are; your mission is to fully unfold that, and when you do so, it feels like you really hit the 'sweet spot' of life itself. The moment you strike a resonant note of this sweet nectar, it feels as if your life has true meaning - it has been fulfilled up to that point.

Just like the honey bee, flying tirelessly from flower to flower, the soul in you is yearning for this perfection of expression. So, not only does the Resurrection open you more fully into higher dimensional vehicles, but it will also guide you into situations to expose the last vestiges of inner tightness arising from your previous attachments to the external drama. It is no longer that you are contracting within this tightness – because you are no longer reacting to the drama – however, you are infusing higher levels of consciousness and to do so, you will need a 'wider pipe' of expression. So at times, if any old fragments of behaviourisms – any micro-expressions – kick in, the internal superhighway will feel constricted. You have to fully open your wings - to open out through these contracted 'hotspots'. You may well feel heat, like electricity flowing through an overburdened fuse.

So in the Resurrection, the soul will manifest new situations to expose these hotspots, in order to expand the pipe, that the electricity of new beingness can flow unhindered through. The tendency is then to recreate similar situations from much earlier in your journey, even from your pre-Awakened state. It can feel a bit like reliving aspects of your life again.

Imagine, for example, you had some kind of pre-Awakened attachment to being in relationship with a partner. Perhaps now that seemingly perfect partner shows up to reactivate all the old memories, mental images and emotional patterns from past relationships that have been stored in your subconscious mind. Once more, you get to see, taste and feel the same old tightness arising from the original need for a particular outcome – although this time, it will no longer be a reactive contraction you feel, but instead a compression, as the soul flows through these previous channels...

> *It could be at this point, that a soul mate shows up, drawn effortlessly by your inflowing beingness. But do not expect it to be all rosy; the purposeful mirror they present will touch all those inner hotspots that you must work through.*

Understandably, you may feel like the Enlightenment process has begun all over again! The difference this time, is that you have an inner recognition that the behaviours are merely fragments of the old conditioning – *compressions to authentic behaviour* - and so you no longer give in to them: acting as the soul – you are no longer sucked into identity. Instead, as you feel them activating, you must stay in the behavioural action, *and open out through them*. This is the most productive way to complete the Resurrection.

What will greatly help you during this phase, is to look for the "feedback loops" within any given moment. The soul is working tirelessly to unveil itself. This can be greatly supported by resonant frequencies in the external world, which could be within another person. When each magnifies and reflects authentic beingness to the other, the energy begins to escalate; both will feel it building inside themselves, and this infusing beingness then begins to shape the world in a most profound way. Unity Consciousness is deeply creative and shaping of the external drama, but you must channel and harness it for it to be truly effective in any given location or situation.

However, you do not have to be in partnership for this to happen. You could be building such joyful feedback loops in nature – by witnessing your own reflections in the natural beauty that you see. Or else it could be a higher dimensional relationship that gives you the feedback, whereby you are witnessing the synchronistic interplay – you are being spoken to and supported by a telepathic knowing exchange, but through the lower density.

The Multi-Dimensional landscape

You begin to walk through a multi-dimensional landscape in this way. So the 3D world still looks much the same – do not necessarily expect that to change in the short term. However, how you now appreciate it, and act through it, greatly changes; every movement and action takes on a deeper significance, and you are at the centre of this unfolding story.

This is where 'active attention' is essential, rather than 'controlling intention'. In the spiritual mainstream, you will likely often have heard about the requirement to 'set your intentions' with regard to how you approach the circumstances of your life. Whilst such focus can indeed manifest results, because you begin to control flows of consciousness, it is totally counterproductive to your full, resurrected, multi-dimensional being. Who is it that is wanting to control the flow? It can only be an identity still. And in trying to establish how it should be, or how you should be in it, not only do you override the natural flow (thus suppressing and retarding it), but also the tendency is to dissolve authentic beingness.

Thus 'setting intentions' is counterproductive to your full unfolding.

However, 'active attention' is fully supportive to becoming who you truly are, and also, working hand-in-hand with the divine. Benevolence will bring all its power to bear, in any given situation, to support the unfolding of your multi-dimensional self.

Active attention functions by working to be completely open to the moment, without intention, instead reading the flow of the underlying, authentic reality. You allow your consciousness to be 'spiked' to the deeper meaning. It could be a particular word in any given sentence, it could be the sign on a billboard, an animal sound in nature, or even the lyrics of a song. Benevolence works best by giving energy to what needs to be focussed on now. In this way, the flow through you is accelerated; you may feel any compressing hotspots within, and then open out through them with your new, emerging gifts of beingness.

For example, I have discovered that in working with people, their soul will frequently provide the answer to problems they are currently facing – especially deeply buried and concealed source pain. This can be the hardest to get to and activate. But often, the soul will talk about it through the person. They will give away micro-expressions. As a healer, if you can pick up on these words and subtleties with your active attention, and feed them back to the person - for example, "Tell me what the word 'unsupported' means to you?" - then often this can be enough to get them into the source pain. And this is where benevolence will help you, by spiking in your awareness these multi-dimensional touch points.

So, your life is by now becoming increasingly multi-dimensional. The Resurrection facilitates your final attunement to the inherent qualities of the soul, expressed through the bodymind. As the final vestiges of redundant neural pathways begin to dissolve and your subconscious mind becomes ever clearer, you find yourself increasingly aligned with higher guidance; you are naturally attuning to inherent beingness. Action is now mostly spontaneous and authentic, arising from your at-one-ment with the natural flow of the universe in the moment. If questions do arise, they are those arising authentically from the soul, and are more pointers, as to where your consciousness is now being directed. You become able to trust more, that the answers will always become apparent.

During Gateway 5, you will unveil a profound capacity to see and read the deeper meaning behind all events, both for yourself, the people you work with, and the activities across our planet as a whole. You come to recognise physical manifestation as being primarily symbolic of your inner state of consciousness, and you align more to the patterning of events, thereby rendering yourself a willing and malleable tool of Benevolent Consciousness.

Furthermore, you become increasingly surrendered to the Divine Purpose - *helping all sentient life align with the natural flow* - and are therefore trusted with ever greater support and resources to bring the Right Action of the universe into fruition. You become increasingly able to read the truth of the moment and what is being invited. At the same time, you are totally accepting of everyone's free will to choose, realising that not everyone will feel, or align with, Right Action.

A deep realisation may dawn, that in this plane of consciousness, Right Action is frequently thwarted - there is, as yet, simply too much distortion. But the ceaseless downward flow of unconditional love from Benevolent Consciousness, ensures that synchronicities – *'spikes' in the flow* - are continually updated, presenting ever changing mirrors, encouraging wayward souls to come willingly back into alignment. So whilst you may not always accurately prophesy, you become able to read likely scenarios; although you may not foresee the future exactly, you can intuitively read the next step you are being invited to take.

The Resurrection is the final purification and rejuvenation process in this current chapter of the human story. It leads to humanity's evolution into the next divine form (what I feel given to call Divinicus). This phase is of vital importance if you are to fulfill your role as a multi-faceted, multi-dimensional being of service to the Divine Purpose. Our planetary system is ascending, and lightworkers will be engaged in this process, facilitating the retrieval, healing and Ascension of other souls. We will be required to transmute dense energies that are prevalent in the Earth's field, and help realign her energy grid, so the shift into the higher consciousness can happen more smoothly.

In order to do this, we must be absolutely familiar with multi-dimensional experience; we must be living day-by-day within the deeper meaning – the underlying flow. There must be no internal blockages, attachments nor compressions that might restrict your capacity to fulfill the Divine Purpose. Right now, the world needs you, the absolute fullness of you!

At Resurrection you are fast becoming a 'tantric master' in the wider sense: able to completely submerge yourself in full-embodied experience, and yet not at all be lost in it.

With this capability, increasingly, you gain access to at least three dimensional planes of existence: the Third, the material one in which many have been engrossed for countless lifetimes; the Fourth, the bridge between higher and lower worlds; and the Fifth, the New World of higher etheric vibrations, founded on unconditional love, joy and mutual respect for all life.

Actually, what is happening, is that you are unfolding as a bridge between two worlds; able to express and live the next higher realm, whilst existing in this lower one. Thus you become a channel for the New Paradigm, infusing it here, all around you, inspiring others to make that journey too.

Early in your spiritual unfolding, you will have become aware of these different realms – *the two worlds* - although you may not necessarily have been able to define their experiences. Indeed, it is not necessary to do so. You may simply be enjoying the experiences and unfolding into them, without the need to explain or to rationalise. For those moving towards such multi-dimensional living, it is also important to realise that you do not have to leave your body and go 'elsewhere' to experience it; rather you may unfold those inner experiences here into your daily – *physical* - life. All dimensions can and **are** experienced here and now. They are done so through your seven bodily vehicles of expression (what we may collectively term the "bodymind").

The Seven Bodily Vehicles of Expression

So what are these vehicles through which the dimensions are experienced? According to the Divine Design for humanity, the soul flows downwards through ever decreasing vibrational planes of existence, like a stream flowing down a mountain from its source. The stream of our soul, interacts with the dimensions at various consciousness exchange points (what we call the chakras). These are where Unity Consciousness, as the soul, flows into Separation Consciousness as the bodily vehicles. The overriding purpose is to initiate divine acts of creativity - *Right Action* - by which to experience, and fully express, who you really are.

This is the main purpose of life: to fully express yourself as a unique experience of the One. There is nothing else to know, and nothing else going on. The One – "God" - is seeking to reveal itself through You!

Understanding the purpose of the bodily vehicles and how they work, is of profound benefit to unveiling your multi-faceted capability, fulfilling your life in the most superlative ways. You unveil and reveal gifts you probably never dreamt possible.

Here then, is my personal overview of what those vehicles are, how they function together, and what they're capable of. I have listed them in what you might consider reverse order – from the top down. Because when functioning as designed and intended, the light of divine creativity flows downwards from the Source, through ever decreasing dimensional frequencies. As before, this is my interpretation, intended merely as a guide, to assist you in your own unfolding…

7. Spirit-Light-Body (merkaba): *the spirit-light-body is designed to harness soul consciousness, flowing in through the crown chakra, to align your being with the right dimensional activity, which is at one with your higher purpose.*

Through the spirit-light-body, the soul has the capacity to act through multiple planes of consciousness simultaneously. It connects you with all other sentient life, and is able to harmonise with the co-creative impulse of other souls in your sphere of influence. Your divine purpose could be channelling in the harmonistic light of the Fifth Density, to which humanity is ascending; it could be counteracting Opposing Consciousness in the Fourth Density, to prevent distortional interference; alternatively, it could be bringing absolute presence into the Third Density, to connect with, and inspire, those not yet fully awakened. Thus the spirit-light-body shines the light of your soul inter-dimensionally.

6. Celestial Body: *the celestial body harnesses and stores reflections of your soul-ray-harmonic through the countless lifetimes you have experienced. Its purpose is to help you align with true aspects of your beingness.*

The downward shining light of the soul is next received into the third eye chakra, which 'looks' into the outer world, comparing what it sees, to the reflections of the soul in the celestial body. When the soul notices its own brilliance, it helps you align with, and unfold, those aspects of beingness that are most becoming of you in that given moment – *what you feel 'given' to express.* You 'settle into your groove' so to speak. It is that feeling of complete self-belief, self-confidence, self-acceptance and contentment. When we can notice ourselves manifested in the outer world through our own authentic inner reflection, that is when we are truly living. We are frequently reduced to tears at the seemingly simplest of things, because we are fulfilling our divine purpose. When we are fully aligned with who we are, it feels just like hitting the 'sweet spot' of life itself.

5. Higher Mind: *from authentic being arises authentic creation. The purpose of higher mind is to harmonise with the divine flow of synchronicity, and initiate Right Action aligned with the universe.*

Now is the time to experience your beingness through creative impulse. At this stage, the creative movement is quite abstract and undefined; the purpose is more about exploring questions about the nature of reality and co-creating evolutionary growth with other sentient life, rather than an actual creation itself. Souls come together and resonate concordant frequencies between them, that start to weave together a co-creative exploration of life's deeper meaning: the beginnings of a new reality that encourages each soul to evolve and grow, to become more self-realised. In my view, this is where the idea of the 'sacred contract' has arisen from. It is not necessarily that a soul 'agrees to carry out such and such', it is more that there's synergy on what needs to be explored and learned. And so the soul now acts through higher mind contemplations, gathering together 'elementals of consciousness', which form a directional flow of Right Action, like swirling clouds in the heavens.

4. Causal Body: *the causal body is where your karma is held. It is the cause of your incarnation; it creates the agenda for your learning experience, based on past-life attachments through which you need to evolve.*

As the soul ignites beams of creative light, shining down from the higher vehicles, your causal body (also known as the "energy body") works within the universal Law of Attraction, weaving together life's experiences with other souls and circumstances. You are now beginning to create the energetic blueprint – *the landscape* – through which your physical existence will flow. It is here where your karma casts shadows of attachment through the lower vehicles and into your outer reality. The causal body now attracts, and manifests, exactly the right conditions to unveil the learning experiences required for this particular step of your evolution. You are invited to confront and dissolve, the obscuring clouds of karma by fulfillment of non-judgmental Right Action. We perceive this directing influence as a pull through the Heart Centre - "this is the way to go now".

3. Lower Mind: *the lower mind is designed to receive, interpret and process higher channelled knowing through your clairvoyant, clairaudient and clairsentient (psychic) skills.*

So now, due to the gathering energies of the downward flowing creative spark, you know what to you are given to do - the question is, how to do it? If your authentic creative action does not get sidetracked (by Opposing Consciousness for example), the gathering energies are next passed into your subconscious or "lower mind". Lower mind then helps you to 'connect the dots' within the co-creative weave. Through the clairvoyant, clairaudient and clairsentient skills of lower mind, you begin to pick up rhythms and patterns of synchronicity in your "consciousness landscape" and have clear visions of the 'garment' to be created. As Right Action draws together the threads of reality, moment by moment, it becomes abundantly clear what you are being invited to do and how to do it. Through lower mind, the universe is helping you to align with your highest purpose.

2. Emotional Body: *the emotional body builds energy, sensitivity, passion and conviction around your behaviours, to bring your creative Right Action into fruition.*

The creative process has now gathered together the right fabric of elementals for your creation, but it next has to be woven into form. The soul now utilises the emotional body to garner more consciousness elementals, and weaves emotion around the creative impulse: it provides a multi-coloured palette of experience that brings the garment to life; it makes the illusionary reality feel very real, yielding meaning and sense of purpose to life. Emotional content is what adds essential vibrancy to your creation – it gives a sense of purpose, motivation and traction in this often dense physical realm. It adds sensitivity to your experience of life. However, once the creative action has come to fruition, the weave of the garment is meant to quickly unwind again, so that something else may be created. It is not intended, within the human design, that you hang onto emotions and build identities around them, as is so often the case.

1. Physical Body: *the physical body provides the ultimate vehicle to bring the creative downward flowing process into full expression.*

Too many people are too controlling of their physicality, or else too insensitive to the subtle, descending impulses through it. Paradoxically, it is often because they are too attached to physical phenomena. Yet when we can fully let go, then internal sensitivity increases astronomically - you light the beacon of the emergent soul. As the master weaver, your brain reads the pattern that has been crafted through your higher bodily vehicles and then orchestrates a magical symphony of activity throughout your billions of material cells. The physical body finally brings into life the creative, expressive, evolutionary purpose, in the myriad of human possibility. The physical body is a multifaceted mirror of higher creative intent. It is the jewel in the crown - it brings manifested reality to our original, abstract contemplation. Finally, when the channels are fully open, the Divine Purpose comes fully into being, manifested here and now, in all its glory, unleashed through the physical realm.

So from my perspective, this is the Divine Design for humanity - how the creative process is supposed to happen. Why is it then that most people do not experience the magical flow of life in this way?

The Matrix of Mass Human Subconsciousness

As I have alluded to continually throughout this book, we live in a system of control – *metaphored graphically, of course, in the film trilogy "The Matrix"*. The lower mind, emotional and physical bodily vehicles are over-stimulated with constant, disharmonious distraction. Unnatural lifestyles have been created and are propagated constantly through TV, newspapers, radio and other media. The surrounding energy field is bombarded with electromagnetic interference through mobile phones, satellites, gadgetry, microwaves, and Wi-Fi. Food in the industrial food chain is deliberately infused with addictive substances, such as processed sugar and sweeteners, MSG (monosodium glutamate) and gluten; many mainstream foods have artificial colourings, pesticides, antibiotics and hormones; not to mention the propensity for alcohol, caffeine and nicotine in our society. Our water has been contaminated with energetically harmful fluorides and the vast quantities of corporate, so-called 'medicinal' drugs, that end up being continually recirculated in the water system. The average home has constant, residual electric fields, due to overuse of electronic gadgetry. Most houses are awash with toxic chemicals used to clean and disinfect, which in actual fact, damages and lowers one's energetic sensitivity. The same can be said for the unnatural polyesters and other oil-based compounds used to make clothing.

So it would seem, that our society has been perfectly configured to desensitise people's energy bodies and condition souls to conform to lower patterns of behavioural lifestyles. In this way, the downward flowing soul is typically truncated at the level of the solar plexus. It is no coincidence that this happens to be one of the most unprotected and sensitive areas of the body; it is intended to be open to all external inflows of energy, but this source of people's psychic sensitivity, has been closed down by deliberate over-stimulation...

for the majority of people, the subconscious mind has been conditioned like a maze - a roundabout with no exits.

This is why it has been so easy for people to develop addictive, conditioned behaviours, which trap, fragment and dissipate the flow of the soul into continual, repetitive eddy currents. Just like software on a computer, the neural webs of fixed behaviours, of which I have spoken in the earlier Gateways, take root in the brain, locking the soul into a false self-identity. It is this that creates a lower based lifestyle, which can be readily controlled by the illusionary fears, false ambitions and manipulating agendas of Opposing Consciousness. So perfect is this system of control, that many awakening people are left with the inescapable conclusion, that it was designed and perpetuated that way to enslave people.

Now however, after centuries of incarnation and getting continually lost in this artificial – *synthetic* - drama, humanity is being gifted a wonderful opportunity: an enlightening wave of higher consciousness is beginning to activate within people's hearts. This "Christ Consciousness" as some call it (although not of a religious nature), has been dispatched and intensified to liberate those who are ready to step out of the maze. This energy works by sounding a note - a vibration - through your energy field, which resonates with, and therefore amplifies, the sound of your soul, that it may be heard once more above the outer din of society. This helps people reintegrate the soul within their being, and then cleanse the lower bodily vehicles (as I have outlined in this book), so that more of humanity may resurrect their inherent human beingness.

Now, at this crucial juncture in the Earth's evolutionary story, the matrix of dense frequencies is being challenged through the field and broken down. Increasingly, heightened awareness is bringing the destructive ways of the past, into the light. This cleansing process – this Great Realignment – is not going to be an easy journey as the light separates out from the density. The old world fabric – the matrix – will steadily break down over time.

This is why it is often so confusing for people in spiritual circles at this time. You feel the lightness flooding into your heart, but wonder why the outer world does not look the same. Why is it still in such darkness? It is because the crusted bed of the stream is being stirred up and broken down, so that it may be washed away. Do not worry therefore if it looks increasingly cloudy before it clears.

As you purify the physical, emotional and lower mind vehicles, your soul begins to unfold into the causal body, thereby enabling you to process your karma. Following that, you begin to embrace the awesome creative capacity of higher mind, which can effortlessly shape the immediate circumstances of your life according to your higher evolutionary purpose. When the lower vehicles are clear from the distorting influence of Opposing Consciousness, the creative flow from higher knowing to lower realisation and authentic manifestation, becomes seamless, without tightness, tension or internal grasping. In this way, you are liberated to see clear, undistorted reflections of yourself within the celestial body.

Your own purification

Despite the darkness within society at this time, you are deeply encouraged to focus on your own purification – far from being selfish, this actually speeds up the cleansing process of the Great Realignment that the Earth is now engaged in (fully explained in DIVINICUS). As you purge yourself of the outdated density, you become able to 'step into' and utilise the spirit-light-body. This yields a more complete experience of multi-dimensionality. You can still feel the Third Dimension with all its intensity, but you are now able to go inwards and transcend it, to ride on the more etheric planes. As you transition Gateway 5, experiences are configured to help you move effortlessly between the dimensions, sometimes projecting strength, love or presence in the Third; perhaps countering the negative effects of Opposing Consciousness in the Fourth; or alternatively, enjoying the synchronistic interplay of the Fifth. As you unfold your spiritual service (in whatever guise that comes), this multi-dimensional capability, facilitated by your spirit-light-body, will become of paramount importance.

The Resurrection then, finally unveils your divine purpose for this incarnation, and you become increasingly trusted with the resources of Benevolent Consciousness to fulfill that role. Furthermore, by complete inner purification, you will have dispatched from your being, the malevolent impact of Opposing

Consciousness, which has so unceremoniously shunted humanity out of his complete and rightful expression. Having resurrected all seven bodily vehicles, you are now a fully fledged lightwarrior, bringing into fruition, where possible, the Right Action of the universe. Upon completion of your divine purpose here, you are finally liberated from lower, physical form, to make your glorious Ascension into the next vibrational realm – the "New Paradigm".

Transitioning Gateway 5
- essential tools -

1. **Reconfront past behaviour patterns:** *continually surrender to the unfolding pathway, inviting you to reveal and reconfront, fragments of past behaviourisms. Ride the flow of streaming synchronicity.*

2. **Unfold divine gifts of beingness:** *notice that as you open out through any compressions, new gifts of beingness start to emerge. Let these grow by giving plenty of attention and energy to them.*

3. **Unleash your full potential through sacred sexuality:** *explore the sacredness and sensuality of your inherent sexuality. This has great potential to raise your vibration and harness creative potential, to unleash benevolently into the world.*

4. **Cultivate a strong Twin Flame connection:** *begin to notice, and frequently connect with, the sense of your Twin Flame in your consciousness landscape. Build feedback loops, grow your energy.*

5. **Fully live your multi-dimensionality - become a positive force for change:** *notice that you are afforded constant opportunities to transform the surrounding energy field.*

1.Reconfront past behaviour patterns: *continually surrender to the unfolding pathway, inviting you to reveal and reconfront, fragments of past behaviourisms. Ride the flow of streaming synchronicity.*

As an enlightened being, you will now be acting from entirely higher self motivation. All impetus in life arises directly from the Source, carried on the wings of the now fully reconnected soul. However, the soul is still not yet able to radiate its full splendour through the seven bodily vehicles of expression. At the Transfiguration, the inner child and inner teenager identities would have been broken apart, leaving behind fragments of fixed neural pathways. Whilst you may no longer get lost in them, because any attachment is gone, your divine flow might still 'compress' through them – *like electricity through a fuse.* In other words, your creative channel, although authentic, is still being constrained and constricted to a degree. To finally overcome these compressions, you must reconfront the situations that activate them, and then open out into them...

> *You become so sensitive, that you are literally able to feel the fragments of the past behaviourisms as subtle degrees of tightness within you as 'micro-expressions'; it even becomes possible to feel the neural pathways themselves. By placing your attention in these, you become able to expand through them with your soul consciousness. You literally open out through the compressions.*

So it is likely that you will be guided back into society to recreate circumstances with many parallels to your former, non-spiritual life. Although you no longer get stuck, it may feel like you are compressed down in certain situations and circumstances. By staying centred and present in the compressions, the tightness begins to unwind as you open out through them. Thus, the final fragments of conditioning break apart, and your energy greatly strengthens, as more of the soul can infuse.

As you break through these compressions, you will feel the stronger inflow of light; you now have a greater capacity to build uplifting feedback loops around you. By always looking for the divine light and majesty of beingness everywhere, in everyone, you amplify the soul and its higher purpose - you are bringing out the best in yourself and others.

In so doing, you flush through your subconscious mind by always attuning to the lightness in situations. Although you must be continually careful not to be creating illusionary realities, it is an inherent quality of the soul to look for, and express, the natural lightness of positivity in all circumstances. And because any retarding density has cleared, subconscious activities move much more into your consciousness...

As you keep opening out into any compressions, you are continually unleashing the divine flow through you; you start living within a streaming flow of synchronicity, reading the deeper meaning of events 'on the hoof'.

2. Unfold new gifts of beingness: *notice that as you open out through any compressions, new gifts of beingness start to emerge. Let these grow by giving plenty of attention and energy to them.*

As your bodily vehicles reactivate, and the soul fully infuses through them, you will begin to notice that new talents and capabilities appear. They may be tentative at first, you may only get a slight sense – like reading someone's karma for example – but keep persisting; you are 'pulling the thread' of new possibility, and as you give energy to this potential, it will likely grow and unfold, in ways you could not previously have imagined.

You might have a profound capability to read the flow, for yourself and others; you might find your natural consciousness has an uplifting affect on your environment, without apparently doing anything; you might uncover skills that have a catalytic or empathic affect on people.

These will be authentic expressions of beingness, as determined by the configuration of your soul-ray-harmonic: your unique blend of the Seven Rays of Consciousness. To facilitate this unfolding, you must notice the opportunities to express the new talents, and attune to them at every given opportunity – *to give energy to them.* The more you express them, the stronger these divine gifts will become.

To help in this process of fully embodied expression, you will likely find this "Golden Light Meditation", outlined below, of benefit...

Golden Light Meditation

- *begin by sitting quietly and noticing your breathing*
- *after a few moments, centre your attention above the crown and with every in-breath, concentrate on the downward flow of higher consciousness, experienced as golden light*
- *move to the crown chakra, relax and bring the energy down into the front of it, harnessing the golden light with each in-breath*
- *now, with every out-breath, relax deeply, and feel the flow of light into and throughout the spirit-light-body (the highest subtle layer of lightness you can perceive – simply have your attention in that)*
- *after several cycles through the crown chakra, move awareness down to the third eye, and with each in-breath, breathe into the front of the chakra feeling the inward flow of golden light*
- *once more, with each out-breath, feel the flow of energy into the corresponding bodily vehicle, in this case the celestial body (to locate it, simply work with the sense of the next lower frequency feeling of lightness)*
- *work progressively down through all the chakras, infusing each bodily vehicle in turn*

- *once fully illuminated in this way, with each in-breath, now concentrate on filling **all** the chakras with golden light and with each out-breath, feel the energy flowing from the chakras into their respective bodily vehicles of expression. Fully infuse each with golden light - healing, rejuvenating and resurrecting*

- *finally, notice how the chakras now disappear, as your entire body is consumed within the experience of golden light.*

As more and more higher consciousness infuses your being, you will also gain increasing access to multi-dimensional existence, and the skill to flow between dimensions as Right Action dictates.

The key to perfecting this gift, is to continually notice the influence of the various dimensions in your life: for example, the interplay of streaming, spontaneous synchronicity from the Fifth Dimension or the effects of some kind of interference (psychic attack) by Opposing Consciousness in the Fourth. It may be that you infuse an uplifting, motivational affect on people with charismatic action in the Third Density. You may then more readily harness and enhance these effects by noticing them, opening out through them, and fully unleashing them into the world – basically, more strongly attuning them.

Do not hide your light under a bushel – the world needs it!

3. Unleash your full potential through sacred sexuality: *explore the sacredness and sensuality of your inherent sexuality. This has great potential to raise your vibration and harness creative potential to unleash benevolently into the world.*

Our sacred sexuality has become much maligned, in a controlling world. Like no other subject, it has created enormous taboo - trigger points in our psyche. Yet harnessing the divine nature of this immensely creative energy, is one of the greatest gifts available to you. Sexual energy is not only joyous and deeply liberating, but also connective into the higher dimensions, and can generate incredible creative capacity in your life.

When worked with in an aligned way, sacred sexuality can unleash the fullness of kundalini energy through your being, which then has a naturally magnetic effect through your outer environment.

Clearly, in our very distorted and repressed society, in many cases, sexual intimacy has been degraded to very physical, basic, 'intercourse'. It need not be that way! And neither does it matter if you are in relationship or not - you can still open up the fullness of this creative potential if on your own. It is definitely something to be encouraged. The question is... how?

Here is a basic, bare-bones, 3 step approach:

i. **Confronting taboo and repression:** the first thing is to recognise where you might have been repressed in your sexuality, and work through any contractions caused by distorted behaviours, in the way described in the 9 step process in Gateway 3. Essentially, you must regress yourself into the senses and feelings – *any source pain* – related to sexual intimacy. This may take some considerable time, patience, persistence and sensitivity with yourself. Even if you find it very challenging, and perhaps you would prefer not to go there, nevertheless, it is important to explore and fully delve into your sexuality.

ii. **Building sensuality:** as you have cleared much of these taboo areas, the next step is to increase your level of gentle sensitivity – touching your skin lightly for example (and that of your partner if you have one). This can build into more sensual massage – but, in the beginning at least, avoiding the erogenous zones.

This second step may take weeks and months to build upon. It is definitely not something to be rushed. After a while, you will find yourself becoming increasingly sensual. Then begin to explore the erogenous zones with this gentle sensuality. Allow your soul to be guided. Let any remnants of taboo conditioning fall away – this is a divinely sacred gift, and the stimulation of sexual energy in this way greatly heightens your energy.

iii. **Harnessing sacred sexual energy:** the next step, is to focus on building and harnessing sacred sexual energy within you – as a general way of being. Not that you will always be overtly sexual – not at all! The energy has been greatly misunderstood. Yes, sexual energy can be deeply pleasurable of course, but the *consciousness itself* can be especially creative in your landscape. *It is about activating and harnessing that energy for your greatest creative good, and all life around you.*

So you may begin to build the energy through sacred sexual intimacy, either by yourself or with a partner. It is vitally important that whilst you increasingly enjoy this, you do not get lost in it: specifically, I mean not losing your sense of centre and self, within the action – which, in a non-aligned state, is easily done!

In terms of releasing – ejaculation – many have said that especially for men, the sexual juices should be retained within the body for maximum energetic potential. For me, this is a misunderstanding and a limiting distortion. It is the energy itself that needs to be harnessed within the body, not necessarily the juices. In fact allowing the juices to release, builds the energy in a climactic way (of course); the key is, not to lose yourself in the release…

So in the moment of release, importantly, work not to get lost in the physical expression itself. Enjoy it yes, but switch focus to the energy – the consciousness – of the release, and bring it up through your body, as you might during a kundalini raising meditation. If you are with a partner, then bring the energy up through and around both of you: at the point of release, focus on the loving connection between you, and this will naturally happen.

Here, I have been necessarily brief (sexual intimacy deserves an entire book of its own!). But there are many benevolent tantric practices out there, which I would encourage you to explore. As always, allow your intuition, and own inner knowing, to develop, rather than simply taking on the beliefs of others. Be inspired yes, but let your own unfettered soul take the lead.

In harnessing sacred sexual energy in this way, and not always immediately acting on sexual impulses, but rather holding the energy of it within, then you will find yourself building increasing creative potential – your ability to manifest in line with the divine flow greatly intensifies…

You find yourself naturally creating miracles and magic!

4. Cultivate a strong Twin Flame connection: *begin to notice, and frequently connect with, the sense of your Twin Flame in your consciousness landscape. Build feedback loops, grow your energy.*

Again, the Twin Flame phenomenon is another area of much misunderstanding within the spiritual mainstream. Getting right relation with it, will once more, greatly enhance your energetic power in life and creative potential. Let us be clear…

*The Twin Flame **does not** incarnate! So it is self-defeating to be looking for them as some physical manifestation – although reflections of them will manifest. And it is these reflections which can be harnessed within, building uplifting feedback loops.*

At the Source, as the soul comes into being, it notionally divides into two. Actually what really happens, is that a polarity is created: one part embarks upon its journey through the relativistic universe; the other stays close to the Source, acting as a natural polarity, drawing the soul to ever higher vibrations and sense of self-realisation.

In the beginning, your Twin Flame will be difficult to see and pick up. You will get the sense of influence and guidance by a higher power, but before the Transfiguration, this will more likely be coming from your higher self. It is only when lower and higher self have merged as one (following kundalini activation), that the Twin Flame can be fully felt.

The presence of too much karmic density may also distract, so it is really as you unfold into the Fifth Density, that you will start to get a real taste of your Twin Flame experience...

It is as though there is a benevolent being, all around you, and through you, beginning to act for you in the outer world. The Twin Flame acts within your consciousness landscape. By witnessing their reflections, and bringing their energy back inside yourself, you create incredible energetic feedback loops with the world.

So as this starts to happen, notice Twin Flame reflections in your environment: it could be the twinkle in someone's eyes, cloud formations at sunrise, the way the waves roll up onto the beach, or a creature that comes close to you, generating a sense of well-being inside. It becomes like constantly living within a lucid dream, where you are being deeply supported and cherished by the beauty around you. When this transition during the Resurrection begins to happen, with a deeper sense of meaning and feeling to life, it is likely your Twin Flame is connecting with you.

And when there is no neediness, you will most likely benefit from the reflection of your Twin Flame acting through a soul mate. The soul mate is not your Twin Flame, but a very close vibration to them.

The essential thing, is not to be needing your Twin Flame to appear in a particular guise (like a soul mate for example), because if not, *they can appear everywhere!* And the connection becomes deeply sublime, building much energy within, which once again, manifests increasing creative potential through your outer world.

5. Fully live your multi-dimensionality - become a positive force for change: *notice that you are afforded constant opportunities to transform the surrounding energy field.*

By now, you will most likely be fully aware that the surrounding energy field is awash with Opposing Consciousness, distorting and restricting authentic beingness. Thus it is retarding many millions of people from possible awakening. As a fully fledged lightwarrior, you are now a potent, positive force for change, able to negate the effects of Opposing Consciousness. Thus we break down the surrounding field, and help others escape the restriction in order to flourish and grow.

> *You are now very much invited to watch for opportunities to transmute the surrounding energy field, opening gaps for others, to break through and break out.*

It will always become abundantly clear, through your direct connection to the place of 'all knowing', what action is required, how best to proceed, and when. This is not to say that our Right Action will always result in Right Outcome (one which is aligned to the universal flow). Each person is free to choose, and a true lightwarrior will never manipulate, control or intentionally change the path of another. You simply extend an 'open hand', then, if invited, it becomes abundantly clear what function and act of beingness, will best facilitate the situation.

The more you follow your unfolding path of light, the more an inner landscape of synchronistic action forms: you hold pieces of an incomplete jigsaw, with a variety of possible outcomes. You are now witnessing the unfolding of a continually updating Divine Purpose: which is to liberate as many people as possible, who are ready, willing and able. It is important however, that you do not try to pre-empt the outcome of any particular engagement, otherwise you risk distorting the incoming energy, and once more, build false realities. It is better that you hold your continually evolving vision of the Purpose lightly, allowing it to move, reshape and adapt...

Within your expansion through Gateway 5, learn to hold the space more; trust in your building energy, that it has the capacity to shape and change the situation for the higher good of all.

You must remember that your every thought, word and deed, can, and does, affect the unfolding of the Divine Purpose. When it becomes absolutely clear what is meant to happen, then you may summon every thought, feeling and expression around your actions to ensure they manifest in accordance with the natural flow of the universe. In so doing, you unfold new skills in shaping the surrounding energy field through the power of feeling and highly focussed inner will. Always, our purpose is to transmute the denser energies and rebuild higher congruence with the natural order of life. Whilst you have mastered becoming 'as-nothing' in the presence of Opposing Consciousness, thereby rendering you increasingly immune, your access to the place of all-knowing will provide the necessary approach to negate this consciousness, so that you may bring maximum upliftment to all sentient life.

You are now becoming a very positive force for change in the world – humbly accept, celebrate and engage with that. It is your birthright!

So watch for the Divine Purpose to unfold, holding it deeply in your awareness, and, at every opportunity, harmonise with it.

You notice that increasingly, you are breaking down the denser energies through the field, blocking Opposing Consciousness and catalysing change, weaving together higher congruent realities. Of course many will not be reading from the same script. Even so, selflessly we continue to perform Right Action, always trusting in the infinite organising power of higher consciousness, flowing as a continual stream of benevolence through our lives.

Steadily, as your energy intensifies, Right Action more frequently comes to fruition, and more of those who are ready to be helped can be liberated.

Transitioning Gateway 5
- general misconceptions -

1. You are starting the Ascension process all over again!

As an enlightened being, you can be of enormous help to the ever unfolding Divine Purpose, the central motivation of which, is to help those who have become stuck in the eddy currents of life. You can fulfill your divine role by re-engaging with society, and, as required, going back into the Matrix of Mass Human Subconsciousness, helping people break free.

In order to do so, you must entirely free yourself from the conditioning of your previous life. Whilst you may have broken your attachments to reality and dissolved any false identities, the last vestiges of the conditioned behaviours will still exist – you will likely be feeling them as compressions – micro-expressions – within your bodily field. Hence your soul guides you on a pathway to confront all the old circumstances and patterns. It is as though you are moving into a period of 'on the job' training, helping others, whilst at the same time, exposing remaining inner compressions and quickly expanding out through them. In some ways, it may feel like you are beginning the Ascension process all over again, but rest assured, you are not...

> *In essence, you are finally preparing your vehicles of expression so that you may now move fully into divine service - that which also supports the joy of complete expression of who you truly are, as a way of life.*

2. That you will be recognised by all others

As a resurrected being, you will be flowing with Right Action, and able to quickly discern where others might be stuck or are not following the path that best serves them. If not already, in Gateway 5, you soon realise that you hold many keys to the unfolding of others...

You begin to recognise the situations where others are drawn to you, to receive some kind of resonance or transmission, that can unleash aspects of their soul.

However, we are living in very difficult and confusing times where few recognise the truth when they see or feel it. Even if they do, frequently people go into denial, not wanting to embrace responsibility for their problems and the invitation to change. As a fully enlightened being, you are acting as a very effective mirror, and frequently people do not like what they see - they may blame the mirror rather than seeing their own reflection. Hence it is likely that only a few will recognise what you are being, and how you are helping...

Do not be put off by lack of recognition - it is not necessary that you are seen by others in order to help them. If this is the case, take your feedback for supportive action from elsewhere – be it synchronicity in the surrounding environment, or else the sense of support from higher dimensions.

Always trust, that those you are destined to help, will somehow find their way to your door, and in the multi-dimensional dance of souls, the right transmission will activate and be received. This is what increasingly takes place, as you resurrect your full complement of divine beingness.

3. That you will have an overtly measurable effect in the 3D

You are now acting as a beacon of light in this lower realm: a conduit for higher consciousness through every engagement and interaction. However, you should not automatically assume that your effect will be somehow unilaterally observable or even measurable – neither is there a requirement for thanks!

Each individual has the liberty of choice and expression. Benevolent Consciousness will not manipulate or control people; each person is entitled to their own self-realisation. It is not your (authentic) task to realise for another.

Having said this, we are moving through a major shift of human consciousness, or put more accurately, a growing section of the population is awakening and ascending. So our effect within this community, is likely to be profound and will be felt within the field of consciousness, even if the recipient is unaware of its source.

Neither should we gauge our effect by the amount of our work; rather it should be by the quality. It could indeed be your role only to directly influence one other person, and yet still have a profound effect on the whole. In my view, selfless service has no measure.

4. That all your actions are now 'perfect'

Based on philosophical writings about so called "Enlightened" or "Ascended Masters", it seems to be a general misconception, that when you reach the state of Enlightenment, all your actions are 'perfect'. In one sense they may be, in so far as you are acting perfectly authentically in accordance with the energies flowing through your being, and your perception of Right Action. However, to me, a true master would likely realise that all experience is a distortion of perfection - *of Absolute* - and would therefore continually seek to improve their ability to manifest an increasingly sophisticated expression...

> You may have dealt with distortions, source pain and karma, however, there is always something to learn: as a resurrected being, it will likely be how best to apply your gifts; how best to attune your inner frequencies – your soul-ray-harmonic – for the most uplifting external impact.

No matter how evolved you might feel you are, there is always something to be mastered. Therefore, to me, there is no such thing as an "Enlightened Master". Instead you arrive at the place where you recognise yourself as an eternal student.

5. That Ascension means to 'leave the planet'

It seems to be a general misconception that Ascension means to 'leave the planet' - this is incorrect! Firstly, upon completion of the

Five Gateways, you will be ascended, yet probably stay in the body in this plane, to assist in the Ascension of others. Upon completion of your purpose in this density, you are indeed freed from the need to reincarnate here in physical form.

Your centre of consciousness ultimately shifts into the next realm of existence, where a higher vibrational form of humanity is currently being born, as an integral part of a Renewed Earth.

The New Paradigm exists here and now, within you, and you begin to live it; but most people, are as yet, unable to tune into this higher energetic presence. This final transition to the higher vibration is known as an "Ascending Realm Shift". In other words you 'step out of' this realm and into the next higher one; you shake off the old skin and 'put on' a glorious body of light – *your spirit-light-body.* You are still on Planet Earth, it is just that you are now occupying a higher vibrational form of it.

Ultimately, you are joining what some have referred to as... "The Golden Age". Unfold into it, inside yourself. Live it, here and now, and it will become a reality for you.

Transitioning Gateway 5
- indicators of beginning -

As you step into the corridor of Gateway 5, you may be forgiven for thinking you have just begun the Enlightenment process all over again. Suddenly, patterns of behaviour are recreated, mirroring previous experiences and engagements. You may notice tightness arising once more in the various bodily vehicles of expression. This time however, they have a different quality to them: you notice that there is no internal attachment, indeed there is no contraction (for the soul does not react to events anymore), rather it feels more like a compression, as your soul is seeking to burst through...

You will likely find it entirely natural to want to open out through these compressions. When this starts happening, it is a sure sign that you have stepped into the Resurrection phase of your evolution – into Gateway 5.

You will also notice that you have stopped processing past-life karma. Although at some point, you will likely start to engage Higher Dimensional Karma. Unlike before, this is not of a personal nature, although you may respond personally in an emotive way. Higher Dimensional Karma is where you are working at a group consciousness level – perhaps helping heal the divine masculine energy for example. In which case, you may feel this in a personal way – *you may experience compressions around it* – but in dealing with it inside yourself, you receive some synchronisitic feedback, that you are now working at the higher level.

This may occur as the continual noticing and alignment to synchronistic flow, except it is not happening intentionally. You are simply flowing as the soul, and noticing that you seem to be at the centre of co-creative Right Action. Increasingly, you will be experiencing the surrounding energy field, and its impact on everyone's lives. You will also be noticing your inherent ability to transmute the denser energies, thereby creating breathing space for other souls to flourish. You will likely have a strong connection to your Twin Flame, acting in and through your creative actions.

Here is a summary of the indications that the Gateway 5 transition has begun in earnest...

- *you notice that past-life regressions have ceased, although Higher Dimensional Karma may activate later on, but with a different, more selfless quality to it*

- *you re-engage with patterns of conditioned behaviours similar to those you have previously encountered in your life, but this time, it is clear you are no longer reactive; rather you begin to open out through the recognisable compressions*

- *you may experience frequent 'flashbacks' of negative experiences earlier in this lifetime, as your subconscious mind cleanses out*

- *you will notice new skills and facets of beingness yearning to unfold, as your various bodily vehicles of expression reactivate*

- *your actions are beginning to have quite a powerful effect on the surrounding field (although this may not always be observable by others or measurable by yourself)*

- *frequently, you may find yourself in a position where you have the right gifts to be able to help another and provide a key to their unfolding*

- *the relationship with higher guidance becomes much stronger*

- *perhaps for the first time, your Twin Flame will become active in your life, experienced as reflections in people, nature and general circumstances*

- *you begin to experience quite powerful 'downloads' of higher knowing and inflows of energy, often of a prophetic nature.*

Transitioning Gateway 5
- indicators of completion -

At the completion of Gateway 5, at some particular point, you will notice that the Divine Purpose and your own, have become perfectly aligned. Multi-dimensionality has become a way of life. You sense, and automatically attune to, the downward flowing essence of higher consciousness. You can interpret symbolically – *or directly integrate* - all phenomenal experiences from your assessment of absolute authentic reality. You live in a multi-dimensional, yet seamlessly integrated, "consciousness landscape", which you hold lightly within your bodily vehicles of expression.

> *The energy of your soul flows automatically through this consciousness landscape, performing Right Action for the benefit of all. You are now truly at one with the co-creative process of higher consciousness, intuitively knowing your part within it.*

When Gateway 5 is complete, you will simply know yourself as a fully resurrected being, that only remains in a particular place, because of a deeper, divine purpose. If you stay here, it will be because you are consciously choosing to remain in the body, to help in the Ascension process of our planetary system.

What is more, you will be tasting your divine connection with your Twin Flame constantly, mirrored through the multi-dimensional circumstances of your life, yet seamlessly integrated within...

> *When fully resurrected, it is as if your Twin Flame is actively talking to you, a good deal of the time.*

In summary, these are some of the indications that you have completed the Gateway 5 Resurrection:

- *all behaviours have become completely selfless with no regard for personal gain, other than unlimited higher self expression*

- *choices are made according to the natural flow of the soul, through your inner consciousness landscape*

- *internal 'compressions' will still be happening, but there is an immediate and recognisable opening out into them*

- *the purpose for your incarnation is now fully clear to you*

- *you live within the experience of streaming synchronicity*

- *you exist within multiple planes of reality, with greatly expanded awareness of the vast array of influences*

- *you experience the sense of immortality and timelessness*

- *your ability to read the full depth of the moment heightens greatly*

- *your Twin Flame is an active part of your life, helping to build the polarity of energy, that it may flow into your creations.*

Gateway 5
- summary-

We stand at the dawn of a miraculous new evolution for mankind - a Golden Age - of which some are becoming increasingly aware, yet perhaps dare not fully hope exists as a possibility. The idea that we may ascend into a higher vibrational reality, will seem to many like science fiction fantasy, yet even to the most hardened sceptic, quantum theory must now be opening doorways of possibility through limited thinking. Matter and consciousness are one - there is no such thing as denseness, solidity and separation, except as phenomena made real in often fragile minds...

> *"All arises from the background field of oneness*
> *and flows back to it as the unbridled soul.*
> *Temporarily the ego takes possession and creates*
> *attachment – identification with the physicality –*
> *making you feel less than the greatness that you truly are.*
> *So create from the separation yes, enjoy it fully yes,*
> *but seek not to confuse yourself with the creation itself.*
> *That is to try to hold in place the Seer in you,*
> *which is ultimately fruitless, because it is placeless.*
> *And the fullness of you cannot be indefinitely controlled,*
> *restricted nor constrained."*
> *Openhand*

Quantum theory is also frequently misunderstood, and especially, it seems, in spiritual circles. When we gain the partial understanding that our reality is influenced by what we believe it to be, there tends to arise, in some circles, an attempt to shape that reality according to limited hopes, desires or fears. Alternatively, in the beginning, when you encounter something you do not like, there may also be the denial that your inner state of consciousness has created it in the first place.

To truly shape reality as you might want it to be, you would have to know the intended outcome within **every cell of your being**. It is not just about holding a vision within your mind. Oh sure, some may be able to access the Fourth Dimension and temporarily shape the immediate circumstances of their lives. However, this is only temporary: our separate existence is a mere microcosm in a vast ocean of consciousness, which has a natural design and inherent purpose all of its own. In one sense, the universe has breathed out and is simultaneously breathing back in again. In my view, humanity has now turned the corner. Our purpose is to align with the movement back to the Source - it is our innermost longing. Efforting to create something else, simply removes you from this natural flow like the proverbial fish out of water.

At the Resurrection, you open the floodgates of higher consciousness into your bodily vehicles and fill with the universe. Not only are you the Seer of all things, but the energy of the Seer now flows through you. You are being the Seer and a separated creation of that, at the same time.

You experience this amidst a multi-dimensional landscape – gone are the bounds of a limited 3D reality, where everything appears to happen randomly, which somehow, you must try to control. Instead, you have surrendered to the divine flow, which you continually read and/or readily integrate the deeper meaning of. You are now constantly building mutually supportive energetic feedback loops with the outer world and other sentient life in it. This becomes magically uplifting for all.

You are no longer controlling the flow, or even trying to, but instead harnessing it, and building the energy of it in your location - for the higher good both of your own soul and all other sentient life around you.

This is the true purpose of divine guidance in your life then. It is not to manifest some particular outcome, although you will abundantly manifest many things. Rather, divine guidance 'speaks through you', inviting you to see your authentic beingness in the people, other sentient life, and the situations you automatically shape around yourself. You literally feel, and instantly integrate, the reflections to unleash who you truly are. You are then radiating this beingness through every interaction. The corresponding feedback loops build a divine dance, which has no measure nor equal.

> *Meanwhile, your Twin Flame is dancing through this sensual reality, guiding you ever higher to the fullest expression of who you truly are. What could be better?*

Still resisting the flow (a while longer), and trying to divert souls from it, is Opposing Consciousness, which is acting like a parasitic virus in the field. You observe it through the rampant consumption, the desperate temptation to control life, or the pain of existence experienced by separation from the divine (I go on to explain this fully in DIVINICUS).

This Opposing Consciousness is temporarily trapped within the confines of the Fourth Density, as it has not yet processed out its final attachment to identity. It is clear, that its intrinsic desire to manipulate and control the evolution of another species, has established separation from the Source, and therefore created a barrier between itself and the natural order of life. As it hangs in limbo, it is deceiving awakening people who can be lured into using distorted spiritual laws, attaching them to a desired outcome…

> *This is the synthetic reality – the "Matrix" - that still exists on lower dimensional Earth for a while longer; it is one that is progressively being unwound by expanded, higher consciousness beings, acting through the field.*

Indeed the deception of Opposing Consciousness will not persist indefinitely. Enough people are beginning to see straight through the fabric of this limited reality, so that the fire of transformation is already taking hold and spreading throughout the physical realm. As the Resurrection for humanity unfolds further, more souls will rediscover their profound ability to act inter-dimensionally to nullify the effects of Opposing Consciousness. We are thereby providing breathing space for others to break through the shackles of limiting beliefs and conditioned thinking…

The Resurrection is the final chapter of the human journey in this plane of existence – for those ready to embrace it.

Benevolent Consciousness is here for all. It always has been, speaking through the weave of the fabric of life that we call reality. At Resurrection, you willingly conform to that miraculous weave, and whether Right Action comes to fruition in this plane or not, you still keep flowing in the only direction of real choice – that aligned with the universe. The ego can only deny the flow for so long. At some point, there is no escape, no hiding from the mirror of absolute truth. Eventually, no matter how long it takes, truth unwinds all distortion in its path.

At Resurrection, we become the flow of Right Action – the flow of truth. The soul is fully integrated, unfolded, and flowing freely through your being. You have reclaimed your divine birthright, and now join the movement into the Higher Paradigm, inspiring as many as possible, in whatever way available, to join us there.

Life becomes the magical existence it was always meant to be!

Conclusion

*"There will come a time when you believe everything is ending.
That will be the beginning."*

Louis L'amour

Conclusion

The Past

Just like yours, my journey here has not been an easy one. I can feel the energy of those drawn to this text, and the Openhand work in general. You tend to be pathfinders and way-showers; mavericks who challenge the tired old ways of doing things. You have chosen to come to a challenging place in the universe; yes a beautiful one, but also a dense one, where it is all too easy to lose connection to the divine. As souls, many of you will have come from across the cosmos, from different constellations, with amazing gifts to offer in these very challenging times. Most people tend to forget the immediate details of their past history, but at some point, one fine day, a vibration fires up in the heart...

> *It is an undeniable calling: to ascend the spiritual mountain, break through the density, unveil the fullness of your divine self, then guide others on the journey of rediscovery too.*

Personally, I recall the sense of lostness and rediscovery all too well! Like a person recovering from amnesia, like you, at first I felt very disconnected, a stranger in a strange place, the proverbial 'fish out of water'. But as it is for all of us, the hand of benevolence was never far away, and was clearly speaking to me, in signs and synchronicity, through the weave of the fabric of life – a mystical siren, resonating core frequencies deep within me. How could I deny it? To me, this made all the sense in the world. In a confusing place, it stood out strong and clear, like a home-calling beacon. I was guided on a journey of discovery: the intricate parts of a universal jigsaw steadily dropped into place, painting a multi-dimensional picture, of just what is really happening here on Earth right now...

Why is there so much disharmony and struggling? Why are people generally so out of alignment with the natural flow of life? These were questions that perplexed me, to which I could not rest, until the answers were clear.

Ultimately, I was to rediscover that mankind's wound is a deep-rooted one. Benevolence was wasting no time refamiliarising me with the full picture. But just like it is for you, it could not be one that I was simply told. I had to feel it for myself, activate it within my cellular memory. The synchronistic pull firing in my heart, guided me one day to see the "Oracle" – in this case a shopping centre in the UK. I was drawn into a well-known book store, and caused to gaze upon the latest bestselling book titles. By then, I had already remembered how to open my mind and allow higher guidance to 'spike' my awareness to signs and symbols – clicking together patterns of higher knowing.

As I scanned the titles, it was as if every combination of words gifted me answers to questions I had been inwardly asking. I was moved to tears by the miraculous and benevolent presence of a heavenly consciousness – I could feel it in the field all around me, deeply caring and supportive. However, one combination of words stopped me dead in my tracks, with both shock and recognition – a dim and distant truth, inconvenient, almost too earth-shattering to uncover...

"Homo Sapiens... a correctable mistake"

What could that possibly mean? It was a question that reverberated around inside me, one that would not rest. Later, in the quietness of my own space, the question suddenly snagged on something deep within, pulling on a thread of exposed consciousness. I found myself compelled into a lucid dream. I was having flashbacks to a previous incarnation many thousands of years ago. We, as highly evolved humans, were walking the planes of a stunningly beautiful bygone land, what some might call the "Garden of Eden".

It was a profoundly moving experience, with the absolute feeling of joy and at-one-ment with all things. The ceaseless, flowing river of Unity Consciousness enlightened my being, and in my mind existed crystal clear clarity. There was a depth of peace and stillness, which surpassed any human experience I have since had.

Then suddenly, the dream became a nightmare. Somehow, fear had been induced within me, and my awareness of Universal Life Energy had evaporated. I had been rapidly removed from my divine birthright. Whereas before, there had been no fear of death whatsoever, now it seemed that danger lurked behind every boulder and I was deeply afraid. I was afraid for the safety of my partner, my children and myself, afraid of not finding food or safe shelter. It seemed I was afraid of my very own shadow. My body became tight and closed down, as if the very life force was being drained from me. This was the experience I have come to know as "Homo Sapiens".

Where did it all go wrong? How did humanity's make-up so suddenly and drastically change? It is not within the scope of this book to explore humanity's true origins - I have felt not to complicate things at this stage. It has been my purpose more to provide a routemap of self discovery, to give energy to the way forward. In which case, people will mostly discover the truth for themselves – it will unfold in front of them. Suffice it to say for now, as I go on to explore fully in DIVINICUS, I have absolute heartfelt conviction, that the beginning of mankind's so called 'modern' civilisation, some twelve thousand years ago, was not nearly as straightforward as the history books would have you believe. What I will say right now, is that it is clear to me beyond a shadow of a doubt, that the Original Humans existed as highly evolved, fully integrated and multi-dimensional beings, totally at one with their interconnected divinity. That was until an inter-dimensional life force – *like a virus* - intervened.

How was this Opposing Consciousness able to influence people? As hard as it may be to imagine, I am convinced that genetic manipulation has played a key role in diluting and limiting original human beingness. It seems the human genetic code is littered with fallibility, past which most other creatures have long since evolved. To me, it feels like humanity has been softened to accept conditioning and limitation. But if we observe and acknowledge this, we still have the intrinsic power to negate the interference. 5GATEWAYS is a means to do this.

What is clear, is that humanity's multi-dimensionality has been closed down into limiting channels - which is why most only perceive the lower plane of consciousness. And it is hard to imagine, that not all your thoughts and emotions might be your own; that you might have been conditioned to accept lower behaviourisms.

It is only when you start challenging the patterning of modern life, that the audacious scope of this Intervention comes into view: you feel it, see it and taste it, as your soul works to break free from it.

Benevolent Consciousness has been helping humanity since the Intervention began. It has been providing a continually evolving mirror, so that you may connect with your true centre and see more clearly through the mind's frequently hazy delusions. It has generated countless synchronistic experiences, delivered an abundance of leaders, guides, scriptures and writings. Many of the teachings have, over time, been distorted, but with an enquiring mind and the razor edge of profound self-honesty, everyone has the intrinsic capacity to sort the wheat from the chaff.

Consider, for example, the biblical story of Jesus. Those familiar with the story may have recognised that the expansions of consciousness termed in this book as the 5GATEWAYS, closely parallel the evolutionary milestones of Jesus (the Buddha too in fact). Did Jesus really exist? Are the events described in the Bible true? To me, the key is not whether the story is true, it is the story itself that counts - this is the real gift from Benevolent Consciousness...

It is a story which billions of people across our planet know – especially when you include that of the Buddha too. But it is not just the story of the occasional master, it is the story of what you yourself are capable of, what you can attain, and what milestones you must pass in order to get there.

In my view, the Jesus story represents a powerful metaphor told through the life of an ordinary man - "the son of God" - just as we are all the sons and daughters of God (where God is the Source – the now ever-present Seer). It is the story of a man who awakens to the presence of his soul at an early age, is then baptised in the river Jordan and realigns to follow the path of his soul. His heart leads him to the desert, to fight with inner and outer demons, generating attachment to the need for an outcome in the external drama of life. Maybe his attachments were to self-sacrificing service, but they were attachments nevertheless, which needed to be overcome, just as every person eventually must.

This journey led to his Transfiguration, where the 'Holy Spirit descended upon him'. In other words, his soul was fully reconnected and reintegrated with Unity Consciousness. Yet he was still not fully purified, still not fully liberated. An inner shadow (the false prophet perhaps?) caused identification with the bodymind of Jesus. Only an extreme event - a crucifixion - could expose this shadow. "Why hast thou forsaken me, Father?" This is what Jesus supposedly cries out from the cross. Were it true, it would not be the enlightened being calling, for in Enlightenment, there is always awareness of divine union, irrespective of what is happening. We know that to taste everlasting union with the absolute – the 'Father' - we must also know abandonment, for we cannot truly know one thing, in the absence of its opposite.

So in the moment that Jesus called out, the shadow was exposed, self-realisation dawned and the darkness of the shadow dissolved. "It is accomplished", the Seer – the Father - was finally liberated as an invisible surfer, riding the wave of the soul through the bodymind. No longer was there the restriction of identification with the ego. There remained the absolute, divine experience of non-localised presence, acting through a bodymind. He was being both the father, and the son, *at the same time.*

In the story, after the crucifixion, the bodymind of Jesus was later resurrected. This final purification is depicted by the cleansing of his dead body. To me, this is a metaphor, supporting the need to cleanse, reactivate and re-energise the various bodily vehicles of expression that defines the Resurrection itself – the resurrection into a Higher Paradigm of being.

We are not limited to a singular reality. The event was demonstrating the possibility that is open to everyone; it is just that the story has been coloured and glamourised to seem beyond reach of a 'mere mortal' – it is not! The original story was always intended as an inspiration. It is time to reclaim it as our own, through the journey that we write in day-to-day life.

The Present

So exactly how does this story help us in our current predicament, as we seem to be moving into ever more turbulent times? In my truth, the story provides a priceless routemap, a profound gift to humanity. Although veiled in distorted and dogmatic thinking, its legacy stands the test of time, as proved by others who have previously walked the path, and today, by many thousands around the world, who are also living testament to it. It clearly indicates the transitions we are all being invited to take.

> *It was never meant to be about just one man, nor just one religion. It was never meant to exclude people. We are **all** the sons and daughters of God! If you have the courage to go inwards and follow the unfolding pathway, **everyone** has the capability to transition the 5GATEWAYS.*

As challenging as these transitions may at times be, through the doorway marked "Fear", is to be found immense joy, freedom and liberation - the 'rewards' for your courage, commitment and trust. We are truly blessed to be alive in these times of planetary Ascension. Those tuned in to the energies of higher consciousness, are already beginning to witness one of the most spectacular, most magical, most miraculous phenomena in the cosmos - a planetary rebirth. Many are already centred in this divine flow of expanded consciousness - a Golden Age - of profound harmony and unconditional love.

So what of the difficulty and darkness we see all around us? Yes indeed, just as the light is intensifying, so too is the darkness. Personally, I have come to accept this as a necessary 'evil'. As we each attune to the light within, then the darkness all around becomes ever more obvious. As our planetary system is ascending, the denser energies must be transmuted; in other words, you must process out your karma. This does not mean to simply 'ditch it', for this creates identity once more - an identity which is avoiding it. Rather, it means to relive your karma, but this time, without fear or attachment. It takes courage and profound self-honesty, but ultimately it does dissolve.

If you resist, as many across our planet currently are doing, then you hold within yourself a limiting relationship to the denser energies, expressed as a sense of separation, desire, fear or worry. As people continue to hold this negative energy, then the polarity between the higher plane and the lower intensifies, creating an ever growing potential energy difference. This is exactly how tornadoes are created, and we witness their destructive force wreaking havoc, as the energy is transmuted, in other words discharged.

So each person has a choice:

Either to venture inwards now, process out your karma and become as one again with the higher vibrations of our planetary system, in which case, the transition will be a relatively smooth one; or, if too many resist the changes, it will create growing tension, with a much more chaotic and turbulent transition.

Whichever it is though, whatever happens in the lower world, remember, that we each have the ultimate choice as to how we experience it – how we live our lives through it. Amidst the greatest challenge, lies the greatest opportunity. Spiritual mastery is open to every one.

The Future

So which is it likely to be: the smooth transition or the turbulent one? In my truth, what lies ahead cannot be foretold with absolute certainty, for each of us has free will, and we create the future by the choices we make in the present. Indeed, our divine birthright is freedom of choice, and yet even so, we are also currently acting as one, where every single thought, word, feeling and deed, affects the outcome of the whole.

So, in my view, it is counterproductive to get too attached to prophecy. A productive alternative however, is to look at the pattern of events leading up to this moment, and to see where the wave of human consciousness seems to be heading. If we do this, we observe guidances of what could happen, if the mainstream continues in the direction it is currently moving. This provides the opportunity to look into the mirror of external experience, feel the impact inside yourself, embrace your part in the co-creation, then change what no longer serves you.

When I look into humanity's mirror right now, I observe the following:

1. *There is a rapid acceleration of spiritual evolution for some - a "quickening" - the intended solution to get humanity back on his destined evolutionary pathway.*

2. *The majority are still resistant to change. Their seemingly growing attachment to, manipulation and rampant exploitation of, our earthly resources, is bringing them ever closer to the precipice of their own self destruction.*

This raises a dichotomy. We are all one, and yet appear to be moving in increasingly divergent directions. If this continues, it would seem practically certain that the society we live in will become increasingly unsustainable, until it implodes, causing catastrophe for millions. In fact, do we not already witness this beginning to happen all around us, with accelerating climate change, financial crisis, dwindling natural resources, poverty, starvation, disease and violence? In an increasingly globalised society, the effects are ever more likely to be felt by all, not just the impoverished.

Yet, even amongst all of this, I see the eternal presence of divine light, a benevolent 'open hand' offering help to those prepared to listen. I believe passionately, that those open to hearing will be offered a safe passage through the turbulence, and just as for Moses in the Biblical story, the "Red Sea" (the Fourth Density) will part before you. If you follow the path of the soul and its magical journey, you will find a safe shore, return more to your roots, learn how to be more self-sustaining, and then rediscover the divine birthright that was so tragically taken from you...

> *"Yea, though I walk through the val-*
> *ley of the shadow of death,*
> *I will fear no evil: for thou art with me; thy rod and thy staff*
> *they comfort me. Thou preparest a table before me*
> *in the presence of mine enemies: thou anointest*
> *my head with oil; my cup runneth over.*
> *Surely goodness and mercy shall follow me all the days of*
> *my life: and I will dwell in the house of the Lord forever."*
> *Psalm 23 The Bible*

What will be the circumstances of your remaining time here? No one else can say but you. It is your hidden story, which only you can uncover. In the chaotic times unfolding all around us, as the old world reality steadily breaks down, it could lead to anything - for Jesus it led to his physical crucifixion. Not a very pleasant fate you might think, but that would be a judgment. In the story, it was exactly what Jesus needed to master his shadow, liberate his soul, and in so doing, he left a powerful message, which has spanned the passage of time.

The point being, that you are capable of mastering any circumstance that befalls you. You are not this body, not this mind, you are not something that is meant to pass away into oblivion. You are a child of the universe, with the potential for an immortal soul. Live that way, and live it now!

If another growing trend of awakening souls is followed through, it is likely that some will let go of their attachment to the precarious crutches of a crumbling society, and find a way of living more at one with Mother Earth - perhaps in self-sufficient communities. Alternatively, you may feel your destiny is best served by remaining in the Matrix to shine the light for others. We each have a destiny and glorious story to fulfill. In fact, the intensity and uncertainty of the current situation, creates even more fertile ground in which your being may evolve and grow.

Whatever the hands of time hold in store, you can be sure of one thing: the path that offers the greatest sense of fulfillment, the greatest expression of being, the greatest liberation, will be that guided by your soul...

"It doesn't interest me if there is one God or many gods.
I want to know if you belong or feel abandoned.
If you know despair or can see it in others.
I want to know if you are prepared to live in the world
with its harsh need to change you.
If you can look back with firm eyes
saying this is where I stand.
I want to know if you know how to melt
into that fierce heat of living
falling toward the centre of your longing.
I want to know if you are willing
to live, day by day, with the consequence of love
and the bitter unwanted passion of your sure defeat.
*I have heard, in **that** fierce embrace,*
even the gods speak of God."
David Whyte

Whether we know it or not, we will each play a part in the Ascension of Mother Earth - *we cannot avoid it* - but how we experience it, how we transition it, is entirely up to us. We are each gifted the divine right of free will: we can either attune to the density and darkness - the part that is dying - and fight with each other to control ever dwindling natural resources; or we can surrender to the internal super-highway, evolve our consciousness and attune to the lighter energies of unconditional love, joy and mutual respect for all life.

Yes, that invitation is open to every single one of us. We are free to become as one with the Divine Will - our very own higher purpose - and follow the unfolding pathway through the 5GATEWAYS into the New Paradigm.

Will you be one of those who makes that choice?

Glossary

Terms commonly used in this book are listed below.

Ascension: when a sentient life form moves from one vibrational state of existence to the next, higher one.

Attachment: when a soul becomes identified with the physical 'drama' in some particular way.

Bodily vehicles of expression: the human bodily vehicles formed from Separation Consciousness (collectively termed the "bodymind") through which the soul expresses.

The seven bodily vehicles are outlined here...

Spirit-light-body: facilitates multi-dimensional experience. Also known as the "merkaba" (connected via the crown chakra).

Celestial body: holds, stimulates and reflects authentic recognition of the soul (connected via the third eye).

Higher mind: harmonises with the divine flow and manifests the conditions for higher education, expression and evolutionary growth (connected via the throat chakra).

Causal body: (the energy body) retains karma - the blueprint for each incarnation (connected via the heart chakra).

Subconscious mind: interprets abstract wisdom of higher mind, and facilitates psychic skills in a Third Density way (connected via the solar plexus chakra).

Emotional body: holds, processes and expresses one's emotional state (connected via the sacral chakra).

Physical Body: the sum collection of consciousness cells forming the physical body (connected via the base chakra).

Chakra: an etheric location within a human being where Soul Consciousness infuses into the bodily vehicles of expression.

The seven main chakras are outlined below:

Base chakra: the etheric centre where Soul Consciousness infuses into the physical body. Positioned at the coccyx and also known as the "root chakra".

Sacral chakra: the etheric centre where Soul Consciousness infuses into the emotional body. Positioned roughly where the spine and pelvis meet.

Solar plexus chakra: the etheric centre infusing Soul Consciousness into the subconscious mind.

Heart chakra: where Soul Consciousness infuses into the causal body. Located on the spine at the general level of the heart.

Throat chakra: the etheric centre where Soul Consciousness infuses into the "higher mind" bodily vehicle of expression.

Third eye: the general centre of core consciousness for the soul within a human being. Located in the centre of the head at the pineal gland. Also known as "the soul centre".

Crown chakra: the etheric centre where Soul Consciousness infuses into the spirit-light-body.

Consciousness: awareness of relativistic experience - life itself.

The key consciousness terms used in this book are as follows...

Benevolent Consciousness: a benevolent life form assisting in the natural evolutionary process of another life form. Also frequently referred to as "Higher Guiding Consciousness" or "benevolence".

Opposing Consciousness: a non benevolent life form, opposing the natural evolutionary process of another for its own benefit.

Separation Consciousness: generates the relativistic sense of separation between sentient life forms.

Unity Consciousness: connects all sentient life forms and draws them back to ever higher levels of unity.

Consciousness landscape: an interconnected pattern of information, held within our consciousness, formed by observing external signs and symbols. When lightly held and referenced within the bodymind, it forms the landscape through which the soul flows.

Conditioned behaviour patterns: these are either closed 'programs' of behavioural activity caused by an attachment in the false self, or they are 'distortions' of authentic soul-inspired behaviours. Society tends to program these within people, according to generally accepted social, political, religious or scientific attitudes.

Dimension/Density: a vibrational state or energetic frequency level, within the universe (not to be confused with x,y,z dimensions, which define a locational position in the physical realm).

Dimensional realm: a grouping of dimensions forming one plane of existence - for example the 'Lower Dimensional Realm' consisting of the first, second and third dimensions.

Divine Purpose: the naturally benevolent and compassionate shaping purpose of the universe, bringing sentient life to perfection.

Earth-bound soul: a soul that has left the body and yet remains in the Third Dimensional Realm, due to over attachment to this plane.

Enlightened state: when a sentient life form is experiencing itself as what it truly is - the Seer - non-identified presence.

Enlightenment: when a sentient life form is constantly experiencing itself as the Seer.

Ego: where the soul has attached to, and formed an identity with, the bodymind.

Gateways of Light: transition points from one level or state of consciousness (from one Density) to a higher, more expanded one.

The five key expansions of consciousness are outlined below...

Awakening: connecting to the magic of the soul and one's interconnectedness with all life.

Realignment: surrendering to the supreme governance of the soul in one's life - alignment with the Divine Purpose.

Transfiguration: the dramatic shift of perception, from identification with the false self, to being the Seer, expressed as the soul, through the bodymind.

Enlightenment: the soul confronts and releases all karmic filters – finally dissolving any shadow identities. The soul becomes fully integrated within one's being.

Resurrection: where all seven bodily vehicles of expression are finally cleansed, reactivated and re-energised. The soul unfolds into multi-dimensional living.

Identity: where the soul (your unique personality) builds a web of conditioned behaviours within the bodymind and identifies with them - the soul is attached, leading to a false self ego.

The key identities referred to in this book are listed below...

Inner child identity: a complex web of fixed neural pathways formed in early childhood.

Inner teenager identity: a complex web of fixed neural pathways formed at, or shortly after, puberty.

Shadow identity: where the soul is being filtered (and distorted) by karma. Also known as the "shadow" or "imposter".

Karma: an attachment formed by the soul to a particular experience in a past life, which then regenerates a similar experience in the current incarnation, in order to release the attachment (also referred to as "source pain" or "karmic source pain").

Right Action: action which is at one with the natural directional flow of the universe as a whole.

Right Outcome: when Right Action is made manifest.

Sentient life form: a separate, identifiable life form.

Soul: a unique expression of the Seer, animating a sentient life form.

Soul family: a group of closely related souls, all vibrating on a similarly aligned harmonic, and assisting each other in their spiritual evolution.

Soul-ray-harmonic: the unique blend of the Seven Rays of consciousness that forms the characteristics of your soul. Otherwise known as your inherent 'personality'.

Synchronicity: when seemingly random occurrences gather together in a definable pattern, thereby rendering a deeper meaning or story.

The Observer: an aspect of mind - a temporary inner identity - formed from the intention to observe thoughts, emotions, motivations, feelings and behaviours.

The Heart Centre: a more expanded evolution of the Observer. The place where you feel and surrender to the natural pull of your soul.

The Seer: non-identified presence - the one True Self existing throughout the universe. Also referred to as "Pure Presence", "The Absolute" and "God".

The Source: the centre of consciousness from which the phenomenal universe arose.

Openhand

Purpose
Openhand is a Higher Benevolent Presence, the purpose of which, is to catalyse spiritual evolution, by helping people dissolve conditioned behaviour patterns and limiting beliefs. Openhand empowers people to find their true beingness and ascend into a magical new reality, based on unconditional love, joy and unity with all life.

Openhand Ventures
Openhand Ventures is an organisation led by Open, based in Glastonbury in the UK, which operates as a not-for-profit company. Its purpose is to harness and express the energy of Openhand, here in this realm, for the benefit of evolving people.

Worldwide Seminars, Workshops and Courses
We are given to spread the message, tools and advice contained within this book, as far and wide as possible. In line with this calling, we conduct seminars, courses, workshops and retreats around the world. If you would like us to run a seminar or course for your organisation or private group, email courses@Openhandweb.org

Join our growing community - Openhandweb
It brings great joy to our hearts to witness the miraculous expansion of consciousness taking place across the planet. It is within our purpose to join together a virtual community of ascending people to share advice, resources, transformational tools, philosophy and above all, a common bond of unconditional love. Our website provides a platform for this growing community.

To find out more, visit...

www.Openhandweb.org

Other publications by Openhand

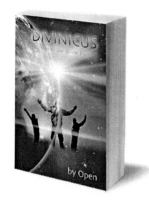

DIVINICUS: rise of the divine human

Where did humanity really come from? And where is he going to? DIVINICUS explains through a journey of rediscovery, just exactly why the situation on Earth right now is so challenging. What is mankind's destiny? The book will captivate you on an enthralling journey, from the deserts of Arizona to the plains of South Africa; from the Garden of Eden to the Big Apple; from ancient Lemuria to submerged Atlantis. Travel inter-dimensionally to the Divine Human in you.

Trinity's Conscious Kitchen

The first Openhand recipe book, designed to inspire soul through compassionate and conscious cuisine. In the spirit of raising consciousness, all recipes are original, animal-free, wheat-free and free from refined sugar. Most people who eat this way, not only experience optimal health, but also greater spiritual, mental and emotional clarity.

Guided Meditations, Enlightening Articles

Openhandweb is packed with tools and resources for your evolution. Check out our guided meditations, which you can download, plus our extensive library of enlightening articles and inspirational videos.

For all publications above, visit our web community:
www.Openhandweb.org

Lightning Source UK Ltd.
Milton Keynes UK
UKOW01f0656070216

267832UK00002B/100/P